Pharmacoeconomics and Outcome Assessment: A Global Issue

Pharmacoeconomics and Outcome Assessment: A Global Issue

Editor: Dr Sam Salek,

University of Wales,Cardiff

Euromed Communications Ltd

Haslemere, UK

Learning Resources
Centre

1 2 3 1 3 4 2 4

ISBN 1 899 015 23X

Printed and bound in the United Kingdom by Redvine

Contents

PREFACE   Sam Salek

FOREWORD   Michael F Drummond

LIST OF CONTRIBUTORS

CHAPTER 1   The impact of health economics on
health policy, health services and
decision-making

David Cohen   1

CHAPTER 2   Pharmacoeconomics: what's in a name?

Mo Malek   19

CHAPTER 3   Pharmacoeconomic education in schools
of pharmacy

*Karen Rascati, JoLaine Draugalis,
Therese Connor and David Sclar*   25

CHAPTER 4   Methodologies used to evaluate and measure
the economic outcomes of drug treatments

Clive Pritchard and Adrian Towse   33

CHAPTER 5   Case studies in pharmacoeconomics and
assessment of outcomes

*Bradley Martin, F Lamar Pritchard,
Jeffrey Kotzan, Matthew Perri III and David Sclar*   53

CHAPTER 6   The use of interactive computer models to present pharmacoeconomic data

Andy Duggan   73

CHAPTER 7   Pharmacoeconomics and clinical drug research

Jeff Lee, Jane Osterhaus and Ray Townsend   85

CHAPTER 8   The potential and limitations of pharmacoeconomic research in the pharmaceutical industry

Ray Churnside and Patrick Hopkinson   103

CHAPTER 9   The role of pharmacoeconomics in response to globalization and increased competition in the pharmaceutical industry

Gregory Hess, Marc Watrous, David Strutton and Anthony Bower   119

CHAPTER 10 Pharmacoeconomics and the future of the pharmaceutical industry. Should they be encouraged to establish a pharmacoeconomic team?

David Jones   143

Preface

This book is founded upon the growing global importance of the discipline of pharmacoeconomics as the method of assessing the economic outcomes of drug therapy. Among many others, I have a genuine concern over the existing confusion between 'health economics' and 'pharmacoeconomics'. Are these just two different names with the same meaning, which do the same things? Or are they two different disciplines with common boundaries? Other questions arising from this argument are: does the pharmaceutical industry's perception of pharmacoeconomics in searching for a panacea in the present climate of outcomes assessment, value for money and reimbursement match the academics' pursuit; should the pharmaceutical industry establish in-house pharmacoeconomic expertise as a response to globalization; and should the discipline of pharmacoeconomics be fully claimed by schools of pharmacy and form part of their core undergraduate and postgraduate curriculum?

In an attempt to openly debate these issues of concern, a team of leading authorities from both academia and the pharmaceutical industry are brought together in this book. The chapters are carefully selected to develop a systematic approach to the debate and at the same time to foster the way of thinking and a set of techniques in order to make the book of interest to a wider audience. Moreover, some of the visionary views expressed by the authors should undisputedly place the book next to those in the reading list of students pursuing degrees in health and social policy, marketing, economics, pharmacy, health management, medicines management, clinical research, pharmaceutical medicine and those already working in these fields.

It is envisaged that subsequent editions will be prepared at short intervals to reflect the timely dissemination of the continuing change in this growing field to the readers.

I enjoyed working with the authors of the chapters and I gratefully acknowledge their hard work and support. I also thank the publishing team at Euromed Communications for their patience and understanding during rather a long preparation period for this book. My heartfelt thanks goes to my family and friends for their support, love and especially their help and understanding during final stages of completing this task.

Sam Salek
Centre for Socioeconomic Research
Welsh School of Pharmacy
University of Wales, Cardiff, UK
May 1999

Foreword

The terms 'pharmacoeconomics' and 'outcomes assessment' have become common currency in recent years. A new journal, 'PharmacoEconomics' was launched in 1992 and a new society, the International Society for Pharmacoeconomic and Outcomes Research, is growing rapidly.

The birth of a new field of study inevitably raises many issues: why has pharmacoeconomics suddenly become so important; does it really differ from health economics; is it something pharmacists need to embrace; what are the immediate and long term implications for the pharmaceutical industry? This new book, edited by Sam Salek, greatly informs our understanding of these issues.

Pharmacoeconomics and outcomes assessment has gained prominence owing to a changing healthcare environment. Pressures on healthcare budgets mean that all items of expenditure, including those on pharmaceuticals, have come under greater scrutiny. Therefore, manufacturers of pharmaceuticals have come under greater pressure to generate evidence on the value for money from use of their products.

Whilst, in general, this change in the healthcare environment was not welcomed by the industry, considerable effort and resource has been devoted to the production of cost-effectiveness evidence. In some cases, such as in Australia and Ontario, this has been because governments have required it.

In a much greater number of countries, including the USA, the pharmaceutical industry has produced economic data as part of a broader marketing effort. Indeed some companies have sought to achieve a competitive advantage by developing their capacity in pharmacoeconomics.

Many of the methodologies used in pharmacoeconomics and outcomes assessment mirror those used in health economics more generally, in particular economic evaluation. Therefore, pharmacoeconomics is properly viewed as a sub-set of health economics, but, over time, the field may be responsible for the development of new methodologies which would make it more distinctive. There is already evidence that the field covers activities that go beyond the economic evaluation of individual pharmaceutical products.

Since the relationship between the pharmaceutical industry, government and the healthcare system needs to be based on trust, the quality of pharmacoeconomic studies is crucially important. In several jurisdictions methodological guidelines for undertaking studies have been specified and most major pharmaceutical companies recognise that it is important to maintain high standards.

One of the most critical methodological debates centres on whether pharmacoeconomic studies should be conducted alongside clinical trials, or whether modelling approaches will suffice. Given the lack of effectiveness data at the time pharmaceutical products are launched, most analysts believe that modelling studies are an unavoidable fact of life.

The final issue relates to the impact that this new field will have on the major parties. Certainly pharmacoeconomics and outcomes assessment will have a major impact on the role of pharmacists and it is important that it is adequately covered in school of pharmacy curricula. First impressions suggest that this issue has been addressed more fully in the USA than elsewhere.

However, the major impact is likely to be on the pharmaceutical industry itself. If taken seriously, pharmacoeconomics and outcomes assessment will have profound implications for the clinical research programme, both in terms of the design of individual clinical studies and in the selection of compounds for clinical development. Companies have already made major investments in the establishment of pharmacoeconomics departments and this trend is likely to continue.

This new book on pharmacoeconomics and outcomes assessment is to be welcomed. It will not be the last!

Michael F Drummond
Centre for Health Economics
University of York
England

List of Contributors

Anthony G Bower
SmithKline Beecham Pharmaceuticals, Collegeville, PA, USA

Ray Churnside
Central Research Division, Pfizer, Sandwich, Kent, UK

David Cohen
University of Glamorgan Business School, UK

Therese M Connor
College of Pharmacy, University of Texas, USA

JoLaine R Draugalis
College of Pharmacy, University of Arizona, USA

Michael Drummond
Centre for Health Economics, University of York, UK

Andy Duggan
Abacus International, Bicester, Oxfordshire, UK

Gregory Hess
SmithKline Beecham Pharmaceuticals, Collegeville, PA, USA

Patrick K Hopkinson
Glaxo Wellcome, Greenford, Middlesex, UK

David Jones
SmithKline Beecham Pharmaceuticals, Welwyn Garden City, Hertfordshire, UK

Jeffrey A Kotzan
College of Pharmacy, University of Georgia, USA

Jeff Lee
Advanced Health Outcomes, Franklin, TN, USA

Mo Malek
University of St Andrews, UK

Bradley C Martin
College of Pharmacy, University of Georgia, USA

Jane T Osterhaus
Global Health Outcomes, Skokie, IL, USA

Matthew Perri III
College of Pharmacy, University of Georgia, USA

Clive Pritchard
Office of Health Economics, London, UK

F Lamar Pritchard
College of Pharmacy, University of Georgia, USA

Karen L Rascati
College of Pharmacy, University of Texas, USA

David A Sclar
Pharmacoeconomics and Pharmacoepidemiology Research Unit, Washington State University, USA

David R Strutton
SmithKline Beecham Pharmaceuticals, Collegeville, PA, USA

Ray Townsend
Strategic Outcomes Services, Research Triangle Park, NC, USA

Adrian Towse
Office of Health Economics, London, UK

Marc L Watrous
SmithKline Beecham Pharmaceuticals, Collegeville, PA, USA

1

The impact of health economics on health policy, health services and decision-making

D Cohen

INTRODUCTION

New pharmaceutical and other technological advances mean that health services are now able to do more for people than was ever possible before. Continuing new development means that this potential for people to benefit from treatment is increasing year on year. This is unquestionably a positive achievement.

On the other hand, achievement normally comes at a price. While some new technologies may allow the same or more to be done at less cost, for example where a new chemotherapy regimen allows treatment at home which previously required hospitalisation, most produce previously unobtainable benefits at a positive cost. The fact that these benefits come at a cost is not a bad thing *per se*. What matters is whether this extra health can be justified by the cost of achieving it. In an ideal world of infinite resources such considerations would not be necessary. In the real world of finite resources pursuing benefits while ignoring costs is no longer an option.

Acceptance of this way of viewing the world is quite new. Until recently, the concern with new pharmaceutical and other technological developments was almost wholly with issues of efficacy and safety. Demonstrating that something was either safer or more effective than whatever it would replace was normally sufficient to ensure that the new technology would be taken up and would rapidly diffuse throughout the healthcare system.

In recent years, however, rapidly rising healthcare costs have increased awareness world-wide of the economist's contention that the resources available for healthcare will always be scarce relative to the demands made on them. This is true regardless of the nature of the healthcare system, the relative priority given to healthcare versus other areas of economic activity or even the absolute amount of spending on healthcare. Resource allocation choices are inescapable. Accordingly, there is an increasing expectation that clinical trials and other forms of evaluation will provide evidence of cost effectiveness in addition to that on efficacy and safety.

At the same time there is a natural desire by doctors and other health professionals to want to do what is 'best' i.e. clinically most effective, for their patients. This desire tends in particular to become reality in publicly funded or insurance based systems where patients do not pay directly for the cost of their treatment. Thus if resource allocation decisions are left solely to the medical profession it is understandable that a shift of focus from safety and efficacy alone to safety, efficacy and cost effectiveness will not happen. As Rutten and Haan[1] have stated

> "It seems necessary to organise a countervailing force at least in certain areas of our healthcare system, so as to provide some guarantees that on the one hand cost effective procedures are introduced more rapidly, and on the other the diffusion of procedures with an unfavourable cost effectiveness ratio is tempered."(p:30)

The aim of this introductory chapter is to consider what some of these 'countervailing forces' might be, and to give examples of their use in several countries. As will be seen, some of these forces are direct measures such as making economic evaluation of a condition for getting a new drug listed for public reimbursement. Others are far more subtle involving, for example, broad organisational changes aimed at making resource allocation decision-making more amenable to economic thinking.

Before discussing specific measures, however, it is important to understand what it is that these measures are trying to do. Considering them as 'cost containment' would wholly misrepresent what the drive for greater efficiency in healthcare is really about. Accordingly, the chapter begins with a brief explanation of some basic principles of health economics. This is followed by examples, mainly from the UK, of institutional changes undertaken specifically to improve the efficiency of health service delivery. The issue of how the results of economic evaluations have impacted on health policy and clinical decision-making will then be addressed.

WHAT IS HEALTH ECONOMICS?

Economics is *about* the allocation of resources to production and the distribution of the outputs which result. Economics exists as a discipline because the resources available globally, nationally, regionally or to any industry, organisation or individual are finite. At the same time it would appear that no amount of output could ever satisfy all human wants and desires. Taken together, this means that *choices* about what level of resources to allocate to various sectors of the economy or to the production of specific outputs within those sectors are inescapable. Similarly choices about distribution cannot be avoided. Economics is the science of making choices — regardless of whether those choices are made collectively through some form of central planning or are left to market forces.

Health economics is the application of the *discipline* of economics to the *topic* of health[2]. When viewed as an application, health economics becomes first and foremost a *way of thinking* based on the principles of scarcity and the need for choice. While the techniques of economic appraisal are the principal way that the discipline gets applied, they are merely the 'toolkit'. Use of these tools without a proper understanding of the principles upon which they are based can be ineffective, misleading and/or positively dangerous.

THREE KEY PRINCIPLES OF HEALTH ECONOMICS: OUTPUT, COST AND EFFICIENCY

What is the output of healthcare?

Healthcare services are not normally provided for their own sake. Apart from those suffering from Munchausen syndrome, few people receive any utility (satisfaction) directly from consuming healthcare. Rather, these services are demanded because of an expectation that they will actually have a positive impact on present or future health.

Viewed this way, the principal output of healthcare is 'health' — although this need not be the only output. The inverted commas are used to reflect the fact that many interventions, for example palliative care of the terminally ill, are not intended to raise health status as such. However, if 'health' is perceived in the broad sense of well-being then, if effective, interventions will make people better off than they would have been in the absence of the interventions. In other words effective interventions will normally increase the length of life, improve the quality of life or achieve some combination of the two.

The practical difficulties of viewing output in terms of health achieved is that health is notoriously difficult to define, measure and value. Broad definitions, such as that by the World Health Organisation[3] of health as a

"state of complete physical, mental and social well-being."

are unhelpful when trying to compare the effectiveness of alternative therapies or to compare the health gain from either of these with that from some wholly unrelated area of healthcare.

In practice therefore, *intermediate* measures of output are often used as proxies for *final* (health) outputs. This is acceptable so long as the link between the proxy measure and health are established. Thus evidence that a reduction in smoking prevalence will result in a reduction in smoking-related morbidity and mortality, means that 'number of quitters' is an acceptable output measure even though smoking is not a disease and quitting is not in itself a health gain. The less well established is the link between the proxy and health, the less useful is the proxy.

What is the cost of producing health?

By definition, resources are those things that contribute to the production of output. In terms of health services, the output 'health' is produced using resources such as doctors, nurses, hospital beds, operating theatres, equipment and drugs. Money is needed in order to provide a command over these resources but, according to the above definition, money is not itself a resource since it only becomes productive if used to hire doctors, buy drugs and so on. Similarly, according to the definition above resources can include the time of volunteers, informal carers or anything else which does not involve money payment but which nevertheless contributes to the production of health.

A focus on resource use rather than money leads to a fundamental difference in how 'cost' is viewed in economics. Since resources are scarce, the commitment of resources to any one use means sacrificing the benefits that could have been achieved if these resources had been used in some alternative (strictly, the next best) way. In economics, cost is thus equated with 'sacrifice' and the term 'opportunity cost' is used to emphasise this notion of an opportunity foregone. Money cost and opportunity cost may coincide — or they may not.

On what basis should resource allocation choices be made?

Scarcity of resources means that it is not possible to do everything that we would like to do. Regardless of what level of resources are currently devoted to healthcare, it will always be possible to do more. This is partly due to the rapid development of new technologies including pharmaceuticals which allows more and more to be done year on year, but also to the fact that resources devoted to healthcare incur opportunity costs elsewhere. The multiplicity of human wants means that better health is not the only good thing that a society desires and there are limits to how much of other potential benefits society is willing to sacrifice in the pursuit of better health.

Scarcity means that resource allocation choices cannot be avoided. If this is accepted, then it is clear that the basis on which these choices are made should be explicit. Economists do not claim to have the only — or indeed necessarily the best-in-all-circumstances criteria for choice, but at the very least economic criteria are explicit and therefore subject to criticism and debate.

The principle criterion used in economic thinking is efficiency which is about maximising the benefits from available resources. It concerns the **relationship** between inputs and outputs i.e. most benefit at least cost. Being efficient means getting as much health as is possible from available resources. Being inefficient means getting less. Viewed this way there is an ethical justification for the pursuit of efficiency, although clearly equity and other considerations have a legitimate place as well.

The likelihood of efficiency happening in the absence of its explicit pursuit is small. Sheldon and Vanoli[4] point out

> "The current allocation of resources to technologies is unlikely to be optimal. It reflects a range of influences such as historical patterns, commercial pressure, professional

interest, enthusiasms and beliefs, consumer demands and political wishes. None of these by themselves is likely to result in an efficient allocation." (p:53)

There are two fundamentally different types of efficiency. *Allocative efficiency* concerns what gets produced and in what quantities i.e. what level of resources should be allocated to the production of X. Technical efficiency addresses the much narrower question of 'how' to produce X given that a decision has already been taken to produce it. Technical efficiency issues are not concerned with whether or to what extent X should be produced.

As will be seen below, the vast majority of economic appraisals have addressed questions of technical efficiency. Since the focus of this chapter is on the impact of health economics, as well as the impact of economic evaluation — we will turn first to allocative efficiency issues with a necessary emphasis on economic thinking rather than economic evaluation.

GETTING HEALTH ECONOMIC THINKING INTO PRACTICE

Accepting scarcity

A prerequisite to the use of health economic thinking is an acceptance that no healthcare system can possibly do all things for all people. This means recognising explicitly that some form of prioritising is necessary and unavoidable. Such recognition has been slowly emerging over the past decade or so.

In the UK, annual expenditure on the National Health Service (NHS) is mainly determined by government during public expenditure negotiations. Health services are provided according to need and at zero price at the point of use. Until quite recently there has tended to be an implicit belief that the role of the NHS was to use this money (strictly, to use the resources which this money could command) to meet all health needs. Words like rationing were eschewed in all official documents.

At a recent conference organised by the British Medical Association and others, a motion that

"This house believes that rationing in healthcare is inevitable"[5]

was carried.

It is unlikely that such a motion would have even been debated, let alone carried, had it been considered at a similar conference ten years ago.

Why the change in attitude and why not just call for bigger budgets? Christine Hancock, secretary of the Royal College of Nursing, was one of those at the conference who offered vocal opposition when she said[5]

"If doctors and nurses are seduced by the idea of rationing they give politicians the perfect excuse not to increase resources"

Many in the UK who accept the need for rationing would also no doubt like to see additional resources devoted to the NHS. They are increasingly coming to the realisation, however, that while extra funding will ease the problem it cannot make it go away. If 'need' is perceived as 'capacity to benefit from treatment' then clearly each new technological advance is increasing need. Premature babies born with low birthweights that were previously incompatible with life became 'in need' only when the technology of neonatal intensive care allowed them to be saved. Need is clearly a dynamic concept. As the pace of technological advance is unlikely to decrease, the gap between met need (what we are achieving) and total need (what we could achieve in a world of infinite resources) will widen. Constantly increasing funding is therefore needed just to keep the gap from widening further and as long as society has other needs as well (for education, defence, law and order, etc., not to mention private consumption needs) closing the health needs gap completely will not be possible.

As a result of this growing acceptance of scarcity, explicit prioritisation is becoming an increasingly common feature of the British NHS. In recent years several Health Authorities have gone so far as to remove certain interventions such as tattoo removal, cosmetic surgery or gender reorientation from the list of services which they will fund and others such as fertility treatment are currently being considered.

Shifting the focus from health services (effort/activity) to health (output/achievement)

Health economic thinking is based on the idea that as a society we value health and are thus willing to divert resources from the production of other valued things to its production. Viewed this way, the objective of any health service is better described in terms of health achievement than as the provision of health services. While ineffective interventions are clearly a waste of resources, effective interventions can vary enormously with regard to how much health they produce and how efficiently they produce it.

The introduction of economic thinking to health policy requires such a shift in focus from activity to achievement. This shift appeared formally for the first time in England with the strategy document The Health of the Nation[6] and in Wales with Strategic Intent and Direction for Wales[7]. Both documents had a health focus and with targets set in terms of health gain rather than activity.

The advantage of this approach can be illustrated using the Welsh example. Here, the strategy was given additional weight by instructions from Welsh Office for all Districts to set up multi-disciplinary 'health gain teams' for each of the 'health gain areas' identified in the document. Each area covered the full range of services relevant to that area. For example, the cancer area would include every type of activity that could produce cancer health gain including primary and secondary prevention as well as treatment of existing illness in the community, and in primary care as well as hospitals. This allowed Districts to concentrate on the needs of a group — including those at risk — the full range of interventions available to increase health in that group and the relative efficiency of one intervention *vis-à-vis* another.

Mid Glamorgan was the first District to make formal use of an economic framework for intra-area resource reallocation across the full range of health areas. A series of 'marginal analysis' exercises were conducted. Priority investments were identified together with areas for disinvestment which would free resources to support the investments on the principle that every investment would involve a marginal gain in health benefit and every disinvestment would involve a marginal loss of health benefit. If candidates for investment and disinvestment could be found so that the marginal gain could exceed the marginal loss, then an overall health gain would be identified at no net increase in cost. The result was a **resource neutral** shift in the balance of expenditure which, it was agreed, represented a more beneficial (health gaining) use of existing resources and hence an improvement in efficiency.[8]

Initiatives to raise awareness of opportunity cost

According to economic thinking, all resource commitments incur opportunity costs. Efficiency is pursued by comparing the anticipated benefits from any resource commitment against the benefits that will have to be foregone. In the past, the pursuit of efficiency was hampered by the fact that those who made the decisions had little incentive to consider opportunity cost. Indeed there has been a long tradition of clinician hostility to the idea on the grounds that it is unethical to take 'cost' into account when considering patients' health[9].

Clinical budgeting

An early UK attempt to introduce opportunity cost considerations in resource allocation decision-making was the introduction in the 1980s of 'clinical budgeting' in hospitals. Traditionally, budgets had been allocated to specific hospital functions such as pharmacy, radiography and physiotherapy. One major disadvantage to this system was that the people responsible for managing the functional budgets were not the ones who generated the costs. For example, chief pharmacists had only limited influence over the hospital doctors who prescribed the drugs — and doctors had little concern for the budgetary consequences of their prescribing. A second problem was that planning — including priority setting — had never been undertaken on a functional basis but rather on a client group or a disease group basis. The idea behind clinical budgeting was that 'clinical directorates' would be set up around clinical services (e.g. cardiology or paediatrics). Directorates would be headed by senior clinicians who would have responsibility for a budget from which functional inputs would be 'charged'.

Under the old system consultants wanting a new piece of equipment would base the request solely on anticipated benefit. Under the new system they would also have to convince their clinical colleagues that these anticipated benefits will outweigh other benefits that will have to be foregone because the money will no longer be available for these other uses. This system became known as the Resource Management Initiative and was successfully in place in many hospitals before the introduction of the 'internal market' in 1991.

Increasing competition by creating internal markets

The principles of economics can be applied in any political context. The policies which emerge, however, cannot be considered independently of the political setting within which they were developed. In the UK, the Conservative Party came to power in 1979 committed to an ideology of reducing government interference in all aspects of life. From an economic perspective this involves a preference for leaving the problems of resource allocation and output distribution to market forces — essentially the interplay of supply and demand. At the same time the Government pledged itself to retaining the NHS as a publicly funded, zero price at point of use service. The use of market forces as a means of introducing health economic thinking in the UK health service must be seen in this context.

The Labour Party has recently formed a new government committed to abolishing the internal market. At the time of writing, no indications have as yet been given as to how this will be done, or what will replace the internal market.

Very briefly, introducing an internal market involved giving Health Authorities responsibility for assessing the needs of a defined population and for **purchasing** healthcare services out of a fixed budget to meet those needs. Hospital and other **providers** of healthcare became NHS Trusts or Directly Managed Units of the Health Authorities. In either case, they earn income by selling healthcare services and that income is used to pay their staff and cover other costs.

One of the main objectives of the change was to increase *technical efficiency* by making providers compete with each other for business. According to the basic economic principles of market forces, competition provides an incentive for firms to find more efficient production methods i.e. methods which allow unit costs to fall. Lower unit costs allow firms to increase sales by lowering prices while still allowing profit to be made. Inefficient firms will go out of business as price falls below their unit costs. There is thus a constant drive for all firms to seek to be as technically efficient as possible.

There are however, many features of healthcare which make it unlikely that such a simple analysis would describe provider behaviour. In the case of new technologies for example, Rutten and Haan[1] have stated;

> "Managers of healthcare institutions are expected to keep a clear eye on the efficiency of new technologies, but in practice they value advanced technologies in the hospital as a way of increasing the attractiveness of their institution and in directing patient flow."

Similarly, Robinson and Luft[10] have observed that in the United States,

> "increased competition among hospitals for patients will take the form of

inflationary increases in the technological intensity of hospital services or a 'medical arms race', rather than price reductions aimed at patients."

The extent to which technical efficiency in the UK improves as a result of the introduction of an internal market remains to be seen. A second idea behind the change, however, was that an internal market would increase *allocative efficiency* on the basis of the following economic arguments.

Purchasers will realise that their budgets are insufficient to buy enough healthcare to fully meet the needs of the population they serve. This will increase their awareness of opportunity cost as it will become evident that more spent on one group of patients leaves less in the budget to spend on others. The 'cost' of one patient's health improvement will thus be seen in terms of other patients' potential health improvement foregone. This will encourage allocative efficiency, as one of a purchaser's main objectives will be to maximise the total health benefit for the population they serve.

It would appear that this change in purchaser's thinking is taking place. Reallocations of resources away from certain services, for example tattoo removal or gender re-orientation, are being defended with reference to the (more highly valued) needs of others, rather than by claiming that those receiving these services don't benefit, or simply that "we can't afford them".

THE IMPACT OF ECONOMIC EVALUATIONS ON POLICY AND CLINICAL DECISION-MAKING

The number of economic evaluations has increased dramatically in recent years from 111 applied studies in 1992 to 1053 in 1996.[11]

While it is encouraging to see the number of economic studies increasing, a more important question is what influence these studies are having on health policy and resource allocation decision-making. Unfortunately, it is notoriously difficult to examine the extent to which studies influence practice by simply looking at cause and effect. As Selby Smith[12] has pointed out

"... the relationship between research and public sector decision-making is rarely direct and immediate. The relationship tends rather to be interactive, cumulative and related to a range of other variables. The simple view that a particular research study results (or does not result) in a particular decision, action or use is generally wrong." p:241.

Recently, Rutten and Drummond[13] claimed that

"decision-makers often despair about their lack of ability to influence the diffusion and use of health technologies" (p:88)

9

and argued that in reality the range of available options is considerable. They identified eight policy instruments which they felt could be influenced by the information from economic appraisal. These were:

- planning specialist facilities — for example using economic information to inform on optimum size of facilities and implications for patient borne costs
- excluding technologies from public reimbursement — for example via the methods used in Australia and Canada for restricting lists of drugs to those shown to be cost effective (see below)
- reforming payment schemes for healthcare institutions — for example by adapting the diagnostic related group (DRG) reimbursement scheme operated by Medicare in the USA to take account of evidence of cost-effectiveness of alternative treatments
- encouraging budgetary reform within institutions — for example to inform the UK's system of clinical budgeting (see above)
- changing payment systems for healthcare professionals — for example to correct any existing incentives in fee-for-service payment systems which encourage inappropriate use of technologies
- developing medical audit — especially for the production of guidelines
- introducing co-payment for users — possibly by offering patients the opportunity to pay an excess charge if they wish to have a non-cost effective drug prescribed
- encouraging competitive arrangements in healthcare systems — for example by providing information to help the UK NHS internal market (see above)

The demand for and supply of economic evaluations

Clearly, the importance of each policy instrument will vary between countries depending on a host of factors. Evidence suggests that the impact of economic evaluation on health policy varies considerably between countries and depends to a large extent on the institutions which exist and the nature of the 'interactive' relationship mentioned above.

There is also a somewhat circular momentum that can be set in place. In the case of the UK for example, one effect of recent organisational changes, has been an increase in the demand for evidence of cost effectiveness. The UK bodies which fund health services research have responded by emphasising the need to address economic issues, where appropriate, in the design of studies submitted to them for funding. This in turn will increase the amount of cost effectiveness evidence available to help relevant audiences in their pursuit of greater efficiency.

It is also possible that the production of cost effectiveness evidence can itself give momentum to the cycle. In her review of the impact of economic appraisals in Denmark, Alban[14] stated

"However, as this article stresses, economic appraisals have also been used to

introduce the economic appraisal approach as a way of thinking, as a road to efficiency within the health services. This has led to the incorporation of economic appraisals into committee work ...., the issuing of guidelines to local health authorities including efficiency, and to some acceptance of the efficiency term among health professionals." (p:1647)

Presumably the greater the acceptance of the need for efficiency, the greater will be the demand for relevant information to help in the pursuit of this aim.

In the Netherlands, the Health Insurance and Executive Board (HEIB) has placed economic evaluation firmly in its strategy. Healthcare in the Netherlands operates under a system of compulsory insurance which covers the whole population for chronic care and about 60% for acute care. The remaining 40% rely on private insurance for acute care. HEIB plays a major role in regulating prices and quantity of services financed by either insurance system.

Conventionally, interventions were added to existing benefit packages simply on the basis of whether or not they were accepted by the medical profession. A growing awareness of resource scarcity in the mid 1980s led HEIB to introduce a strategy which would give it more control and, where appropriate, allow efficiency issues to influence what was and what was not to be included in the packages. The addition of new technologies to the benefit packages would now be conditional on the results of a medical technology assessment. This was later extended to strengthen the importance of evidence of cost-effectiveness in that assessment.

In order to help with policy making, HEIB together with the Ministries of Health and Education and Science funded an evaluation programme in 1988 which contained a strong element of economic appraisal. After five years, an assessment of the scheme concluded that economic evaluations conducted as part of the evaluation programme were beginning to contribute to the decisions of the government and were being used in professional agreements which formulate treatment protocols[15]. While in the past HEIB has asked for evidence of cost-effectiveness prior to the reimbursement of some new drugs, the authors predicted that the Netherlands was likely follow the lead of Australia and Canada in using economic appraisal to determine the reimbursement of drugs.

The experience of other countries would seem to confirm that economic appraisal has had a greater effect on policy than on clinical decision-making. In Denmark, Alban[14] concluded

"The use of economic appraisals in Denmark has not yet caught on at the clinical decision-making level" (p:1651)

but pointed out that at policy level economic appraisals can have a major influence if those to whom the appraisals are directed are also involved in the process. In Australia, a similar situation was found with the effect economic appraisal results on policy apparently much more evident than on clinical decision-making[16].

It is evident that different countries have different ideas about whether, to what extent and how results of economic studies should influence policy and decision-making. This is not surprising given the variations in systems of healthcare delivery and differences in socio-economic and political make up.

It is also true that interpretation of the results must be dependent on relevant local consideration. When commenting on how economic evaluations of drugs can influence resource allocation decisions, Buxton[17] stated

> "The decision-context, local costs, differences in existing practice, different potential alternative uses of available resources, local values — each or any one might logically lead to a different local view as to whether, and in what circumstances a drug was cost-effective. Cost-effectiveness is not an inherent feature of the drug's pharmacodynamics but of the way a drug impacts within the context of a particular healthcare system." (p:24)

Why has economic evaluation had so little influence on clinical decision-making? Medical ethics versus social ethics

It is natural for doctors and other health professionals to want to do what is best for their patients. Where patients have to pay directly for the full cost of their treatments, the doctor will, of course, also have to take cost into consideration when making decisions about how to manage the patient.

Direct payment at point of use, however, is not a common means of health service delivery even in systems which are essentially private. In the United States, for example there is still a large element of public provision, and most of those not eligible are covered by occupational based or other insurance schemes. Where patients do not pay directly for treatment, then the doctor's desire to consider costs will be much reduced when making decisions about patient management.

Doctors have always practised under a system of medical ethics which has conventionally focused on the two ethical theories of 'virtue' and 'duty'[18]. These are *individualistic* ethics based on the doctor's responsibility for the individual patient and a guiding principle has long been that it is unethical to do anything which does more harm than good.

More recently, and due to an increasing awareness of scarcity of resources, ethicists have begun to focus on a third ethical theory; that of the 'common good'[2]. This is a *social* ethic based on responsibility for the health of populations. Here the guiding principle of only doing those things which do more good than harm still applies, but the terms are used from a social perspective. On this basis any intervention which yields only small benefit to the patient but involves large opportunity costs (sacrifices) elsewhere, will from a social perspective be doing more harm than good.

Given that a doctor's first duty will inevitably be to his or her patient, the reluctance of the medical profession to enthusiastically endorse social ethics is hardly surprising. Accordingly a doctor's preference for making clinical decisions on the basis evidence of effective rather than cost-effectiveness is equally understandable.

Nevertheless, those responsible for health policy making and for broad resource allocation decisions have to see their duty as being to the whole population — including potential future consumers of healthcare. A decision to put additional resources into developing neonatal intensive care units will be made before any of the babies who will benefit from them have been conceived. Similarly it is not possible to identify the individuals who will benefit from increasing the level of resources going to mass screening or immunisation campaigns.

Reconciling individual and social ethics. The case of General Practitioner fundholding

There are many ways that clinicians can be encouraged to become more cost effective and hence to be more dependent on the results of economic evaluations. Guidelines are an obvious example but more fundamental structural changes can also bring about the desired change.

The UK reforms which brought in an internal market also introduced a system of general practice fundholding whereby general practitioners would take on essentially the same role as Health Authorities i.e. they would be given a budget out of which they would purchase healthcare for their own patients. The principles were the same as for purchasing health authorities only here it would be more likely that the GP would have a more personal knowledge of the needs of his or her patients. Thus when choosing between alternative drugs, a non-fundholder would consider relative effectiveness and prescribe the drug which is best for the patient. A fundholder would also take account of differences in cost and question whether the extra cost of the more effective drug can be justified by the extra effectiveness, given the notion of opportunity cost. Put another way, only the fundholder would want to know which drug is more cost-effective.

The importance of dissemination

Any country which wishes to see information from economic studies used in clinical decision-making will first have to ensure that such information is brought to the attention of the relevant people. A recent survey[19] of the impact of economic appraisals on decision-making in 10 European Union countries identified four principal means of disseminating results as shown in **Table 1**.

The most striking feature of the table is that those studies whose results were the subject of newspaper and other media reports were far more likely to have an impact on decision-making than where dissemination was by any other means. The authors point out that this could be due to many factors including the fact that media coverage reaches a greater number of relevant decision-makers or that the topics addressed by media reported studies were more politically sensitive or of greater public concern. In addition they propose that the greater impact may have been due to the simple fact that mass media reports tend to be less technical and thus easier to understand. This important point is discussed over.

Table 1: Methods of dissemination of results		
	Number (%) of studies*	% of studies having having an impact
Publication	55 (74)	29
Presentation at seminar/conference	33 (72)	39
Newspaper/media	10 (20)	80
Newsletter	23 (77)	26
* most studies used more than one method of dissemination		
Source[19]		

Perhaps more important, however, than the results of individual and hence potentially rogue studies, is information from systematic reviews which summarise what is known, express it in non-technical language and preferably include some form of critical analysis.

In January 1994 the UK NHS Centre for Reviews and Dissemination (CRD) was established specifically to carry out and commission reviews of effectiveness and cost effectiveness, maintain a database of past and ongoing reviews, and provide a mechanism whereby information could be efficiently disseminated to relevant audiences[20].

CRD reviews cover both clinical and organisational issues. In addition to its database on reviews of clinical effectiveness, CRD maintains a database specific to economic evaluations. It conducts its dissemination role mainly through two regular publications; *Effective Healthcare* and *Effectiveness Matters* and through summaries written for publications which are read by clinicians and health service managers.

Compulsory economic evaluation: the ultimate measure

The most extreme way of ensuring that economic evaluations are undertaken and that the results impact on service delivery is to make economic appraisal a compulsory part of the process of getting the intervention approved for practice. There are two recent examples where pharmacoeconomic evaluations have for all intents and purposes been made mandatory.

Australia

Australia was the first country to introduce an element of compulsion. In order to be eligible for public reimbursement, pharmaceutical products must be included on the Pharmaceutical Benefits Schedule list. Since January 1993, new products could only be added to the list if the submission for listing included the results of a pharmacoeconomic evaluation. While the issue of public reimbursement is strictly independent of the process of licensing,

"... public subsidy is an essential requirement for the successful marketing of most products".[21]

Thus while not a requirement for licensing, economic evaluation essentially became compulsory.

The process involves making a submission to the Pharmaceutical Benefits Advisory Committee (PBAC) who recommend or do not recommend, listing. The PBAC also uses the results of the study to determine whether or not the drug is cost-effective at the submitted price and can also recommend a range within which the drug would be cost effective. This information is passed on to the Pharmaceutical Benefits Pricing Authority and is used together with other factors to determine the price at which the product is listed.

Clearly, in order to make such judgements, PBAC require that the economic evaluations be undertaken in a consistent matter. Guidelines produced in 1992 (revised in 1995) specify the types of clinical and economic data that need to be collected, how they should be analysed and how the results should be presented[22].

Canada

In 1995, the Canadian province of Ontario made the submission of an economic/ pharmacoeconomic evaluation — or justification for why such an evaluation was absent — a requirement for getting new pharmaceuticals listed in the Provincial formulary and for obtaining a reimbursement price. Again, judgements about the economic aspects of the drug could only be made if the evaluations were conducted in a consistent manner and so in the previous year Ontario issued guidelines on how to conduct an economic appraisals of drugs[23].

In Canada, healthcare is a provincial matter and each province has a separate healthcare system. In order to assist other provinces who might wish to follow the Ontario lead, the Canadian Central Co-ordinating Office for Health Technology Assessment (CCOHTA) issued their own guidelines which could be used in any other province which wished to follow Ontario's lead[24].

CONCLUSION

New technologies — including pharmaceuticals — have greatly increased the capacity of healthcare systems to produce health benefits, but have at the same time contributed to rapidly rising costs. This in turn has increased awareness of the need to make resource allocation choices, of the opportunity costs associated with every resource commitment, and of the need to ensure that policies and organisational structures are conducive to the pursuit of efficiency.

The impact of health economics as a way of thinking appears to have been much greater at the level of policy and organisation than it has been at the level of clinical decision-making. This is understandable given the doctor's natural concern for the welfare of the individual patient and the planner/policy maker's concern for populations. Nevertheless, examples such as clinical budgeting and general practitioner fundholding in the UK have shown that it is possible to influence clinical decision-making by creating an environment conducive to economic thinking. Effective systems of critical review and dissemination are a prerequisite to successful use of economic thinking at this level. Clinical guidelines which take account of economic issues are helpful as well.

The more policies and structures are set in place which use economic thinking, the greater will be the pressure on the research community to provide the required economic information. Policy measures such as making economic evaluation a requirement for getting a drug on a reimbursement list are an extreme way of ensuring that pharmacoeconomic evaluations get undertaken and their results used.

This chapter has not addressed a number of issues which arguably are relevant. For example there is an ongoing debate concerning the balance of economic studies which produce data alongside clinical trials, and those which use the results of trials and other information to build models. Further there are specific problems about the methodologies employed and the issue of who funds/conducts the evaluations. These issues will be addressed in subsequent chapters.

References

1. Rutten F and Haan G. (1990) Cost effective use of medical technology: regulatory instruments and economic incentives. In Jonsson B, Rutten F, and Vang J. (eds) *Policy Making in Healthcare: Changing Goals and New Tools.* Linköping Collaborating Centre, Linköping.
2. Mooney G. (1992) *Economics, Medicine and Healthcare* (2nd ed) Wheatsheaf, Hemel Hempstead.
3. World Health Organisation (1958) *The Constitution of the World Health Organisation: Annex 1.* The First Ten Years of the World Health Organisation. Geneva.
4. Sheldon T and Vanoli A. (1997) Providing research intelligence to the NHS: the role of the NHS Centre for Reviews and Dissemination. in Towse A (ed) *Guidelines for the Economic Evaluation of Pharmaceuticals.* Office of Health Economics, London.
5. Smith, R (1993) News Report. *British Medical Journal;* **306:**737.
6. Department of Health. (1991) *Health of the Nation* HMSO
7. Welsh Office. (1989) *Strategic Intent and Direction for Wales.* Welsh Health Planning Forum. Cardiff
8. Cohen D. (1994) Marginal Analysis in practice: an alternative to needs assessment for contracting healthcare. *British Medical Journal.* **309:** 781–5.
9. Loewy EL, (1980) Letter. *New England Journal of Medicine* **302,** 1970.
10. Robinson J and Luft J. (1985) The impact of hospital market structure. *Journal of Health Economics* **4:** 333–356.
11. Pritchard, C. (1998) Trends in Economic Evaluation. Office of Health Economics, London.
12. Selby Smith C. (1994) From research to action: Does economic evaluation affect health policy or practice? In Jonsson B, Rutten F, and Vang J. (eds) *Policy Making in Healthcare: Changing Goals and New Tools.* Linköping Collaborating Centre, Linköping.
13. Rutten F and Drummond D. (1994) *Making Decisions about Health Technologies: A Cost Effectiveness Perspective.* University of York, Centre for Health Economics. York.
14. Alban A (1994) The role of economic appraisal in Denmark. *Social Science and Medicine* **38** (12) 1647–1652.
15. Rutten F and van der Linden J. Economic appraisal in health insurance system: the case of the Netherlands. *Social Science and Medicine* **38(12)** 1607–1612.

16. Selby Smith C, Hailey D and Drummond M. (1994) The role of economic appraisal in health technology assessment: the Australian case. *Social Science and Medicine* **38(12)** 1653–1662.
17. Buxton M. (1997) The Canadian experience: Step change or gradual evolution? in Towse A (ed) *Guidelines for the Economic Evaluation of Pharmaceuticals.* Office of Health Economics, London.
18. Jonsen A and Hellegers A.(1987) Conceptual foundations for an ethics of medical care. in Tancredi L. (ed) *Ethics of Healthcare.* National Academy of Sciences. Washington.
19. Davies L, Coyle D and Drummond M.(1994) Current status of economic appraisal of health technology in the European Community: Report of the Network. *Social Science and Medicine* **38**(12) 1601–1607
20. Glanville J. (1994) Evidence based practice: the role of the NHS Centre for Reviews and dissemination. *Health Libraries Review* **11,** 243–251.
21. Drummond M. and Aristedes M. (1997) The Australian cost effectiveness guidelines: An update. in Towse A (ed) *Guidelines for the Economic Evaluation of Pharmaceuticals.* Office of Health Economics, London.
22. Commonwealth of Australia. (1992) *Guidelines for the pharmaceutical industry on preparation of submissions to the Pharmaceutical Benefits Advisory Committee: including submissions involving economic analyses.* Canberra. Australian Government Printing Office. (revised 1995)
23. Ministry of Health .(1994) *Ontario Guidelines for Economic Analysis of Pharmaceutical Products.* Ministry of Health Toronto.
24. CCOHTA. (1994) *Guidelines for Economic Evaluation of Pharmaceuticals: Canada.* Canadian Coordinating Office for Health Technology Assessment, Ottawa.

2

Pharmacoeconomics: what's in a name?

M Malek

INTRODUCTION

It is nearly 15 years since the term pharmacoeconomics was used first in industry and then in academic departments around the world. Nowadays it is being used interchangeably with the likes of 'health economics', 'outcomes research', 'policy research' and a few more depending on who is using it and the context in which it is being used. In fact, the emergence of pharmacoeconomics as an independent discipline is a bit like that of Management during the 1960s and 1970s. Indeed it is the hallmark of all postmodern areas of enquiry which fall between two (or more) established disciplines. Management as a discipline is firmly based within other social and behavioural sciences, like economics, sociology and psychology, to mention but a few. Within academia Management was received with extreme suspicion and outright hostility by the 'mainstream' economists. The general view was that "what is academically respectable in Management we already teach in economics in the form of industrial and/or business economics, and what we don't teach is not worth teaching". Most of these 'new' areas are 'applied' disciplines with the specific condition that more than any other area of enquiry they are subject to endorsements of the 'customers'. As such, the main justification, indeed their raison d'être, is their 'relevance' to the immediate needs of their customers. Their research is 'near market' research and entirely customer driven whose experience of the single established discipline handling their problem successfully has been rather disappointing and have been attracted by the multi-disciplinary, multi-functionality of the new discipline.

The tensions created by the new discipline is both exciting and constructive or, in Schumpetrian terminology, constructively destructive as it opens up the frontiers which hitherto had remained under-explored or totally ignored. But at the same time it also raises the uncomfortable issues associated with the 'identity', 'ownership' and 'genealogy' of the new arrival. The hotly contested areas are the 'boundaries' of the enquiry and the methodology adopted by the new disciplines.

All these were present when pharmacoeconomics emerged in the early 1980s, and some of them are still the subject of heated debates.

PHARMACOECONOMICS: THE BIRTH

As a discipline pharmacoeconomics had a difficult birth. It was one of the rare occasions when the perceived needs of the public sector and industry conjecturally coincided and the academia had the ability to step in and satisfy the need. In its early days of development it was virtually indistinguishable from health economics. Both the industry and the public health sector became interested in the development and application of pharmacoeconomics/health economics for their own particular needs. The government/public sector and the third party payers were interested because of the need for cost containment and the potential of economic evaluation to curb the costs and a means to delay the use of 'inappropriate' and 'expensive' health technology, where increase in the marginal effectiveness are not large enough to justify the premium price claimed by the new products. The industry saw this as an additional marketing weapon in an increasingly competitive market. At this point narrowly defined pharmacoeconomics was synonymously used as economic evaluation.

Meanwhile within the industry and academia there were voices of dissent against this narrow definition of pharmacoeconomics. The argument, quite justifiably in my opinion, was that if pharmacoeconomics is the same as economic evaluation why should we bother to have a new terminology. The feeling was that any meaningful definition of pharmacoeconomics should be broad enough to encompass the entire spectrum of the value chain in the production, distribution, and utilisation of the pharmaceutical products and devices. The most comprehensive remit maintained:

"Pharmacoeconomics is the study of how people and society end up choosing to employ scarce productive resources that could have alternative uses, to produce various drugs and other pharmaceutical products and distribute them among various people and groups in society to enhance quantity and quality of life. It analyses the costs and benefits of improving patterns of resource allocation in production, distribution and consumption of such products." [1]

This definition is simply application (or if you wish plagiarism!) of Samuelson's celebrated definition of economics as applied to the pharmaceutical products and devices. From the point of view of the consumers (patients, Government, third party payers etc.), this definition encompasses the narrow definition and deals with the questions of economically rational prescribing. Indeed one could argue that this perspective enables governments to make decisions which are 'locally' optimal depending on the status of their ethical pharmaceutical industry and its contribution to the local treasury. Seen from this viewpoint we can see, for example, that the attitudes of both the British and Australian governments are locally 'optimal', although they are distinctly at the opposite ends of the spectrum.

20

From the industry's point of view, given the complexity and the lead-time involved in the process of the drug development, it would be vital to incorporate and use pharmacoeconomic data from the start. This would require the 'economic dossier' of the drug to accompany the medical counterpart throughout the entire life cycle of the drug (see **Figure 1**). The nature of pharmacoeconomics advice, contribution and skills of those involved according to this definition would vary and go beyond those of the health economics. The internal customers for

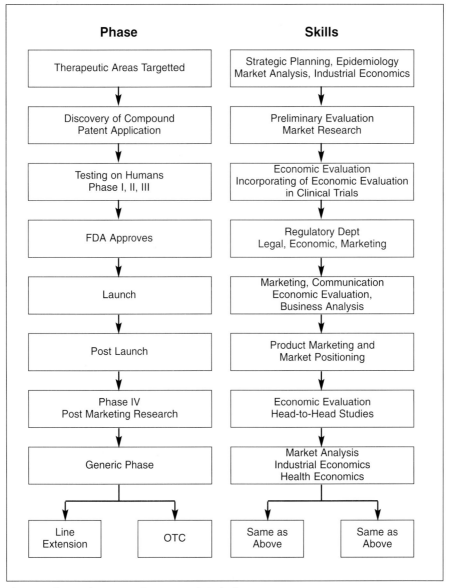

Figure 1: Phases of Drug Development and Marketing

pharmacoeconomics research will be also different and include those engaged in the strategic planning, corporate research and development, corporate marketing, operational marketing as well as all those involved at the consumer end of the value chain.[2] Pharmacoeconomic models (and not just economic evaluation models) are now being used as a tool for portfolio management in pharmaceutical companies. A recent survey of 28 pharmaceutical companies shows that only four companies regarded health economics data as being of great benefit or essential when managing pre-clinical development.[3] In contrast pharmacoeconomic models (broad definition) are used to provide the information that justifies the level of investment in projects. Pharmacoeconomics influences research and development investment decisions as part of the marketing mix from the very beginning when robust decisions are required to decide whether to enter into a therapeutic area or not. This influence remains through the whole process of drug development and marketing. The skill-mix requirements of the pharmacoeconomic team changes and only at the consumer end coincides with that of health economics (see **Figures 1** and **2**).

SKILL REQUIREMENTS

From the point of view of the pharmaceutical companies, pharmacoeconomics is at the interface between research and development and marketing. The interface is at the organisational as well as the strategic levels and covers the entire product lifecycle as well as scientific and commercial planning skills. As the process of drug development proceeds there are several audiences with different interests asking different questions.[4] The pharmaceutical industry was notoriously lacking a department which would bring different interest groups together. This was especially more visible in the diametrically opposed divisions of research and development on the scientific end and sales and marketing at the other end. The question posed by the research and development departments was whether a chemical compound works and if it does what is its safety and efficacy profile. On the other hand the marketing departments were concerned with commercial issues and the two groups were unaware and at times uninterested in knowing the problems facing the other party. Pharmacoeconomics aims to bridge this gap and answer different questions posed on the way.

As the relevant questions change, different tools/skills are deployed to answer the requirements of the internal and external customers of pharmacoeconomic studies (see **Figures 1** and **2**). The skills required at the early stages when the therapeutic areas are targeted are that of epidemiologist, market analyst and portfolio managers. The decision has to fit in with the long-term strategy of the pharmaceutical company and the team should include an expert in strategic management and scenario analysis. As we move through Phase I/II the questions asked by the internal customers can be answered through simple modelling and the quality of life scales. The expertise required is that of a health economist and/or a modeller.

In Phases IIIa and IIIb the objective of the pharmacoeconomic study is to support the pricing and marketing strategy. To this end, the economic evaluations need to be incorporated into the clinical trials. While the early parts of the strategy combine

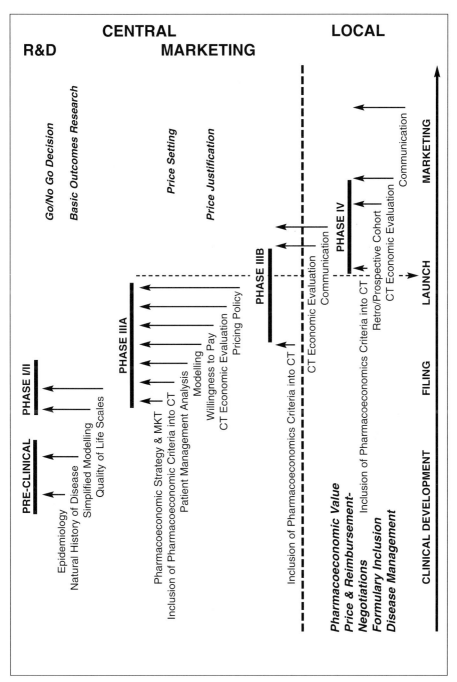

Figure 2: Pharmacoeconomic objectives and tools will vary and complement each other during the life of the product.

strategic market research and scientific interface, the latter parts of pre-launch strategy will need to anticipate regulatory and experimental medical attitudes. Post-launch tactics revolve around an understanding of market dynamics. The skills required are those of industrial and health economics, regulatory affairs and marketing.

Given the partial overlap between health economics and pharmacoeconomics it is understandable why they have been used interchangeably at the consumer end of the product lifestyle. However, the skills required from a pharmacoeconomic division properly constituted within a pharmaceutical company are much broader, more comprehensive than can ever be met by health economists. This partially explains why the term has almost always been interpreted in a 'narrow' context as it would be easier for an individual to acquire the expertise of a health economist, than the pharmacoeconomics which by its very nature is multi-disciplinary and multi-functional.[5]

PHARMACOECONOMICS: THE FUTURE AND THE RESEARCH AGENDA

There is an old Aristotelian principle in which acts are to be distinguished by their respective objects, powers are known by their acts, and substances are defined by their powers.[6] In other words what people (and departments, organisations, institutions,…) do actually defines what they are. Given the applied nature of pharmacoeconomics, what is happening in the pharmaceutical industry and the way pharmacoeconomics is placed within the pharmaceutical companies and the power position of the relevant departments also defines the remit and functional utility of the discipline. Pharmaceutical companies have been quick to recognise the relevance of pharmacoeconomic analysis to strategic planning, both in early phases of drug development and in determining the likely market of future drugs.[7] The academic community, on the other hand, has been slow to recognise either the complexity of factors determining drug pricing or the potential for systematic research in this area. The challenge is to do academic research which is also relevant for managerial decision-making.

REFERENCES

1. Malek, M. 'Pharmacoeconomics: Introduction', *The Pharmaceutical Journal,* Vol. 256, November 1996, pp.759–761.
2. Malek, M. 'Pharmacoeconomics', *Pharmaceutical Forum*, Spring 1995, pp.17–19.
3. See *Pharmacoeconomics and Outcomes News* **189**: 3–4, 21 November 1998 and **190**: 3–4, 28 November 1998 and **191**: 3–4, 5 December 1998.
4. Davey, P. and Malek, M., 1994. 'The impact of pharmacoeconomics on the practitioner and the patient', *PharmacoEconomics* 6(4) pp.298–309.
5. Davey, P., Malek, M. Dodd, T. *et al.* 'Pharmacoeconomics and Drug Prescribing', in Speight, T.M. and Holfora, N.H.G. (eds), *Avery's Drug Treatment,* Auckland 1996, 4th Edition, pp.393–422.
6. Haldane, J., 'Rational and Other Animals', in O'Hear, A. (ed), *Verstehen and Human Understanding,* Cambridge: Cambridge University Press 1996.
7. Clemense, K., Garrison Jr, L.P., Jones, A. *et al.* 1993. 'Strategic Use of Pharmacoeconomic Research in Early Drug Development and Global Pricing', *PharmacoEconomics*, **4**: 315–22.

3

Pharmacoeconomic education in schools of pharmacy

KL Rascati, JR Draugalis, TM Connor and DA Sclar

INTRODUCTION

Pharmacoeconomic (PE) education takes place in many settings by many disciplines. For example, pharmacoeconomic education is offered by the University of York Centre for Health Economics (UK), the McMaster University Faculty of Health Sciences (Canada), and the Leonard Davis Institute of Health Economics (US), to name a few. One association, the International Society for Pharmacoeconomics and Outcomes Research (ISPOR) recently supplied a profile of its members.[1] Educational degrees of ISPOR members were in statistics, nursing, accounting, economics, business administration, public health and other health sciences. Doctoral degrees were in medicine, philosophy, pharmacy, public health, and jurisprudence. The most prevalent degrees were PhD (17%), MS (9%), PharmD (9%) and MD (7%). Therefore, while the authors realise a wide variety of sources offer pharmacoeconomic education, the focus of this chapter is on the pharmacoeconomic education that is offered by colleges or schools of pharmacy.

In 1994, the American Pharmaceutical Association (APhA) held an invitational conference to address six key questions relating to outcomes research.[2] One of these questions was "What are the training needs for developing research skills in pharmaceutical outcomes research?" Some highlights from the discussion of this question include:

1 recommended areas of study include biostatistics, health behaviour, epidemiology, economics, research design and methodologies, analysis and theory, and computer science;
2 skills should be taught via coursework in combination with other opportunities such as practicums;
3 multidisciplinary models are needed;
4 combination degrees (eg masters/fellowship programs) that go outside the

academic framework should be considered;

5   pharmaceutical industry should have a role in developing professionals; and
6   there is a danger of "conflict of interest" issues that should be addressed by exposing students to the concepts of scientific integrity.

A number of continuing education opportunities in pharmaceutical economics exist for practicing pharmacists including printed materials, home study programs, and meeting presentations.[3] The American College of Clinical Pharmacy offers an extensive four-module program titled "Pharmacoeconomics and Outcomes — Applications for Patient Care" while the American Society of Health-System Pharmacists initiated their "The Competitive Edge — Advanced Experiential Training in Conduction and Using Outcomes Studies" program in Fall 1997. These types of initiatives demonstrate that practicing pharmacists need pharmacoeconomic evaluation skills to practice contemporary pharmacy.

In a 1991 paper, Draugalis and Jones-Grizzle provided suggestions for incorporating pharmacoeconomic topics, until such a time when the entire course was deemed necessary.[4] Juergens *et al*[5] examined the level of pharmacy school training in statistical and analytical methods, with an emphasis on pharmacoeconomic issues such as cost-effectiveness analysis, cost-benefit analysis, cost-utility analysis, and quality of life issues. Surveys were sent to all US schools of pharmacy and an 83.8% response rate was achieved (62 of 74). Results indicated that 19.3% of Bachelor of Science (BS) programs and 32.8% of Doctor of Pharmacy (PharmD) programs provided training in pharmacoeconomic analyses in a required course, and an additional 36.1% of BS programs and 22.2% of PharmD programs provided this training in an elective course. About half of the schools planned to expand the scope of these programs in the next three years. Juergens and colleagues concluded that current education is not keeping pace with the skills needed to evaluate pharmacoeconomic literature. Subsequently, Kolassa[6] offered a rationale and syllabus for a basic course in pharmaceutical economics.

Researchers at The University of Arizona held an invitational conference in 1993 to address the roles of colleges of pharmacy in meeting industry's pharmacoeconomic needs.[7] As a result of this conference, surveys were sent to participants from 29 US colleges of pharmacy in order to estimate the number of graduate students being educated to fill this demand.[8] Survey responses indicated that in 1994, 92 individuals were enrolled in US graduate-level pharmacoeconomic education or training programs at 18 institutions and at least two schools planned to initiate graduate pharmacoeconomic programs within the year.

The research cited above suggests there is a high demand for individuals with pharmacoeconomic education and training, and that schools of pharmacy were planning to expand their programs to help fulfil this need. An updated survey of pharmacoeconomic education provided at the undergraduate level is needed to assess the trends. Also, a world-wide or international view of pharmacoeconomic education is warranted. Therefore, the purpose of this research was to assess and summarise pharmacoeconomic education offered in schools of pharmacy around the world in 1997.

METHODS

Sampling and Survey Methods

Due to time and resource constraints, the survey was primarily administered via electronic mail (e-mail). Dr David Temple, from The Welsh School of Pharmacy in the UK, maintains a website that includes a "World List of Pharmacy Schools".[9] Many of the schools on this list have electronic mail addresses or website addresses that may be used to contact someone at each school. The electronic addresses available from this website were used to survey schools of pharmacy outside the US. When an e-mail address was available for a school of pharmacy, this address was used. If no e-mail address was given but a website was listed, the authors contacted the website to locate an e-mail address of an appropriate respondent. In many cases the webmaster at the site was contacted with a request for an e-mail address for a contact at the school of pharmacy.

For US schools of pharmacy, the American Association of Colleges of Pharmacy (AACP) was contacted, and a current list of electronic mail addresses for Deans' offices of US Schools of Pharmacy was forwarded to the authors.[10] If an e-mail address was not listed in the AACP data, a facsimile (FAX) of the survey was sent to a faculty member at the school.

Surveys were sent electronically on June 16, 1997 and responses were included in the analyses if a reply was received by July 6, 1997. Because the results are descriptive in nature, no statistical tests were conducted.

Survey Questions

A definition of pharmacoeconomics was provided at the beginning of the survey. The definition chosen for this survey was "Pharmacoeconomics identifies, measures and compares the costs and consequences of pharmaceutical products and services".[11] The survey consisted of four main questions:

1   Does your school of pharmacy provide pharmacoeconomic education?
2   How many clock hours are devoted to pharmacoeconomic education?
3   Is this education part of the required or elective curriculum? and
4   How many students receive this education per year?

Examples of calculating 'clock hours' were given as: "If your school offers two lectures that are 90 minutes each, your response would be 3 clock hours. If your school offers a class that meets 3 hours a week for 15 weeks, your response would be 45 clock hours." Lastly, respondents were asked to provide any additional comments in the space provided at the end of the survey.

Surveys sent outside of the US asked respondents to answer the four main questions for two levels of students:

1   Professional-level and
2   Graduate-level

The US surveys asked respondents to answer these four main questions for three levels of students:

1   Bachelor of Science (BS) students
2   Doctor of Pharmacy (PharmD) students and
3   Graduate-level students (Master of Science [MS] or Doctor of Philosophy [PhD]) students.

In order to standardise the responses, the US data on BS and PharmD students were collapsed into 'Professional-level' responses. More detailed analysis for the US schools appears elsewhere.[12]

RESULTS

Respondents

Surveys were sent to 191 schools of pharmacy (112 Non-US, 79 US). Responses were received from a total of 98 schools for a 51.3 per cent response rate (41/112 = 36.6% Non-US; 57/79 = 72.2% US). **Table 1** shows the number of pharmacy schools contacted and the number of pharmacy schools responding for each country.

Question 1 — Does your school of pharmacy provide pharmacoeconomic education?

Of the 98 schools providing responses, 67 (68.4%) schools (17 Non-US [41.5%] and 50 US [87.7%]) indicated providing pharmacoeconomic education at some level. **Table 2** summarises the number of schools offering PE education at the professional and/or the graduate level. For US schools, if the school offered the program at the BS and/or PharmD level, they were categorised as providing PE education at the professional level.

Schools were counted as having PE education if the courses were available at the time of the study. In addition to the programs listed in **Table 2**, other respondents indicated PE education was planned to be added to their curriculum in the near future. Seven respondents indicated that some type of PE education would be added between now and the year 2000 (2 in 1998, 4 in 1999, and one in 2000).

Question 2 — How many clock hours are devoted to pharmacoeconomic education?

There was a wide range of answers for this question, and the distribution of responses was not normally distributed. Therefore the range, mean, standard deviation (SD) and median will be presented for each analysis.

In non-US schools, clock hours of PE education ranged from 1 to 100 hours for professional students. The mean number of hours was 17 (SD = 27), and the median

Table 1.

Country	Surveys sent	Responses	Country	Surveys sent	Responses
Argentina	1	1	Mali	1	0
Australia	5	3	N. Ireland	1	0
Austria	2	0	Netherlands	3	1
Belgium	7	0	New Zealand	1	1
Brazil	3	2	Norway	2	1
Canada	9	3	Poland	1	0
Chile	1	0	Portugal	2	0
Costa Rica	1	1	S. Korea	3	0
Denmark	1	1	Scotland	2	1
Egypt	1	0	Slovakia	1	0
Finland	3	0	Slovenia	1	0
France	5	3	Spain	6	2
Germany	7	5	Sudan	1	0
Greece	1	0	Sweden	1	1
Guatemala	1	1	Switzerland	3	1
England	10	4	Taiwan	2	1
Hong Kong	1	0	Thailand	2	1
Hungary	1	1	Turkey	2	1
Iceland	1	0	Uruguay	1	0
Indonesia	1	0	Wales	1	1
Italy	9	1			
Kuwait	1	0	Non US	112	41
Lebanon	1	1	US	79	57
Malaysia	2	2	**Total**	**191**	**98**

Table 2.

Country	n	Professional	Graduate	Country	n	Professional	Graduate
Argentina	1	Yes	No	Norway	1	Yes	Yes
Australia	1	No	Yes	Scotland	1	Yes	Yes
Canada	2	Yes	Yes	Sweden	1	Yes	Yes
Denmark	1	No	Yes	Wales	1	Yes	Yes
England	3	Yes	Yes				
Guatemala	1	No	Yes	Non US	17	13	15
Hungary	1	No	Yes	US	17	Yes	No
Malaysia	1	Yes	No		33	Yes	Yes
Malaysia	1	Yes	Yes	**Total**	**67**	**63**	**48**
New Zealand	1	Yes	Yes				

was 10 hours. For non-US graduate programs the hours ranged from 2 to 70, with a mean of 27 (SD = 21) and a median of 23 hours.

For US schools the numbers of clock hours spent on professional PE education ranged from 2 to 160 hours, with a mean of 26 hours (SD = 26) and a median of 16 hours. For US graduate programs, the clock hours ranged from 15 to 140, with a mean of 48 (SD = 27) and a median of 45 hours.

Question 3 — Is this education part of the required or elective curriculum?

Thirteen respondents from non-US schools indicated PE education was offered to professional students. Of these, 8 indicated the education was in a required course, 4 reported it was offered by an elective course, and 1 school reported both required and elective components of PE education. Respondents from 15 non-US schools indicated PE education was offered at the graduate level. Of these, 8 indicated the education was in a required course and 7 reported it was offered through an elective course.

Respondents from 50 US schools indicated PE education was offered to professional students. Of these, 35 indicated the education was contained in a required course, 3 reported it was offered by an elective course, and 12 schools reported both required and elective components of PE education. Respondents from 33 US schools indicated PE education was offered at the graduate level. Of these, 20 indicated the education was in a required course, 11 reported it was offered through an elective course, and two schools reported offering both required and elective PE education to graduate-level students.

Some respondents reported having difficulty choosing whether PE at the graduate level was offered through a required or elective course. The confusion arose because although PE education may not be required for every graduate student in the program, it was required for those graduate students who "tracked-in" or specialised in a PE-related area.

Question 4 — How many students receive this education per year?

Similar to the results of Question 2, the number of students receiving PE education at each school had a wide range of responses and was not normally distributed. Therefore ranges, means, standard deviations, and medians will be presented for each analysis.

In non-US schools, the number of professional students per school receiving PE education per year ranged from 10 to 120, with a mean of 71 (SD = 39), and a median of 80 students. The number of non-US graduate students per school ranged from 3 to 55, a mean of 16 (SD15), and a median of 10 students.

In US schools, the number of professional students per school receiving PE education per year ranged from 14 to 190, with a mean of 92 (SD = 40), and a median of 90 students. The number of US graduate students per school ranged from 1 to 12, a mean of 5 (SD 3), and a median of 5 students.

Additional Comments

As mentioned in the methods sections, respondents were asked to record any additional comments in the space provided at the end of the survey. Respondents from 27 schools provided comments. As previously stated, respondents from 7 schools reported than PE education is planned for the near future. In addition, one school indicated that PE education will be added to the Medical School curriculum in 1998.

Respondents from 5 schools mentioned that PE education was taught in conjunction with other departments. For example, some students were enrolled in courses taught by professors of medicine, public health, management, economics, and epidemiology, while other students received training from the Health Department. Three respondents reported that PE education was combined with other topics such a financial management, epidemiology, healthcare policy, and the evaluation of pharmacy services. Because of this overlap, some respondents stated that it was difficult to estimate the number of "clock hours". One respondent's school provided post-doctoral training in pharmacoeconomics, but there were no questions about this type of PE education on the survey.

Three respondents used the comments section to specify the breakdown of hours in the elective versus the required courses. Four respondents indicated that they would like the Dean of their school to receive a copy of the study results, in order to increase the number of hours devoted to PE education. Two of these 4 reported that students received only a few clock hours of PE education if there was time at the end of a course they were teaching. Three respondents reported "other" types of comments.

LIMITATIONS

Results should be interpreted with caution due to some limitations. As mentioned in the introduction, PE education is offered by many disciplines. This study focused on education provided at Schools of Pharmacy. Although all 79 US Schools of Pharmacy were contacted, some non-US schools were not contacted because an e-mail address was not available from the database used. A higher response rate may have been achieved if the survey was not conducted during the month of June. Some universities reduce hours during the summer and some faculties may have been on vacation during this time. Also, as with most surveys, responders may differ from non-responders. Lastly, some respondents indicated difficulty estimating the number of clock hours of PE education, some reported PE education was interrelated with other topics and taught by other disciplines, and some respondents were not sure whether the graduate courses at their school should be classified as an elective or required part of PE education.

DISCUSSION AND CONCLUSIONS

It is interesting to note that every US school that offered PE education at the graduate level also provided it at the professional level. Non-US schools had more graduate students per school enrolled in PE education than US schools (Non-US mean = 16, median = 10; US mean = 5, median = 5) while US schools, on average, had more professional students enrolled in their programs than non-US schools (US mean = 92, median = 90; Non-US mean = 71, median = 80).

Direct comparisons of these results with previous studies in the US is difficult, because each survey asked similar, but different, questions. For example, this survey asked about pharmacoeconomic education "offered" to professional and graduate pharmacy students in elective and required course, while Jeurgens et al.[5] asked about specific analytical techniques in professional programs, and Gregor and Draugalis[8] assessed the numbers of graduate students enrolled in programs that "emphasised" pharmacoeconomics.

Although direct comparisons cannot be made, it seems as if there has been a growth in the number of schools offering education in pharmacoeconomics. As mentioned before, 7 respondents indicated that their schools plan to add PE education by the year 2000.

Future research should be aimed at assessing pharmacoeconomic education outside of schools or colleges of pharmacy. This may include surveys of other health professional schools (eg medicine, nursing) as well as economic and public health educators. PE education also takes place outside of universities. Examples include institutes, centres and pharmaceutical companies, as well as continuing education (CE) offerings.

A survey to update this information should be conducted every 2 years. As the use of electronic mail and websites increases, access to this information is easier to collect at the international level.

REFERENCES

1. International Society for Pharmacoeconomics and Outcomes Research, http://www.ispor.org. 12/98.
2. American Pharmaceutical Association. (1994). *Patient Outcomes of Pharmaceutical Interventions: A Scientific Foundation for the Future.* American Pharmaceutical Foundation, 2215 Constitution Ave. NW, Washington DC, USA, p103–119.
3. Draugalis JR. (1994). Updated skills: pharmacoeconomics as continuing education. *Topics in Hospital Pharmacy Management,* **13**(4): 72–76.
4. Draugalis JR, Jones-Grizzle AJ. (1991). Pharmacy education and pharmacoeconomics. *Journal of Pharmacy Teaching,* **2**(2): 3–10.
5. Jeurgens JP, Szeinbach SL, Smith MC. (1992). Will future pharmacists understand pharmacoeconomic research? *American Journal of Pharmaceutical Education,* **56**(2): 135–140.
6. Kolassa EM. (1994). A basic course in pharmaceutical economics: background, rationale, and suggested syllabus. *Journal of Pharmacy Teaching,* **4**(3): 15–27.
7. Draugalis JR, Coons SJ. (1994). The role of colleges of pharmacy in meeting the pharmacoeconomic needs of the pharmaceutical industry: A conference report. *Clinical Therapeutics,* **16**(3): 523–537.
8. Gregor KJ, Draugalis JR. (1994). Graduate pharmacoeconomic education and training programs in US colleges of pharmacy. *American Journal of Pharmaceutical Education,* **58**(4): 378–381.
9. Editor: Temple DJ, Browsable World Wide Web site; http: //www.cf.ac.uk/ uwcc/phrmy/ WWW-WSP.
10. American Association of Colleges of Pharmacy, 1426 Prince Street, Alexandria Va. 22314, USA.
11. Bootman JL, Townsend RJ, McGhan WF. (1996). *Principles of Pharmacoeconomics,* Harvey Whitney Books Co. Cincinnati OH USA, p. 7.
12. Rascati KL, Draugalis JR, Connor TM. (1998) Pharmacoeconomic education in U.S. Schools of Pharmacy. *American Journal of Pharmaceutical Education,* **62**(2): 167–169.

4

Methodologies used to evaluate and measure the economic outcomes of drug treatment

C Pritchard and A Towse

INTRODUCTION

The last decade has seen a heightened level of interest in the use of economic evaluation for decision-making in healthcare, an interest which has manifested itself in the development of a number of official guidelines for the conduct of economic studies. In some cases, these have focused exclusively on the economic evaluation of pharmaceuticals. Most notably, the Australian government has required, since 1993, that pharmaceutical companies submit an economic evaluation in support of a claim for public reimbursement of their products. This requirement has been supported by a set of guidelines initially issued in draft form in January 1990 and subsequently amended, first in 1992 and, most recently, in 1995.[1]

Subsequent to the production of the Australian guidelines, policy makers in the province of Ontario, Canada, have produced a set of guidelines also directed at the pharmaceutical industry, the final version being published in September 1994. Since September 1995, companies' claims for a new drug to be included in the Ontario formulary have been required to include an economic evaluation (or a justification for its absence) for the submission to be regarded as complete. In parallel with the development of these guidelines, a set of guidelines for the whole of Canada was developed to reside with the Canadian Coordinating Office for Health Technology Assessment (CCOHTA), with the latest version appearing in November 1997.[2] Although these were not intended to be linked directly to a formal reimbursement process, they are also specifically concerned with the evaluation of pharmaceuticals.

The UK has been another relatively early participant in the move towards setting guidelines for the economic evaluation of medicines, with the publication of a voluntary checklist jointly by the government and the pharmaceutical industry.[3] More recently, new guidelines have been developed by economists at the Department of Health for use by the National Institute of Clinical Excellence (NICE) when assessing economic evaluations of health technologies generally. Elsewhere,

Alban *et al.*[4] have reported on the introduction of guidelines for economic evaluations of new pharmaceuticals to support a claim for public reimbursement in Denmark. Although initially voluntary, the authors note the potential for the guidelines to become mandatory. Elsewhere, academic led guidelines have been developed for France, Germany and Belgium, while health ministries in Portugal, Norway and the Netherlands are also developing guidelines. Checklists for economic evaluations have also been drawn up to support the peer review process by both the *British Medical Journal*[5] and the *British Journal of Medical Economics*,[6] the latter being based on the Department of Health/ABPI guidelines.[3]

These developments suggest that economic evaluations of pharmaceuticals will increasingly be used by prescribers to inform treatment choices and in pricing and reimbursement negotiations between the pharmaceutical industry, governments and other bodies funding healthcare expenditure. Against this background, the aim of this chapter is to outline methods used for the economic evaluation of healthcare technologies in general, and to highlight some of the issues which are of particular relevance to the evaluation of pharmaceutical products. Section two explains the nature and purpose of economic evaluation, section three describes the main forms of economic evaluation, and section four illustrates how economic evaluations may be used to make decisions in healthcare. Section five then goes on to discuss some of the main methodological and practical issues relevant to the economic evaluation of pharmaceuticals, while section six provides a summary of the chapter. Where appropriate, examples of economic evaluations taken from the HEED database produced by the Office of Health Economics will be used to illustrate the discussion.

WHAT IS ECONOMIC EVALUATION?

Economic evaluation is a tool to assist decision-makers in achieving value for money from a limited budget devoted to healthcare, indicating which treatment decisions should be made in order to achieve maximum health gain from the resources available. Alternatively, if this is not the goal to be pursued in a particular circumstance, it will illustrate the sacrifice in terms of health gain elsewhere which must be made to achieve an alternative objective such as the treatment of a particular priority group of the population. An economic evaluation must, therefore, consider both costs and outcomes and, since it is a tool to inform choices between treatments, must explicitly compare two or more interventions.

As will be seen, different types of economic evaluation take different approaches to the measurement of the outcomes of healthcare. However, all types of evaluation, in principle, may adopt the same approach to measuring and valuing costs. The economic cost of an intervention is the value of the resources used in providing it (e.g. doctors, operating theatres, pharmaceuticals etc.). Since resources are scarce relative to the demands made upon them, using a resource for one purpose means a lost opportunity to use it for another. This is the opportunity cost. Therefore, while resources are normally valued in monetary terms, the use of a resource may not necessarily be associated with a monetary flow. For example, a voluntary carer has an opportunity cost (the value of the other things they could be doing with their time) but does not receive a financial reward.

Measurement of Costs

There are basically two types of costs to consider in an economic evaluation,* direct costs and indirect costs. Direct costs represent those resources which are directly used in treating a patient. These include costs incurred by the health service, such as the use of drugs, doctors' and nurses' time, GP visits and overhead costs associated with hospital stays ('hotel' costs). They also include costs incurred by agencies outside the health service, such as social and voluntary services. When comparing pharmaceutical treatments for a particular indication, therefore, comparison of pharmaceutical costs alone may be a poor guide to the relative overall direct costs of treatment. A higher price pharmaceutical may result in lower total costs if it enables a shorter hospital stay, for example. Also included in direct costs are out of pocket expenses incurred by patients themselves, for example in travelling for treatment, and by friends and relatives, such as those incurred in making hospital visits.

The second type of costs is indirect costs, or productivity costs, which reflect the impact on the time of patients and friends/relatives as a result of treatment. Just as direct costs reflect the use of scarce resources, so patients' time is a scarce resource which can be used for a number of alternative uses. Indirect costs will, therefore, include patients' time in undergoing treatment since this will represent lost opportunities for the patient to engage in work or leisure. Even if the individual does not suffer a financial loss as a result of undergoing treatment, a value can be attached to these lost opportunities (for example the value of the individual's lost output). More significantly, different treatments may have different effects on the individual's longer term ability to work. For example, a pharmaceutical treatment which is more effective than another in providing relief of migraine may allow the sufferer to be more productive in the workplace, resulting in an indirect cost saving.

Which costs are included in an economic evaluation will depend crucially on the perspective of the analysis. It is usually recommended that an economic evaluation intended for a public healthcare decision-maker should take a broad societal perspective. That is, all costs should be included no matter by whom they are incurred (and all benefits no matter to whom they accrue). However, decision-makers seeking to attain value for money from their own particular budgets may have different perspectives. For example, hospital managers are unlikely to be concerned with costs borne by the general practitioner or by social services; indeed, there may well be an incentive for costs to be shifted from secondary care on to other agencies. While central government will be concerned to take all these direct costs into account, it may be felt that indirect costs should be excluded from the analysis. This could be either on the grounds that to include them would discriminate against those not economically active or because they lie outside of concerns about maximising the value obtained from public expenditure.

---

* Intangible costs are also sometimes identified as a type of cost. They are generally defined as the 'cost' of discomfort and anxiety experienced by the patient while undergoing treatment, but are perhaps more appropriately thought of as part of the health effects of treatment. If they are included in an economic evaluation at all, it is most likely to be as part of a cost benefit analysis.

Measuring Outcomes

Clinical Outcome Measures

While the use of resources is generally converted into a monetary cost value in economic evaluation, there are a number of different ways in which outcomes may be measured. Firstly, a clinical variable specific to the disease area of interest may be used. For example, economic evaluations of antihypertensive and lipid lowering drugs have used reductions in blood pressure[7] and changes in low density lipoprotein (LDL) cholesterol,[8] respectively, while drug treatments for asthma have been assessed in terms of measurements of lung function such as peak expiratory flow.[9] Such clinical outcome measures may not, however, be closely related to individuals' subjective well-being. A measure which attempts to capture the impact of an intervention on a patient's quality of life may therefore be more appropriate.

Quality of Life

A number of quality of life measures have, been developed. These may be specific to a particular disease, such as the Arthritis Impact Measurement Scale (AIMS), or generic measures covering all aspects of health, such as the Nottingham Health Profile (NHP) and Short Form 36 (SF-36). Generic measures can be applied to any disease area. For example, Walker et al.[10] review the application of the generic UK Sickness Impact Profile (UKSIP) in the measurement of quality of life in migraine sufferers, but it has also been applied to cardiovascular disease[11] and psoriasis.[12] A distinction can be made between profile measures and index measures. The former can be used to estimate treatment effects for a number of different aspects or 'dimensions' of quality of life without combining the scores on the individual dimensions, whereas index measures yield an overall quality of life score. The UKSIP, for example, is an index measure as it has 12 dimensions which can be weighted together to generate an overall score from 0% to 100% of best possible health, while the SF-36 is a profile measure since it produces separate scores for each of its eight dimensions. The results obtained from a profile measure can cause problems of interpretation when improvements are observed in some dimensions and deteriorations in others, as was the case in the study of medical versus expectant management of women with endometriosis associated infertility by Bodner et al.[13] (see **Table 1**).

In this example, a decline in score represents an improvement in health related quality of life. In order to assess whether quality of life overall has changed, a judgement has to be made concerning the relative importance of the different dimensions and, in particular, whether improvements in some dimensions outweigh the decline in others. Moreover, although it was found that only one of the changes was significant, that on the pain scale for the expectant management group, it is unclear whether the changes on all the dimensions taken together would constitute an overall change in quality of life.

Quality Adjusted Life Years

Depending on the intervention being evaluated, length of life and quality of life may both be important outcomes. In this case, the two may be combined into a quality

Table 1: Changes in SF-36 scores for medical and expectant management of endometriosis associated infertility.

SF-36 Dimension	Change in SF-36 score under:		
	Medical management	Expectant management	Difference: medical minus expectant
Physical functioning	3.6	1.0	2.6
Social functioning	−4.8	−2.0	−2.8
Role-physical	7.1	2.3	4.8
Role-emotional	9.5	1.5	8.0
Mental Health	−5.1	3.4	−8.5
Energy-fatigue	0.7	4.8	−4.1
Pain	−17.5	−15.7	−1.8
General health	−0.4	1.1	−1.5

adjusted life year (QALY). For this purpose, a generic measure is required which yields an index of overall health (rather than separate scores on individual dimensions of health). Generic index measures produce a set of scores referenced to a 0 to 1 scale, with 0 typically being the score for death and 1 the score for perfect health, with negative scores reflecting quality of life worse than death. A measure which has historically been used by health economists in the UK to generate QALYs is the Rosser matrix (see **Table 2**).

The QALY benefits of treatment are simply calculated by multiplying the change in quality of life score by the number of years of survival over which it applies. For example, an improvement from cell DV to cell AI of the matrix is associated with an improvement in quality of life score of 0.3. If experienced over five years, this improvement would yield 1.5 QALYs and, if experienced for a duration of ten years, 3 QALYs.

More recently, the EuroQol EQ-5D scale has been promoted as a means of providing quality of life adjustments when calculating QALYs. As shown in **Table 3**, a self-completion questionnaire has been developed to assess patients' quality of life.

Responses to the questionnaire give descriptive information about quality of life which must be translated into an overall score. This begs the question of whose values are to be used to attach scores to each of the 243, i.e. 3^5, possible levels of quality of life given by the five dimensions with three levels on each. In the case of the Rosser matrix scores produced by Kind et al.,[14] a sample of 70 individuals, made up primarily of patients and healthcare professionals, was used. However, there is a strong argument, particularly in a publicly funded system such as the UK NHS, that resource allocation decisions should incorporate the vales of the general public. Thus, a EuroQol 'tariff' has been produced by Dolan et al.[16] based on values obtained from a representative sample of the general population. This provides an "off the shelf" set of scores which can be applied to any analysis using the EuroQol instrument.

Table 2: The Rosser matrix. Source: Kind *et al.*[14]

Disability Rating	Distress Rating			
	A	B	C	D
I	1.000	0.995	0.990	0.967
II	0.990	0.986	0.973	0.932
III	0.980	0.972	0.956	0.912
IV	0.964	0.956	0.942	0.870
V	0.946	0.935	0.900	0.700
VI	0.875	0.845	0.680	0.000
VII	0.677	0.564	0.000	−1.486
VIII	−1.028	N/A	N/A	N/A

N/A = not applicable

The sample selected for interview was drawn from the non-institutionalised population of England, Scotland and Wales using the national postcode address file, and approximately 3,000 responses were used. The respondents were given descriptions of some of the 243 quality of life states and asked to value them using the time trade-off method, which asks how many years in perfect health is equivalent to a given number of years of being in the less than perfect health state of one of the EQ-5D states. For example, if ten years in the less than perfect state of health was regarded as being equivalent to only five years in perfect health, the score attached to that particular health state would be 0.5, compared with 1 for perfect health and 0 for death. A variety of methods are available for obtaining such values, including the visual analogue scale (VAS) and the standard gamble. The VAS, also known as the 'feeling thermometer', asks respondents to place different levels of quality of life on a 100 point scale, again with the end-points of death and perfect health, such that a health state positioned half way along the line would receive a score of 0.5. The standard gamble, meanwhile, presents the choice between a gamble, on the one hand, with two possible outcomes — perfect health or death — and an alternative option of being in an intermediate health state. The respondent is required to specify the probability of achieving perfect health under the gamble, such that the two options are regarded as equivalent. If a 50-50 gamble is regarded as equivalent to the intermediate health state with certainty, then this health state is given a score of 0.5.

Willingness to Pay

Rather than attaching a QALY value to the outcomes of healthcare, an alternative means of valuation is to value outcomes in monetary terms. This is done by

Table 3: The five dimensions of the EuroQol scale. Source: Brooks, with the EuroQol group[15] (with permission from Elsevier Science).

By placing a tick in one box in each group below, please indicate which statements best describe your own health state today.

Mobility

I have no problems in walking about ☐

I have some problems in walking about ☐

I am confined to bed ☐

Self-Care

I have no problems with self-care ☐

I have some problems washing or dressing myself ☐

I am unable to wash or dress myself ☐

Usual Activities (e.g. work, study, housework, family or leisure activities)

I have no problems with performing my usual activities ☐

I have some problems with performing my usual activities ☐

I am unable to perform my usual activities ☐

Pain/Discomfort

I have no pain or discomfort ☐

I have moderate pain or discomfort ☐

I have extreme pain or discomfort ☐

Anxiety/Depression

I am not anxious or depressed ☐

I am moderately anxious or depressed ☐

I am extremely anxious or depressed ☐

evaluating the willingness to pay (WTP) for healthcare programmes and again the values of the general public can be incorporated into the analysis. For example, a sample of the Norwegian population was asked how much they would be willing to pay, using contingent valuation, in the form of increased taxation to fund three different healthcare programmes (a helicopter ambulance service, more heart operations and more hip replacements).[17] In addition to deriving hypothetical WTP values for overall programmes, monetary values can also be derived for a specific intervention from patients undergoing that intervention. A technique for indirectly measuring WTP is that of conjoint analysis.[18] In this approach, monetary values can be traded with various attributes of the healthcare intervention.

TYPES OF ECONOMIC EVALUATION

The following sections provide a brief overview of how the different approaches to outcome measures are classified into different types of evaluation. We then consider how this information can be used for decision-making purposes.

Cost minimisation analysis

This description is applied to those studies in which the outcomes are equivalent across the interventions being compared and therefore can be thought of as focusing on the least cost alternative. The label may apply whatever the outcome measure or measures used. This form of analysis may be specifically chosen if there is evidence from the literature that the outcomes of the different interventions are equal, and thus the evaluation reduces to a comparison of costs, or it may emerge during the course of the study that outcomes are equal. An example of the latter is the prospective evaluation undertaken alongside a randomised trial[19] of subcutaneous versus intravenous erythropoietin in haemodialysis patients. The study found that there were no significant differences in outcomes between the two groups (visual analogue pain scores, haematocrit level and haemoglobin levels) but that the subcutaneous route of administration was less costly by over $1,100 per patient.

Cost consequences analysis

In this form of evaluation, it is usual for analysts to present results for a range of outcome measures. Some will employ a battery of quality of life measures without focusing on any one as the main outcome of interest. For example, Sacristan et al.[20] used a range of functional and quality of life measures, including the Brief Psychiatric Rating Scale and the Clinical Global Impressions scale, to evaluate olanzapine as treatment for patients with schizophrenia resistant to conventional antipsychotic drugs. In this case, the authors also summarised the changes in the different scales into an overall 'response to treatment', with the response rate for olanzapine being 36% at six weeks and 48% at six months. However, cost consequences analyses can often be difficult for decision-makers to interpret as they must, in general, make their own judgements concerning the relative importance of different outcome measures. Therefore, while cost consequences analyses are the most common form of evaluation, with around half of the original evaluations on the HEED database which were published in 1998 being of this type,* they are perhaps the least useful for decision-making, unless decision-makers are clear about the consequences and costs which interest them and so are happy to discard the rest.

---

* It should be noted that those studies classified as cost consequences analyses in HEED include some studies which do not explicitly incorporate a comparator and are therefore better described as partial analyses, rather than full economic evaluations. The term 'cost-outcome description' has been used by Drummond et al.[21]

Cost effectiveness analysis

This description is applied to those studies which use a single primary outcome, or effectiveness, measure expressed in 'natural units', often in the form of a clinical outcome such as those noted in *Clinical Outcome Measures* above. The results of the analysis are expressed in terms of cost per unit of health gain. For example, Maetzel *et al.*[22] estimated the cost-effectiveness of misoprostol for rheumatoid arthritis patients receiving nonsteroidal antiinflammatory drugs in terms of cost per gastrointestinal (GI) event averted. Prophylaxis for all patients with misoprostol, rather than no prophylaxis, was estimated to cost around Can$95,000 per GI event averted. The disadvantage of using such condition-specific outcome measures is that, while the analysis may be able to indicate the most cost-effective means of achieving a particular objective for a particular group of patients, it is not possible to compare the relative cost-effectiveness of different types of interventions for diseases affecting different patient groups. Thus, it would not be possible to compare the relative value for money achieved in health gain from investing resources in the prevention of NSAID-related gastrointestinal events as opposed to, say, investing resources in treating asthma sufferers.

When it would, in principle, be possible to make comparisons across disease areas is when cost-effectiveness analyses (CEAs) present their results in terms of life years gained (around 20% of original CEAs on the HEED database that were published in 1998 did so). However, treatments are not always intended to improve survival, particularly in chronic diseases for which quality of life may be a more important outcome. Cost utility analysis is required to allow for both survival and quality of life.

Cost utility analysis

Cost utility analyses express the outcomes of healthcare in terms of 'utility' units, generally the QALY (although a competitor, the Healthy Years Equivalent, has also been proposed), with results expressed in terms of cost per QALY gained. A recent example is the study by Messori *et al.*[23] who estimated a cost per QALY ratio for the use of lamotrigine in patients with refractory epilepsy. The use of lamotrigine, as opposed to no adjunctive treatment, was estimated to cost around $41,300 per QALY gained. Since all healthcare interventions are arguably intended to improve one or both of survival and quality of life, cost utility analysis can, in principle, be used to compare the value for money of investments in different programme areas. It can therefore be used to make high level resource allocation decisions. However, although it can indicate the most cost-effective way of producing QALYs, it raises the question of how much society thinks it is worth putting into healthcare as opposed to non healthcare uses, to achieve a QALY. Thus, it cannot say whether it is worthwhile using resources to obtain the QALYs offered by an intervention rather than devoting them to an alternative non healthcare use. The question of whether additional taxes should be devoted to healthcare rather than, say, defence cannot be addressed by cost utility analysis, but requires the use of cost benefit analysis.

Cost benefit analysis

In this form of analysis, both resource use and health outcomes are valued in monetary terms, with health outcomes being valued using the willingness to pay approach. The results of the analysis can, therefore, either be expressed as a ratio of monetary benefits to monetary costs or, more appropriately, as net benefits or net costs. The advantage of this approach is that it can indicate whether or not an investment is worth making depending on whether it yields net benefits or net costs. Moreover, in principle, it can be used to compare investments in healthcare resources with investments in other sectors of the economy, such as transport or the environment, where evaluations are normally conducted entirely in monetary terms. It can also allow for the criticism of QALYs that they only take account of the health benefits of healthcare when there may be other aspects of healthcare, such as information provided by screening programmes (e.g. the reassurance of a negative test result), which are valued independently of the health outcomes. Ryan[18] shows how preferences may be obtained towards characteristics of healthcare services such as travelling time, waiting time, choice of doctors and access/parking.

The use of cost benefit analysis should, in principle, give an unambiguous answer as to whether an intervention is worth undertaking or not. An example is the study by Tang et al.[24] who evaluated different options for the timing of ondansetron administration in the prevention of postoperative nausea and vomiting (PONV) by asking patients in their trial to state their willingness to pay to avoid PONV. The study found that patients were willing to pay an average of $117 to prevent PONV which, compared with the cost of PONV management of $21, gave a benefit to cost ratio of 5:1. Assuming that $21 is the correct opportunity cost of providing the service and that additional revenue can be raised, it will therefore be beneficial to adopt the treatment. Despite its theoretical advantages, however, cost benefit analysis is used rarely in practice. Only ten original cost benefit analyses were identified for 1998 from the HEED database. This is in part because of methodological and measurement issues but also because patients rarely pay out of pocket for healthcare and healthcare budgets are usually fixed, hence finding out individual or societal WTP can be seen as unethical or irrelevant.

DECISION-MAKING ON THE BASIS OF AN ECONOMIC EVALUATION

When comparing the relative costs and health benefits of two alternative interventions, there are nine possible results of the comparison, as illustrated below (see **Table 4**). Each of costs and health benefits can either be higher, the same or lower under one alternative relative to the other.

In this diagram, there are six cases in which one alternative is undoubtedly the preferred treatment. Starting with the middle column, where the health benefits are the same under intervention A as under intervention B, then we have cost minimisation analysis, for example, the study by Kaufman et al.[19] mentioned in the section on cost minimisation analysis. Option B is to be preferred when the costs of

A are higher and option A is to be preferred when its costs are lower. When both the costs and health benefits of the two interventions are the same, then the decision-maker will be indifferent between them.

In the top right hand corner, intervention B is again preferred when A has lower health benefits and the same or higher costs. In the latter case, the decision-maker is in the fortunate position of being able to provide greater health benefits at reduced cost by providing B rather than A. Conversely, on the left hand side of **Table 4**, A is preferred to B when A has greater health benefits at the same or lower cost, the latter case enabling an increase in health benefits and a cost saving by providing A rather than B. For example, Davies *et al.*[25] estimated that, in the treatment of schizophrenia, the probability of a favourable outcome with risperidone was 78.9% at the end of two years, compared with 58.9% for haloperidol. In addition, the cost per patient was estimated at $15,549 for risperidone compared with $18,332 for haloperidol.

Often, however, the decision-maker will not be able simply to choose a dominant alternative (one with lower costs and greater benefits). Normally, the bottom right hand cell or top left hand cell of **Table 4** will be appropriate, with one intervention providing greater benefit but also being more costly than the alternative. In this case, the additional, or incremental, cost of the more effective treatment must be compared with its additional, or incremental, health effects. The following section provides illustrations of this incremental calculation in examples of cost-effectiveness and cost-utility analyses.

The incremental cost-effectiveness ratio

The incremental cost-effectiveness ratio gives the ratio of the differences in the costs of two interventions to the differences in health benefits, or effectiveness. If A and B are the two interventions, with C_A and C_B the cost of the two interventions and E_A and E_B indicating their effectiveness, then the incremental cost-effectiveness ratio

Table 4: Nine possible results of comparing interventions A and B.

		Comparative health benefits of treatment A versus treatment B		
		Higher	Same	Lower
	Higher	Not sure	Prefer B	Prefer B
Comparative costs of treatment A versus treatment B	Same	Prefer A	Indifferent	Prefer B
	Lower	Prefer A	Prefer A	Not sure

(assuming that A is the more effective and more costly option) is calculated as:

$$\frac{C_A - C_B}{E_A - E_B}$$

The following example serves to illustrate a calculation of an incremental cost-effectiveness ratio and also highlights some of the problems which can arise in the interpretation of cost-effectiveness ratios. The example is taken from Gupta[26] who estimated the cost-effectiveness of five different oral antifungal regimens for the treatment of dermatophyte onychomycosis of the toenails. These were griseofulvin, itraconazole (continuous), intraconazole (pulse), terbinafine and fluconazole. The results of the analysis, in terms of treatment costs and symptom-free days for each option over a time horizon of three years, are presented in **Table 5**.

The first point to note about these results is that, while it is possible to calculate differences in costs and effectiveness (symptom-free days) between pairs of treatment options, there is no explicit baseline to which the costs and symptom-free days in the first two columns of the table are related. Rather, the implicit assumption of the average cost-effectiveness ratios presented in column four is that there is a hypothetical 'no intervention' option associated with no costs and no symptom-free days. In effect, zeros have been entered in the formula given above for C_B and E_B to calculate the 'average cost-effectiveness ratio' for each of the five treatment options.

An 'average cost-effectiveness ratio' is unlikely to be helpful to the decision-maker, however, since a 'no intervention' option which has zero costs and zero health effects (symptom-free days in this example) may not be a realistic alternative to treatment. There are likely to be some costs associated with a 'no intervention' option and there may also be some symptom-free days even in the absence of treatment. In this case, the author has, correctly, gone on to consider the incremental costs and effects between the five treatments considered. When calculating the incremental changes between treatments, the analysis becomes somewhat simplified in this example because the disaggregated figures for costs and symptom-free days indicate that three treatments are dominated (the two others provide greater benefit and lower cost). A comparison of the remaining two options indicates that terbinafine has an incremental cost of US$9.67 per symptom-free day compared with intraconazole (pulse). A comparison of the fourth and fifth columns in the table indicates that it is important to know whether a cost-effectiveness ratio is an incremental ratio or an 'average' ratio based upon a hypothetical 'no cost, no effects' alternative. While cost-effectiveness analyses should present incremental cost-effectiveness ratios, an average ratio is frequently presented in addition to or in place of the incremental ratio. When considering an incremental cost-effectiveness ratio, it is also important to know whether the comparator intervention is relevant to the decision the evaluation is being used to inform.

In the above example, having established the incremental cost-effectiveness ratio between the two non-dominated treatments, the decision-maker must decide whether he or she is willing to pay an additional $9.67 to achieve an extra

Table 5: Average and incremental cost-effectiveness ratios in the treatment of onychomycosis				
Treatment	Expected cost per patient ($US)	Expected symptom-free days (SFDs)	Average cost per expected SFD	Incremental cost per expected SFD
Griseofulvin	2880	408	7.05	Dominated
Itraconazole				
– continuous	2022	929	2.18	Dominated
– pulse	1182	942	1.26	
Terbinafine	1211	945	1.28	9.67
Fluconazole	1443	680	2.12	Dominated

symptom-free day by the purchase of terbinafine rather than pulse intraconazole. Thus, while the analysis should indicate which treatment options are feasible (i.e. not dominated) and provide the incremental cost-effectiveness ratios appropriate to the decision being made, it is up to the decision-maker to attach a value to the health gains associated with the particular treatment of interest. In this case, a willingness to pay of at least $9.67 will lead to a decision in favour of terbinafine whereas a willingness to pay of less than $9.67 will give pulse itraconazole as the preferred mode of therapy.

The use of QALYs in decision-making

Whether or not the additional investment in the more effective drug is worthwhile from the decision-maker's point of view will depend on their individual circumstances; in general, there is little indication of what society is willing to pay for particular types of outcomes. However, where improvements in survival are concerned, decision-makers may draw on estimates of the value of life normally calculated in a context other than that of healthcare. For example, in their evaluation of rare earth screens to reduce radiation dosage from diagnostic X-ray procedures, Ginsberg et al.[27] valued a year of life as being equivalent to the annual Israeli GNP per capita of $15,085.

When making comparisons across all healthcare programmes, it is not just the value of a life or a year of life that is important but what decision-makers are willing to pay for a quality adjusted life year (QALY). In this context, Laupacis et al.[28] suggest grades of recommendation for healthcare technologies based on the cost per QALY ratio. Among those which are more effective and more costly than the alternative, a grade B technology is one which costs less than $20,000 per QALY, a grade C technology is one which costs between $20,000 and $100,000 per QALY and a grade D technology is one which costs over $100,000. They conclude that grade B technologies are almost universally accepted as an appropriate use of scarce resources, that some technologies in grade C are used routinely but there are questions about their appropriateness in some patient groups and that there are doubts about grade D technologies.

In the UK context, Cleland and Walker[29] suggest, on the basis of previous publications, that treatments costing less than £5,000 per QALY are highly cost-effective and that those costing more than £10,000 per QALY are considered expensive. These thresholds were employed to assist in establishing treatment recommendations for patients with varying degrees of ischaemic heart disease. The study compared surgery with medical therapy (as defined in a previous study on which the analysis was partly based) plus aspirin plus simvastatin, and medical therapy plus aspirin alone. It was found that both the simvastatin and surgery options had incremental cost per QALY ratios in excess of £10,000 for all patients when a five year time horizon was taken. Thus, medical therapy plus aspirin was indicated as the preferred therapy. Over a ten year period, however, the addition of simvastatin to medical therapy plus aspirin had an incremental cost per QALY ratio within the £5,000 threshold for those with poor left ventricular function. At the £10,000 threshold, healthcare purchasers would be prepared to pay for simvastatin in those with mild angina and triple-vessel disease, and for surgery, rather than simvastatin, in patients with severe angina; the treatment recommendations are summarised in **Table 6**.

In order to compare the relative cost-effectiveness of different healthcare programmes, cost per QALY estimates are frequently entered into a 'QALY league table' such as the one presented in **Table 7**.

Using, for example, a limit of £10,000 as the willingness of decision-makers to pay for an extra QALY, a number of interventions would fail the test of cost-effectiveness, including home and hospital haemodialysis. Under a £5,000 per QALY cut-off, breast cancer screening and heart transplantation would fail to be offered. Although such 'league tables' may, in principle, provide useful information for the decision-maker when making resource allocation decisions by indicating those interventions where QALYs can be purchased relatively cheaply (low cost per QALY), they suffer certain drawbacks which limit their usefulness. For example, the results of different studies may be difficult to compare because of differences in methodologies used. Differences in cost per QALY estimates may owe more to methodological differences than true differences in cost-effectiveness. For example, the inclusion or exclusion of indirect costs, different approaches to the measurement of quality of life, the use of varying time horizons, and the treatment of flows of costs and effects over time (the use of different discount rates*) can all influence the results of the analysis. Moreover, it is not always clear whether an incremental cost per QALY ratio has been calculated and, if it has, whether it is calculated relative to a meaningful comparator from the decision-maker's point of view. Prioritisation on

---

* Discounting of future flows of costs and health effects has the opposite effect of compound interest and reflects the idea that benefits (e.g. QALYs) are preferred today rather than in the future and that there is a preference for costs to be incurred in the future rather than today. Future flows of costs and benefits are therefore given lower weight than those occurring in the present.

Table 6: Treatment recommendations in ischaemic heart disease based on cost per QALY thresholds. Source: Cleland and Walker.[29] (with kind permission from Kluwer Academic Publishers).

Patient group	£5,000/QALY cutoff	£10,000/QALY cutoff
Over 5 years		
All cases	Medicine + aspirin	Medicine + aspirin
Mild angina	Medicine + aspirin	Medicine + aspirin
Severe angina	Medicine + aspirin	Medicine + aspirin
Triple-vessel disease	Medicine + aspirin	Medicine + aspirin
Poor left ventricular function	Medicine + aspirin	Medicine + aspirin
Over ten years		
All cases	Medicine + aspirin	Add simvastatin
Mild angina	Medicine + aspirin	Add simvastatin
Severe angina	Medicine + aspirin	Surgery
Triple-vessel disease	Medicine + aspirin	Add simvastatin
Poor left ventricular function	Add simvastatin	Add simvastatin

the basis of the cost per QALY ratio is also inappropriate if decision-makers have objectives other than the maximisation of health gain, such as the desire to ensure an even distribution of health gain or to ensure that treatment is provided to particular groups of patients. These are general reservations about the interpretation and use of the results of economic evaluations. In the context of pharmaceuticals specifically, a number of methodological concerns are of particular interest; these are covered in the following section.

METHODOLOGICAL ISSUES IN THE ECONOMIC EVALUATION OF PHARMACEUTICALS

The principal issue related to the economic evaluation of pharmaceutical products is how to provide valid cost-effectiveness information to the decision-maker when, for regulatory purposes, the evaluation of pharmaceuticals has traditionally been geared towards the demonstration of efficacy. Economists have a choice between basing economic evaluations on randomised phase III trials (pre-launch studies) or synthesising data from a number of different sources, frequently carried out using decision analytic modelling techniques. The advantages of randomised trials are well known, in terms of estimating the therapeutic impact of a drug with minimum bias. However, a number of reservations have been expressed about their ability to provide economic data which is useful for decision-makers. While randomised trials have high internal validity since they give an unbiased measure of a drug's impact

47

Table 7: QALY league table. Source: Maynard.[30] (with kind permission of Royal Economic Society).

Treatment	Cost/QALY (£ Aug 1990)
Cholesterol testing and diet therapy only (all adults aged 40-69)	220
Neurosurgical interventions for head injury	240
Advice to stop smoking from general practitioner	270
Neurosurgical intervention for subarachnoid haemorrhage	490
Antihypertensive treatment to prevent stroke (ages 45-64)	940
Pacemaker implantation	1100
Hip replacement	1180
Valve replacement for aortic stenosis	1140
Cholesterol testing and treatment	1480
Coronary artery bypass graft (left main vessel disease, severe angina)	2090
Kidney transplant	4710
Breast cancer screening	5780
Heart transplantation	7840
Cholesterol testing and treatment (incrementally) of all adults aged 25-39	14150
Home haemodialysis	17260
Coronary artery bypass graft (one vessel disease, moderate angina)	18830
Continuous ambulatory peritoneal dialysis	19870
Hospital haemodialysis	21970
Erythropoietin treatment for anaemia in dialysis patients (assuming 10% reduction in mortality)	54380
Neurosurgical intervention for malignant intracranial tumours	107780
Erythropoietin treatment for anaemia in dialysis patients (assuming no increase in survival)	126290

in the idealised conditions of a trial (efficacy), they may not have good external validity in terms of providing an accurate estimate of a drug's effects in the context of actual clinical practice (effectiveness). The main problems with phase III trials as the basis of economic evaluations are discussed below.

Context

Firstly, the context of the clinical decision is likely to differ from the context of the trial. Patients tend to be enrolled in trials on the basis of strict inclusion criteria which may not correspond well with the patient group with which the decision-maker is concerned. If patients in the trial are healthier than average, the estimate of efficacy may over or under estimate effectiveness in clinical practice. With regard to resource use, the trial protocol may introduce diagnostic procedures or other items of resource use that would not be incurred in clinical practice. These 'protocol-driven' costs will therefore distort the results of the analysis if it is to be used for decision-making purposes. In addition, a drug may be used, in clinical practice, for a wider group of patients than was envisaged at the time of the efficacy trials. The decision-maker must decide whether the trial results are likely to be reliable for his or her own context or whether an alternative form of data collection may be preferable.

Comparators

In deciding whether or not to purchase a particular pharmaceutical product, the decision-maker is likely to want to compare its cost-effectiveness with those alternatives which are commonly used for the indication. The number of potential alternatives will depend on variations in clinical practice, including inter-country variations, and the range of products currently licensed. Ideally, therefore, an economic evaluation will include a range of comparators to enable comparisons of cost-effectiveness to be made across a range of clinical situations. However, the comparator used in a phase III trial may well be a placebo which often will not be the appropriate comparator from the decision-maker's point of view. Moreover, where an active comparator is used, the number of comparators may be limited relative to the number of alternatives the decision-maker would like to compare. It may be of interest to have comparative cost-effectiveness information on five or six new and old drugs used to treat a particular condition, but it is unlikely that a single phase III trial will be designed with this in mind.

Time Horizon of the Study

The time horizon of a clinical trial may well be shorter than is desirable from a decision-maker's point of view. Even in cases where survival is important, a trial will stop well before survival duration has been observed for all the patients in the trial. In some cases, clinical efficacy may be established and the trial stopped before all the data desired for examining cost-effectiveness have been collected.

Choice of end-points

In addition to measuring outcomes over a shorter than ideal time horizon, a trial may be limited to intermediate clinical outcome measures when what is desired is information on quality of life or long term survival. A sample size set to measure a desired change in a particular clinical outcome may be too small to detect small changes in resource use or in broader measures of patients' well-being. Moreover, there may not be a close relationship between short term clinical effects and longer term outcomes.

Alternatives to Phase III trials

There are two main alternatives to the use of phase III trials as the basis of economic evaluations. One is to adapt the design of trials to provide more useful data and the other is to bring together data from a number of sources in a synthesised model. In the first case, trials would be designed with the following features.[31]

i)   enrollment of patients who are typical of the normal caseload

ii)   current care is used as the comparator
iii) settings and physicians are representative of normal practice
iv)   blinding of treatment allocation is not undertaken
v)   patients are followed under routine conditions
vi)   a range of endpoints is measured, not just clinical efficacy

Inclusion of these design features is intended to produce more generalisable results which are more meaningful to decision-makers, in that they attempt to bring the trial closer to clinical practice, with decision-makers likely to be concerned with how a particular intervention compares with their usual practice. However, even with these modifications, there will always be circumstances in which the period of follow-up in a trial or the number of comparators included in the study is less than decision-makers would ideally like. Therefore, modelling approaches which bring together data from a variety of sources will inevitably be required. In some cases, modelling will be necessary; for example, to extrapolate the results of a trial to a twenty or thirty year time horizon and to incorporate a greater number of treatment options than could feasibly be included in a trial. However, controversy remains surrounding the appropriateness of models and the circumstances under which they should be used.

Sheldon[31] argues that models which bring together different types of data, particularly when it is of low internal validity such as observational (rather than randomised trial) data and expert judgement, have a tendency to be biased. He considers that "a model is only necessary when direct observation of the phenomenon is not available and cannot be collected". Buxton et al.[32] believe that modelling can be a useful first step when few data have been collected on the intervention being investigated, to identify the value of further research or to assist in the process of product development, and, as a last resort, when there is no more reliable alternative means of providing information to decision-makers. In contrast, Halpern et al.[33] believe, given the problems of randomised trials and the need to provide timely data to decision-makers, that models should be given a wider role and argue that it may be appropriate to consider models as the gold standard in economic evaluation.

SUMMARY

At the beginning of this chapter, it was suggested that decisions concerning the pricing and reimbursement of pharmaceutical products are likely to be influenced increasingly by the use of economic evaluations to identify the value of the product in treating patients. Various types of economic evaluation appear in the literature, some of which are more useful for decision-making purposes than others. While cost benefit analysis is, in principle, capable of answering the broadest type of resource allocation question, it is rarely used. On the other hand, the type of evaluation most frequently used, cost consequences analysis, is of limited usefulness for decision-making unless there is one intervention which is superior on every outcome and no more costly than the alternative. Cost-effectiveness analysis can indicate to a decision-maker whether an intervention is worth pursuing, by a comparison of the incremental cost-effectiveness ratio and the decision-maker's willingness to pay for additional health gain.

Cost-effectiveness analysis will frequently allow comparisons to be made between interventions within a particular disease area. In order to compare across healthcare programmes, cost utility analysis can be used, with 'QALY league tables' providing a comparison of value for money across a wide range of interventions. However, there are a number of general factors which render these types of comparisons problematic. One set of methodological issues which is perhaps of more relevance to the economic evaluation of pharmaceuticals than of other types of intervention is the use of clinical trials as the basis for economic studies. While randomised trials have high internal validity, they may lack the generalisability desired by decision-makers. Some argue that there is no substitute for the collection of unbiased data through randomised trials, whereas others argue that models are essential to provide decision-makers with timely and relevant information. This is an important issue which policy makers will need to tackle as they seek to obtain value for money in their purchase of pharmaceuticals.

REFERENCES

1. Commonwealth of Australia Department of Human Services and Health (1995). Guidelines for the pharmaceutical industry on preparation of submissions to the Pharmaceutical Benefits Advisory Committee including major submissions involving economic analysis. Canberra: Australian Government Publishing Service.
2. Canadian Coordinating Office for Health Technology Assessment (1997). Guidelines for economic evaluation of pharmaceuticals: Canada. Ottawa: Canadian Coordinating Office for Health Technology Assessment, 2nd edition.
3. Department of Health/ABPI (1994). UK guidance on good practice in the conduct of economic evaluations of medicines. *British Journal of Medical Economics* **7**: 63–64.
4. Alban A, Gyldmark M, Pedersen A V, Søgaard J (1997). The Danish Approach to standards for economic evaluation methodologies. *PharmacoEconomics* **12**(6): 627–636.
5. BMJ Working Party on Economic Evaluation (1996). Guidelines for authors and peer reviewers of economic submissions to the BMJ. *British Medical Journal* **312**: 275–183.
6. Rapier C M, Hutchinson D R (1995). How useful are the UK guidelines for reviewing manuscripts submitted for publication? *British Journal of Medical Economics* **8**(Part 3):vii–xiii.
7. Edwards P R, Lunt D W R, Fehrsen G S *et al.* (1998). Improving cost-effectiveness of hypertension management at a community health centre. *South African Medical Journal* **88**(5): 549–554.
8. Levin L-A, Schmidt A, Schulte K-L *et al.* (1997). A comparison of clinical and pharmacoeconomic properties of fluvastatin and simvastatin in the management of primary hypercholesterolaemia. *British Journal of Medical Economics* **11**: 23–35.
9. Price D B, Appleby J L (1998). Fluticasone propionate: an audit of outcomes and cost-effectiveness in primary care. *Respiratory Medicine* **92**: 351–353.
10. Walker M D, Salek M S, Bayer A J (1998). A review of quality of life in Alzheimer's disease. Part 1: issues in assessing disease impact. *PharmacoEconomics* **14**(5): 499–530.
11. Salek M S, Luscombe D K, Walker S R *et al.* (1988). Cardiovascular disease and quality of life. *British Journal of Clinical Pharmacology* **26**: 628P.
12. Finlay A Y, Khan G K, Luscombe D K and Salek M S (1990). Validation of Sickness Impact Profile and Psoriasis Disability Index in psoriasis. *British Journal of Dermatology* **123**: 751–756.
13. Bodner C, Vale L, Ratcliffe J, Farrar S (1996). Using economics alongside medical audit. A case study of the management of endometriosis.

14. Kind P, Rosser R, Williams A (1982). Valuation of quality of life: some psychometric evidence. In Jones-Lee M W (ed). The Value of Life and Safety, North-Holland Publishing Company.
15. Brooks R, with the EuroQol Group (1996). EuroQol: the current state of play. *Health Policy* **37**: 53–72.
16. Dolan P, Gudex C, Kind P, Williams A (1995). A social tariff for EuroQol: results from a UK general population survey. University of York Centre for Health Economics Discussion Paper 138.
17. Olsen J A, Donaldson C (1998). Helicopters, hearts and hips: using willingness to pay to set priorities for public sector healthcare programmes. *Social Science and Medicine* **46**(1): 1–12.
18. Ryan M (1996). Using consumer preferences in healthcare decision-making: the application of conjoint analysis. London: Office of Health Economics.
19. Kaufman J S, Reda D J, Fye C L *et al.* (1998). Subcutaneous compared with intravenous epoetin in patients receiving hemodialysis. *The New England Journal of Medicine* **339**(9): 578–583.
20. Sacristan J A, Gomez J C, Martin J *et al.* (1998). Pharmacoeconomic assessment of olanzapine in the treatment of refractory schizophrenia based on a pilot clinical study. *Clinical Drug Investigation* **15**(1): 29–35.
21. Drummond M F, O' Brien B, Stoddart G L, Torrance G W (1997). Methods for the economic evaluation of healthcare programmes. New York: Oxford University Press, 2nd edition.
22. Maetzel A, Ferraz M B, Bombardier C (1998). The cost-effectiveness of misoprostol in preventing serious gastrointestinal events associated with the use of nonsteroidal antiinflammatory drugs. *Arthritis and Rheumatism* **41**(1): 16–25.
23. Messori A, Trippoli S, Becagli P *et al.* (1998). Adjunctive lamotrigine therapy in patients with refractory seizures: a lifetime cost-utility analysis. *European Journal of Clinical Pharmacology* **53**: 421–427.
24. Tang J, Wang B, White P F *et al.* (1998). The effect of timing of ondansetron administration on its efficacy, cost-effectiveness, and cost-benefit as a prophylactic antiemetic in the ambulatory care setting. *Anesthesia and Analgesia* **86**: 274–282.
25. Davies A, Langley P C, Keks N A *et al.* (1998). Risperidone versus haloperidol: II. Cost-effectiveness. *Clinical Therapeutics* **20**(1): 196–213.
26. Gupta A K (1998). Pharmacoeconomic analysis of oral antifungal therapies used to treat dermatophyte onychomycosis of the toenails: a US analysis. *PharmacoEconomics* **13**: 243–256.
27. Ginsberg G M, Schlesingel T, Ben-Shlomo A *et al.* (1998). An economic evaluation of the use of rare earth screens to reduce the radiation dose from diagnostic x-ray procedures in Israel. *The British Journal of Radiology* **71**: 406–412.
28. Laupacis A, Feeny D, Destky A S, Tugwell P X (9912). How attractive does a new technology have to be to warrant adoption and utilisation? Tentative guidelines for using clinical and economic evaluations. *Canadian Medical Association Journal* **146**(4): 473–481.
29. Cleland J G F, Walker A (1998). Therapeutic options and cost considerations in the treatment of ischemic heart disease. *Cardiovascular Drugs and Therapy* **12**: 225–232.
30. Maynard A (1991). Developing the healthcare market. *The Economic Journal* **101**: 1277–1286.
31. Sheldon T A (1996). Problems of using modelling in the economic evaluation of healthcare. *Health Economics* **5**: 1–11.
32. Buxton M J, Drummond M F, van Hout B A *et al.* (1997). Modelling in economic evaluation: an unavoidable fact of life. *Health Economics* **6**: 217–227.
33. Halpern M T, McKenna M, Hutton J (1998). Letter to the editor. *Health Economics* **7**: 741–742.

5

Case studies in pharmacoeconomics and assessment of outcomes

BC Martin, FL Pritchard, JA Kotzan,
M Perri III and DA Sclar

INTRODUCTION

Pharmacoeconomics and the assessment of outcomes stemming from new technologies encompass an array of methodologic designs, an assortment of sources of data, and various rubrics for analyses. The most common classification for pharmacoeconomic analyses is the distinction between Cost Minimisation Analysis (CMA), Cost Effectiveness Analysis (CEA), Cost Benefit Analysis (CBA), and Cost Utility Analysis (CUA) with the basis of these analyses grounded in welfare economics and public policy analysis. For standard definitions of these analyses, we would refer readers to Chapter 4 (pages 40–42).

In contrast to selecting cases based upon methodologic criteria, this chapter identifies pharmacoeconomic issues and cases along disease classifications and analyses of new health services offered by health personnel. The selection of cases by disease state was done to illustrate the point that there are unique economic considerations for each patient population suffering from different diseases and / or being exposed to different treatments. Each set of diseases requires enumeration of different costs. Some disease states lend themselves well to conventional analytic approaches, such as CEA, while for other disease states the measurement of outcomes (indices of utility) have not been well researched and often use approaches that attempt to determine if the technologies are cost saving or perform some CEA where the endpoints are based upon clinical measures of outcome rather than quality of life, or mortality.

The first portion of this chapter highlights the economic assessment of osteoporosis. Osteoporosis (as defined as the loss of bone mass) was selected as the disease itself, strictly defined, has no meaningful outcomes. Osteoporosis, however, does significantly predispose persons to fracture which could have a dehabilitating impact on patient functioning, quality of life, medical expenditures, and mortality. The next pharmacoeconomic set of cases is that of a chronic, devastating, severe mental illness, schizophrenia, that in contrast to osteoporosis primarily afflicts persons in their third through their fifth decades of life. Cases presented for schizophrenia are centred around the evaluation of an atypical neuroleptic, clozapine. The next case is the pharmacoeconomic evaluation of therapies for treating peptic ulcer disease. The understanding of this disease has changed drastically in this decade, where new ideas on the pathogenesis of peptic ulcer disease have given way to new treatment strategies with conventional antibiotics in conjunction with antisecretory agents. Finally, the principles of pharmacoeconomics can be used to evaluate health services delivered by various health personnel to a broad range of patient types. The final series of cases are studies that have attempted to evaluate the impact of clinical pharmacy services in the community and hospital settings.

OSTEOPOROSIS

Osteoporosis is a systemic skeletal disease characterised by bone loss and a resultant increase in bone fragility and susceptibility to fracture. It is a disease that presents the pharmacoeconomic researcher with a multitude of issues. The disease is, in itself, not fatal but leads to increased probability of fractures that require intensive medical interventions, pain, and increased risk of death. The lifetime risk for all fractures are 40% for white women and 13% for white men aged 50 years or greater[1]. However, race and ethnicity also are factors relating to bone mass and osteoporosis. Black Americans have greater bone densities, thicker bone cortex and fewer fractures than whites[2]. These physiologic differences present varying risk factors for the final endpoint for osteoporosis, fractures.

Defining osteoporotic post menopausal female patients is problematic. If bone mass were the primary criterion at two standard deviations below the mean for young women, then about 45% of all woman greater than 50 years of age would present one or more sites of osteoporosis[1]. However, not all fractures are necessarily the result of low bone mass. The proportion of females whose fractures can be directly attributed to decreased bone mass may not be determinable. Therefore, the pharmacoeconomic researcher is encouraged to consider measures of bone mass among other covariates of age, race, diet, drug compliance, and ethnicity as necessary components in pharmacoeconomic studies of osteoporosis and fractures.

The relationship between bone mass as measured by bone mineral density and fracture has been established. For example, Nguyen reported that the most important predictor of fractures of the femur is bone density and body sway[3]. However, bone density does not predict all types of fractures with equal precision. Fractures of the forearm are less related to bone density than either fracture of the hip or vertebral column[4]. However, the relationship between forearm fractures and bone density is about twice as powerful for the proximal site compared to the distal forearm site[5]. Spinal fractures were reported to be significantly related to bone mineral density. Melton reported that a one standard deviation decrease in bone density of the lumbar was comparable to a 17 year increase in age[6]. Thus, the relationship between bone density, after adjusting for age, appears to be an important predictor of fractures.

Age, sex, and other demographic factors are related to fractures. Age has been repeatedly reported to be a significant factor relating to fracture. Hip fractures for the very old (95 years of age) were reported to reach 35.4 per 1,000 in a study of 40 million short stay hospital discharges between 1984 and 1987[7]. White females fracture at a much greater rate than do white males, or black males and females at all ages greater than 50. The incidence of fracture doubles at about five year interval[8]. Further, blacks are more likely to present open fractures of the hip than are whites[9]. Women appear to fracture at a rate about double that for men and whites at a rate about double that for all other races. Marital status, a further demographic factor, was reported to be relating to hip fractures. Never married females were more likely to fracture than married females after adjusting for age[10].

The relationship between fractures and death is a further issue for the pharmacoepidemiologist. Between 20% and 40% of patients suffering a hip fracture expire within six months of the injury[10]. Higher risk patients including those who were incapacitated with a systemic life threatening disease, moribund, or experienced non fracture emergency surgery, faced a 49.4% one year mortality rate[11]. A current three year study of post menopausal Medicaid patients suggests that, although black females are less likely to fracture, they are more likely to succumb to death than white females after suffering fracture[12].

The medical costs in 1986 associated with osteoporosis and fractures have been reported at $2.8 billion for inpatient costs and $2.1 billion for nursing home costs[13]. These escalating costs have been associated with decreases in quality of life and increased disabilities for surviving fracture patients[14]. Although fractures directly increase medical cost for inpatient and physician charges, they have a sustained impact on nursing home costs. Nursing home charges were reported to increase during the month of a fracture but do not return to baseline values following fractures[12].

Hormone replacement therapy (HRT) has demonstrated the ability to prevent post menopausal bone loss[15,16]. Increase bone mineral density is associated with decreased risk of fracture and all of the ramification associated with fracture. Unfortunately, HRT in the form of oestrogen prescriptions are not without side effects. Further, post menopausal women associate oestrogen replacement therapy with increased risks of cancer, weight gain, oedema and other symptomatic effects[17]. It is estimated that less than 20% of the post menopausal females in the United States have received an HRT prescription[18]. Those who receive an HRT prescription are not likely to be compliant. The compliance rate has been reported to fall to 79% after six months, 62% after one year, and 40% after two years[19].

There are several important obstacles facing the researcher attempting to associate medical outcomes with oestrogen therapy for post menopausal females. As discussed above, age, race, ethnicity, marital status and other demographic characteristics associated with bone mineral density. All of these covariates should be included in a model to associate oestrogen therapy with bone mineral density. However, bone mineral density, by itself, represents a physiologic state rather than a disease. More important are those outcomes related to the loss of bone minerals. Fractures represent the most significant medical outcomes because they represent a catastrophic medical event that is both costly and often times leads to mortality and is easily measured. However, a reduction in bone mass may take several decades to develop in the post menopausal female. Given these facts, there is little literature to support a direct link between HRT and fractures. It is not surprising since most post menopausal females are not compliant with their therapy.

SCHIZOPHRENIA

Schizophrenia is a disabling condition that afflicts approximately 1 percent of all adults[20] during any year with lifetime prevalence as high as 1.5% of the adult population. The life-course of schizophrenia is such that persons in their third through their fifth decades of life, typically the most productive economically, show the highest prevalence.

Schizophrenia is a heterogenous disease with variable courses and durations of illness. After an initial episode, only 20% of those patients will not experience another exacerbation. Additionally, estimates suggest that approximately 50 percent of persons diagnosed with schizophrenia eventually become significantly and permanently disabled while others will have periods of relative remission interrupted by crisis episodes with extreme symptomology[21].

The most common classification of the symptomology of this illness is the dichotomisation of symptoms by positive and negative symptoms. Positive symptoms of schizophrenia include delusions, hallucinations, formal thought disorders, bizarre behaviour, and inappropriate affect[22]. It is worth noting that cross-cultural difference for symptoms such as delusions and bizarre behaviour may exist since these are based upon behavioural norms for a population and those norms will vary from culture to culture. Negative symptoms consist of affective flattening, alogia, apathy-avolition, anhedonia-associality, and inattentiveness.

Economically, schizophrenia exacts a significant burden to society by impacting so many facets of societal production. The direct costs of this disorder are characterised by the dehabilitative nature of the disease which often requires acute inpatient treatment, an array of outpatient and community based treatments, long term stays at psychiatric institutions, and pharmacologic agents. This disorder also predisposes individuals to significant indirect costs in terms of diminished productivity, and premature death. Other societal indirect costs include time of caregivers, psychological suffering, and expenses associated with incarceration administration of transfer payments, criminal justice, and property and life lost due to the sometimes violent and criminal behaviour associated with the symptoms of schizophrenia.

Research to date on the economic burden of schizophrenia has focused on both aggregate indices of direct costs as well as estimates of indirect costs[23-26]. For example, while prevalence is at approximately 1 percent in the U.S., annual healthcare expenditures are approximately 2.5 percent[21]. Similar discrepancies in prevalence and cost have been identified in other countries including the Netherlands[25] and the United Kingdom[24]. Estimated total economic costs in the United States (as of 1990) have been identified as high as $33 billion per annum[23,27]. The direct medical costs for schizophrenia account for 45% of the total amount with 3.5% of the costs related to research and training. As might be expected, the largest portion of indirect cost associated with this illness is foregone productivity which accounted for 36% of the total. The sum of social welfare administration care by family members amounted for 11% of the total with the balance of the $33 billion annually going towards other indirect costs related to premature death and crime-related expenditures. Because patients who suffer from schizophrenia are in the peak productivity years of their lives, the disorder bears enormous indirect costs to society, primarily in the form of foregone human capital.

Biomedical research has produced some new therapies resulting in dramatic gains in the psychopharmacology of schizophrenia. Pharmaceutical manufacturers now market three "new generation" psychotropics (clozapine, risperidone, olanzapine) in the United States. These new generation psychotropics exhibit superior or equivalent efficacy combined with markedly decreased incidence of dehabilitating side effect such as extrapyramidal symptoms or tardive dyskinesia compared to traditional neuroleptics such a haloperidol. One major limitation to the widespread use of these agents is the high cost of the agents. Also, clozapine is associated agranulocytosis, a fatal blood dyscrasia, which requires intensive hematologic monitoring further adding to the costs associated with the use of the drug.

Because of the high cost of new agents combined with superior efficacy and side effect profiles, there is a compelling need to investigate these drugs in terms of the economics and outcomes. Certainly managers of various programs overseeing the care of the mentally ill are demanding evidence to justify the use of these expensive agents that are capable of dramatically increasing the cost of drug budgets. Some U.S. Medicaid agencies (a major payer for the care of persons suffering from schizophrenia) are restricting the use of these drugs until such economic evidence is firmly established. This is despite evidence by Stephen Soumerai who demonstrated that a broad restriction in prescription reimbursement results in increased emergency mental health services outstripping prescription savings 17 fold[28]. Limiting the use of these drugs has been a highly debated issue in the state of Georgia, U.S.

Given the relatively high cost of these new agents and the potential of these agents to significantly alter the course of the diseases coupled with the tremendous economic and human burden of this illness, these agents are ideally suited for pharmacoeconomic investigation. The costs that require enumeration for pharmacoeconomic investigation will depend largely on the perspective of the study. This is because the indirect portion of total costs can account for such a large portion if the societal perspective is accepted. The selection of the societal perspective, however, presents some methodologic challenges. Measuring these indirect costs is difficult leaving economist to arduously collect data from multiple sources (social security benefits, employment records, caregiver and provider surveys) or make assumptions about such indirect costs based upon symptom rating scales, functional indices, or place of residence.

In terms of outcomes germane to schizophrenia, investigators of the schizophrenia PORT have developed the following target outcomes that could be measured to assess schizophrenia interventions; clinical status (positive and negative symptoms), functional status (capacity to work), access to resources and opportunities (housing), quality of life (life satisfaction), family well being, and patient satisfaction (quality)[29]. There are several quality of life scales that have been used occasionally to ascertain the humanistic outcomes. Quality of Life instruments are summarised by Lehman and Burns[30] and comprehensive instruments include; Oregon Quality of Life Questionnaire, Quality of Life Scale (Heinrichs-Carpenter), Lehman Quality of Life Interview, Quality of Life Self-Assessment Inventory, and the Lancaster Quality of Life Profile. To date, we are not aware of published community based utility-preference measures that have been routinely used in schizophrenia permitting the calculation Quality Adjusted Life Years (QALYs).

The selection of a decision analytic (CMA, CBA, CEA, CUA) will vary from study to study and again depend upon the perspective and the qualities of the particular therapeutic agent. Unfortunately there is no multi-year prospective study like a Framingham study from which intermediate clinical outcomes such as the Brief Psychiatric Rating Scale (BPRS) scores can be definitively modelled to project changes in final outcome such as life years gained or QALYs gained. As previously mentioned, to our knowledge no utility measure has been published specific to persons with schizophrenia thus precluding any cost utility analyses from being performed until such a measure has been produced, tested in multiple settings, and published. The development of a schizophrenia utility measure would have a profound effect in pharmacoeconomics as the determination of QALYs in schizophrenia economic analyses may be an ideal denominator since the course of this disease can have a devastating impact on the quality of life, though modestly impacting the quantity of life. Indeed it is questionable whether new agents can extend life since schizophrenia is not a fatal condition, though the condition may place sufferers at risk of death due to suicide. Agents that alter the course of schizophrenia may be capable of positively impacting the quality of life and in turn increase QALYs since these agents typically have fewer dehabilitating side effects and may be superior in clinical efficacy.

In terms of selecting comparitors for pharmacoeconomic evaluation of the new generation of psychotropics, there is the family of traditional neuroleptics, the most common in many regions of the world is haloperidol. Given the widespread usage of the traditional neuroleptics and the relatively long history associated with these agents, they are clearly the standard by which comparisons should be made.

Below is a selection of studies used to economically evaluate one of the first new generation psychotropics, clozapine. The general approach in evaluating clozapine has been to determine if the agent is cost saving, focusing on direct medical cost.

A portion of the published pharmacoeconomic evidence to date for clozapine has been based upon remnants of open label clinical trials[31,32] where investigators retrospectively identified economic data from medical charts and interviews of refractory schizophrenics previously enrolled in clinical trials. The authors of these studies have concluded that persons who remain on clozapine for at least one year experience decreases in hospital expenditures that generally offset the cost of the clozapine and increases in outpatient care making clozapine cost saving to cost neutral over a two year follow up period. For the approximately one third of refractory schizophrenic patients who drop out of clozapine treatment, the evidence is less clear as one study did not report the utilisation of those persons and the other study reported small non-significant increases in hospital cost. Since the patients were enrolled in clinical trials with non-equivalent or no control groups, these studies have neither the increased generalisability of naturalistic quasi-experimental studies nor the internal validity of randomised controlled trials (RCTs).

To highlight the international focus of this text, we would suggest readers of this chapter read the article by Linda Davies and Michael Drummond on the Assessment of Costs and Benefits of Drug Therapy for Treatment-Resistant Schizophrenia[33]. This study adapted data from a U.S. based retrospective cohort study and supplemented the data with other trials and expert opinion for the purposes of evaluating clozapine in the United Kingdom.

The study was a preliminary cost effectiveness study of clozapine assessing the impact of switching treatment resistant persons from traditional neuroleptics to clozapine who were receiving long term hospital care. Discounted direct medical costs were tabulated for cost of drugs, inpatient and residential care, and outpatient based services and compared to the years of life with mild or no schizophrenia disability. The method used by these authors was a decision tree primarily based upon a sample of subjects in the U.S. based study published by Revicki et al[31]. To adjust for differences between the U.S. and the U.K., a Delphi panel of five U.K. experts was used to determine estimates of the probability of a person with various symptomology, as measured by the BPRS, would reside in the U.K. for treatment of schizophrenia (long term care / discharge from long term care). The BPRS scores obtained from the U.S. based study were then used in conjunction with the Delphi opinions to obtain estimates for the probability of discharge from long term hospital care (discharge to home / sheltered accommodation) and remain in long term hospital care. Cost estimates applied to the utilisation estimates were derived from the National Health Service and previous investigations. Differences were also accounted for the dosage of clozapine between the U.S. and the U.K. In terms of outcome, the authors calculated years of mild disability gained and operationally defined mild to no disability from schizophrenia as a BPRS score less than 35 or a Clinical Global Impression score less than three. The analysis projected annual and lifetime costs and outcomes. Sensitivity analyses were performed to ascertain the robustness of the assumptions and derived probability estimates.

The results indicate that in the base case, clozapine was cost saving (£1,333 / lifetime) and was cost increasing when the following assumptions were varied: dose of clozapine increased, probability of discharge while on clozapine decreased, the probability of discharge for traditional neuroleptics increased, and more outpatients are eligible for clozapine therapy. The threshold at which clozapine switches from cost saving to cost increasing is when the rate of discharge falls from 19% to 16% for clozapine users. The base case increase in years with mild disability was 5.87 patient years for clozapine therapy. Cost effectiveness ratios (marginal cost / years with mild disability gained) was determined for instances in which clozapine was cost increasing.

This preliminary study provides a good case for using trial data across countries where differences in treatment patterns exist and comparative data within the country are not readily available. The novel feature of this study was the utilisation of BPRS clinical indices obtained from trial data in a different country to estimate resource use in a native county using a native Delphi panel. One caveat the authors note is the potential bias of the Delphi panel where the experts may be more optimistic than reality. The authors reported the results as interim findings that need to be tested using more empirical data, preferably from blinded randomised controlled trials. Also the probability of discharge for persons discontinuing clozapine needs to be better elucidated in this study as the lack of economic information in non-responders was a flaw of the published report from which this decision analysis was based.

PEPTIC ULCER DISEASE (PUD)

The Disease

Basically there are two common forms of peptic ulcer disease: duodenal ulcers (DU) and gastric ulcers (GU). In the past PUD was considered to be idiopathic in nature. The treatment involved a chronic therapeutic protocol, aimed at manipulating the pH of the stomach, including such therapeutic components as: antacids, H_2-receptor-antagonists (H2RA), bland diets, decreasing the "stresses" of life (i.e. anxiolytics, life-style changes), etc. However, scientific discoveries, made during the last two decades, have determined that treatment for the majority of PUD cases should be acute rather than chronic.

Today the aetiology of the ulcers associated with PUD have been grouped into three categories: a) acute stress ulcers, which occur in critically ill patients, b) chronic ulcers associated with non-steroidal anti-inflammatory drug (NSAID) therapy, and c) chronic ulcers associated with a bacterial infection caused by *Helicobacter pylori*, or *H. pylori* as it is better known. It is now known that ulcers develop when factors such as NSAID therapy or *H. pylori* infection disrupt the normal mucosal protective mechanisms of the gastro-intestinal (GI) tract[34].

Once a patient is infected with *H. pylori*, evidence suggests that it is a life-long infection unless interventional therapy is instituted. *H. pylori* infection has also been associated with other disease states such as functional dyspepsia[35], gastric adenocarcinoma[36], and gastric lymphoma[37]. However, this chapter will not examine *H. pylori*'s role in these other disease states.

The Societal Costs of PUD

It has been estimated that five million people in the United States currently have peptic ulcer disease[38]. Approximately one in ten Americans will develop a peptic ulcer at some point during their lifetime. It has been estimated that *H. pylori* is present in over 95 percent of DU patients and more than 80 percent of GU patients if you eliminate those patients with gastrinoma, and those patients taking NSAIDs[39]. Traditionally, the economic costs associated with PUD have been similar in nature to other chronic disease states (i.e. direct healthcare costs, as well as indirect costs linked to a patient's associated decline in productivity). Although the disease has low mortality, its morbidity, economic, and human suffering costs are high. It has been estimated that direct and indirect costs associated with DU alone are between $3 and $4 billion per year[40].

Diagnosis of H. *pylori*

The National Institutes of Health recommends treating PUD patients with antibiotic regimens only after having demonstrating a positive test for *H. pylori*[41]. Basically there are two categories of tests used to determine the presence of *H. pylori* in the GI mucosa. The first category are the noninvasive tests. These include serologic testing and a carbon isotope (^{13}C or ^{14}C)-urea breath test.

The serologic tests rely on the presence of a circulating antibody response to *H. pylori* that can be detected by a test such as an enzyme linked immunosorbent assay. The serology test is the least expensive of all the tests, however it is not useful in post treatment eradication follow-up testing since the antibody will still be present regardless of positive or negative eradication.

On the other hand, the carbon isotope urea breath tests are sensitive and specific as a pre and post treatment diagnostic tool, however is more expensive and more difficult to administer than the serology test. The patient ingests urea labelled with a radioactive carbon isotope, upon which *H. pylori* then utilises a unique enzymatic hydrolysis to yield ammonia and labelled carbon dioxide, which is then detected in the expired air of an *H. pylori* positive patient.

Invasive tests include endoscopic biopsy for urease testing, histology with special stains, and culture. While these procedures were commonly used in earlier clinical trials, their future use will be mostly limited to those patients for whom oesophagogastroduodenoscopy is clinically indicated. This is due to the high cost and invasive liabilities associated with GI mucosal biopsy via endoscopy.

Some clinicians believe that a strong case can be made for not performing tests to diagnose *H. pylori* infection in patients with previously diagnosed non-NSAID induced DU, no signs or symptoms of a hypersecretory state, and no history of treatment with antimicrobial agents that might have cured the *H. pylori* infection by coincidence[39]. It is believed by these clinicians that such a test prior to initiation of therapy with antimicrobial drugs would do little other than simply add to the cost of treatment. However, when using antimicrobials with substantial side effects, it is suggested by these clinicians that an inexpensive serologic test confirm *H. pylori* presence before initiating treatment. However in patients with gastric ulcers or duodenal ulcers who have been taking NSAIDS, a diagnostic test is indicated due to a lower prevalence of *H. pylori* in these patients.

Evaluating Therapies for H. *pylori* induced PUD

A relatively new concept in the treatment of PUD involves the aggressive treatment of *H. pylori* with multi-drug regimens. Typically therapeutic regimens designed to treat *H. pylori* induced PUD involve:

• eradication of the organism, and
• the healing of the ulcer itself.

Traditionally the relapse rate of PUD treated with a typical six-week regimen of an H2RA alone is 65 percent during the first six months after treatment and up to 85 percent during the first year. On the other hand, studies involving eradication therapies have demonstrated *H. pylori* eradication rates to range between 60 percent and 90 percent, while relapse rates have been reported to be as low as 10 percent one year after therapy, for patients deemed compliant[42].

There are several problems associated with eradication of the infecting organism:

• *H.pylori* is protected in its own alkaline environment, which makes it difficult for antibiotics to penetrate,
• the organism exhibits a relatively high degree of antibiotic resistance[43], and
• patient medication compliance has been reported to be a major problem. In fact, patient medication compliance has been identified as the single most important predictor of organism eradication. Even though extensive study is lacking in this area of PUD, two factors seem to play a major role in patient medication compliance:
  a) regimen dosing complexity, and
  b) a regimen's side-effect profile. On one hand, there appears to be a positive correlation between *H. pylori* eradication and compliance, whereas a negative correlation exists between compliance and a regimen's dosing complexity/side-effect profile.

Another problem associated with *H. pylori* eradication involves the refractory nature of some physicians to accept new medical breakthroughs. Hirth, *et al.*[44] found that 99.1 percent of gastroenterologists had prescribed antibiotic therapy to eradicate *H. pylori* at least once, while only 64.6 percent of generalists had done so. The researchers concluded that the generalists were less well informed and possessed more conservative practice styles than their specialists counterparts.

A Meta-Analysis

Many studies have examined the pharmacoeconomic side of PUD[38-40,42,43,45,46]. A meta-analysis recently published by Taylor, *et al.*[46] will serve as our foundation for examining the pharmacoeconomic implications of *H. pylori* induced PUD. The researchers included 119 studies enrolling a total of 6,416 patients in the analysis in an attempt to evaluate and compare the costs and outcomes of treatment with eight leading antibiotic regimens with documented activity against *H. pylori* when compared to traditional maintenance therapy with H2RA's.

The eight antibiotic regimens, with their respective highest frequency dosing schedule,included:

- BMT (Bismuth, Metronidazole, and Tetracycline)(4 times a day),
- CMPPI (Clarithromycin, Metronidazole, and a Proton Pump Inhibitor (PPI- either Omeprazole or Lansoprazole))(twice daily),
- BMTPPI (Bismuth, Metronidazole, Tetracycline, and a PPI)(3 times a day),
- MAPPI (Metronidazole, Amoxicillin, and a PPI)(TID),
- BMA (Bismuth, Metronidazole, and Amoxicillin)(4 times a day),
- CAPPI (Clarithromycin, Amoxicillin, and a PPI)(twice daily),
- APPI (Amoxicillin and a PPI)(twice daily),
- CPPI (Clarithromycin and a PPI)(3 times a day).

These therapeutic regimens were administered to patients under optimal clinical conditions in the studies included in the meta-analysis. The argument was made that these studies would not yield "real world" conclusions (effectiveness vs. efficacy) due to differences in therapeutic complexity as it relates to patient medication compliance. Therefore each regimen underwent a "compliance adjustment" based upon applying validated compliance data to each regimen based upon the total number of daily dosage forms to be taken and their respective dosing schedules. For example, for twice daily regimens, it was determined that approximately 66 percent of patients would take at least 60 percent of their medications, while the remaining 34 percent would take less than 60 percent. Published data was then incorporated which demonstrated that patients with DU who take less than 66 percent of their medications had approximately 77 percent of optimal eradication rates. The researchers decremented the eradication rate by 23 percent for all patients who did not take at least 60 percent of their medications. The compliance adjusted rate for each regimen was an average of the meta-analysis rate and the decremented rate, weighted by the proportion of patients who took at least 60 percent of their medications. It is interesting to note that the rank order of the eradication rates of the eight regimens before and after being "compliance-adjusted" differed only in that BMT and CAPPI changed rank.

The researchers then developed a decision analytic model to compare the first year costs and outcomes for each therapeutic regimen. Decision analysis models are very similar to clinical guidelines (**Figure 1**) in that they both use qualitative methods for determining the optimal management strategy under conditions of clinical uncertainty. Data from these comparisons were then used to determine the relative costs and health outcomes of each regimen.

A threshold analysis (examining the total annual costs of *H. pylori* testing and treatment) demonstrated that each of the eight regimens saved annual costs when compared to traditional maintenance treatment with H2RA's. Annual total testing costs for *H. pylori* and antibiotic treatment ranged from $223 to $410 and prevented ulcer recurrence in 70% to 86% of the patients for the eight regimens studied. The H2RA maintenance costs was $425 and prevented recurrence in 72% of patients.

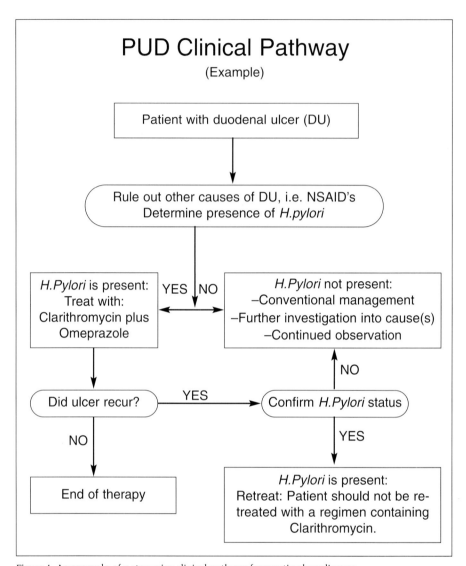

PUD Clinical Pathway

(Example)

Patient with duodenal ulcer (DU)

Rule out other causes of DU, i.e. NSAID's
Determine presence of *H.pylori*

H.Pylori is present:
Treat with:
Clarithromycin plus
Omeprazole

YES | NO

H.Pylori not present:
–Conventional management
–Further investigation into cause(s)
–Continued observation

Did ulcer recur?

YES

Confirm *H.Pylori* status

NO

NO

YES

End of therapy

H.Pylori is present:
Retreat: Patient should not be re-treated with a regimen containing Clarithromycin.

Figure 1: An example of a step-wise clinical pathway for peptic ulcer disease.

After examining the 12 month compliance-adjusted patients without recurrences rate (outcomes measure), the BMT (82%), CMPPI (85%) and BMTPPI (86%) regimens were deemed superior in outcomes (as well as annual costs) to the other five regimens. The compliance-adjusted annual cost for each of the three regimens were $223, $235, and $236 respectively. Since the annual costs of the CMPPI and BMTPPI regimens were approximately the same, the cost-effectiveness of the regimens were analysed incremental to the BMT regimen. After comparing the BMT and BMTPPI regimens (the PPI component consisted of 40 to 60 mg/day for 10 days) it was determined that the BMTPPI regimen cost approximately $13 more per patient and produced a 4% improvement in the number of patients who remained *H. pylori* free for at least 12 months.

If 100 patients were treated with the BMT regimen, the total costs for those 100 patients would be approximately $22,300 for the year. If 100 patients were treated with the BMTPPI regimen, the annual cost would be approximately $23,600, or $1,300 more. Therefore, the BMTPPI regimen would prevent at least a 12 month ulcer recurrence in four patients at an annual cost of $325 per patient. A comparison of the BMT and CMPPI regimens demonstrated that the CMPPI regimen would result in 3 recurrence-free patients at a cost of $400 per patient.

The researchers then performed over 500 monte-carlo simulations of the model where all variables were varied simultaneously. The BMT regimen was the least expensive 72% of the time, the BMTPPI regimen was 15% of the time, and the CMPPI regimen was 13% of the time. The median cost and effectiveness for the BMT regimen was $245 and 82%, the BMTPPI regimen was $258 and 86%, and the CMPPI regimen was $256 and 84%. Head to head regimen comparisons of these three yielded these results: BMT was less expensive than BMTPPI 81% of the time and less expensive than CMPPI 81% of the time as well. CMPPI was less expensive than BMTPPI 52% of the time.

There are several considerations one must use to interpret the results of this meta-analysis. One is that we cannot accurately project cost-effectiveness comparisons beyond one year. Intuition may tell us that the discrepancy between the cost-effectiveness of these eight therapies and maintenance H2RA's would have been greater due to the hypothesis that H2RA use is chronic and perpetuating (extending beyond a year), and the antibiotic regimens are acute and limited.

These types of pharmacoeconomic studies should be ongoing. This is due to the fact that *H. pylori* is not a static entity. The bacteria has already demonstrated a propensity toward antibiotic resistance (especially toward metronidazole) in different parts of the world. Today's optimal therapeutic regimen may not be tomorrow's. There have been discrepancies between results of *H.pylori* outcomes between the United States and Europe that would suggest that patient lifestyles may also play a role in eradication along with differences in bacterial strains.

Co-morbidity issues and variables associated with PUD and *H. pylori* infection (i.e. gastric lymphoma) should be incorporated and controlled for in our pharmacoeconomic models of the future as our data bases mature. Also as we move away from our current "single silos" approach and into a new age of truly integrated healthcare, total resource utilisation cost-effectiveness models may become a reality by virtue of being able to access all data within the system as a whole.

The pharmacoeconomic analyses used in the Taylor *et al* [46] study also did not take into consideration those humanistic variables such a Health Related Quality of Life (HRQOL) and indirect societal costs. Cost and clinical outcomes alone cannot serve as healthcares only judges. We must be able to both quantitatively and qualitatively assess the clinical and economic outcomes of our medical interventions. The humanistic side of HRQOL and human suffering must also be incorporated into our final assessments of which is the optimal therapy of choice.

EVALUATING PHARMACY CLINICAL SERVICES

The principles and practice of pharmaceutical care have stimulated practitioners to develop, implement and evaluate the effect of clinical services on patient outcomes (clinical and economic). Pharmacoeconomic research provides practitioners with information beyond the price of a treatment and thereby seeks to evaluate the overall impact on patient care and well-being. Thus, the evaluation of pharmaceuticals, or other healthcare technologies involves the examination of resources consumed (or costs) and time delineated endpoints of interest (benefits, or consequences).

Community Pharmacy Experience

While it has been generally accepted that community pharmacists perform a variety of interventions that benefit patients and result in saving to the healthcare system there has been relatively little documentation of the cost and saving potential in this practice setting. Some of the first work in this area was conducted by Rupp[47] where he evaluated prescribing errors and pharmacists interventions in the community setting. In this analysis of nearly 6,000 prescriptions a physician and pharmacist deemed to be experts in drug therapy assessed the significance and impact of prescribing errors identified and subsequently corrected by pharmacists interventions. A total of 153 errors were documented, 38 of which both evaluators agreed would have caused harm to the patient if the pharmacist had not intervened. The costs considered in the study included the potential for a hospital admission ($3,015), emergency room visit ($100) or physicians office visit ($26). In this investigation, the estimated value added by the pharmacist across the more than 6,000 prescriptions was $0.19 per prescription screened, $7.15 per intervention and $28.78 per harmful error identified. The cost of the program was determined by assuming a pharmacist's salary of $15 per hour and an average time of 7 minutes per intervention for an average cost of $1.75 per intervention. The cost benefit of these interventions was approximately 1:4 establishing the value of screening for prescribing errors.

In a more recent follow up study Rupp assessed the economic value created by community pharmacists screening for and correcting prescribing errors. Clinical service interventions performed in 89 pharmacies across five states to remedy potential prescribing errors were recorded by a panel of trained observers. These observers documented pharmacy interventions in 623 of the 33,000 new prescription orders observed. This data was then reviewed by a panel of three experts who determined that 28.3% of these problem prescriptions could have caused harm to the patient if the pharmacist had not intervened. A savings of $76,615 was calculated across the 623 problematic new prescriptions, resulting in medical costs savings estimated to be $122.98 per problem prescription.

In this study, the costs measured were limited to the direct medical costs of care that were avoided as a result of the pharmacists interventions. These included emergency room visit and hospitalisation($2,001), emergency room visit ($110), urgent care($60), office visit ($40) and self care. Self care was associated with no direct cost of care. Relevant, but not included in the analysis, were costs attributable to losses in patient productivity, psychosocial costs of pain and suffering to patients and their families, and costs arising from possible litigation against physicians and pharmacists. When distributed across the more than 33,000 new prescriptions dispensed during the study period, this translated into a mean value added of $2.32 per prescription.

In other work, Fincham[48] investigated community pharmacy services by examining 25 pharmacies throughout Kansas where pharmacists documented and evaluated the cost and savings from their pharmacy care interventions. Pharmacists collected self reported data for a four week period including the interventions employed, actions taken and the estimated cost savings. Most pharmacist interventions reported were associated with new prescriptions (68%) followed by refills (15%). The balance of pharmacist reported interventions dealt with over the counter medications and non-prescription related issues. The types of interventions documented by pharmacists included prescribing errors, prescription omissions, drug therapy monitoring and drug interactions. Within each of these categories were more specific types of interventions, for example, prescribing errors included inappropriate drug, indication, dose, regimen, strength, dosage form, quantity, duration, and incorrect patient. Prescription outcomes measured included prescription dispensed as written, prescription clarified and dispensed, prescription changed and dispensed, and prescription not dispensed. The average intervention required approximately 13 additional minutes of the pharmacists time.

Pharmacists documented adverse events potentially avoided by their interventions including, as in the work by Rupp, an emergency room visit, physician visit and hospitalisation. The cost associated with each one of the these adverse effects was estimated and totalled $474, $75 and $5,025 respectively. The hospital costs were determined from the average costs associated with the five DRG classifications that focus on drug reactions or the toxic effects of drugs. The cost assigned to a physician's office visit was derived from the average cost of an office visit in Kansas where the study was performed. The cost of an emergency room visit was determined from the average rates of hospital costs for the West/North-Central region of the United States for state and local government hospitals. The total estimated cost savings attributed to the pharmacists was $490,836 or $1,669 per intervention for the 294 interventions where the pharmacist indicated an adverse event was avoided.

This study did not examine the cost of providing these interventions. However, a limited post hoc analysis reveals that by assuming an hourly rate for pharmacist's time of $30 per hour, the 681 interventions each taking an added 13 minutes of pharmacist time would cost less than $4,500. The cost benefit ratio would be greater than 1 to 100.

All of the above studies attempting to document cost savings of pharmacist interventions used a common approach, where interventions made by the pharmacist were identified, often through self reports, and a panel of experts was used to estimate the likely sequela (emergency room visit, hospitalisation) if the intervention had not been made. The resource utilisation of the sequela were then costed using some estimate of average or prevailing charges for each service rendered (hospitalisation costing $5,025) to compute the cost savings of the studies.

The above general approach to evaluating the cost saving of community pharmacy clinical services have several sources of bias. First these studies do not have control groups where pharmacists intervention rates and event rates for the patients they serve are compared for another set of persons that are not exposed to these pharmacist activities when receiving their prescriptions. Secondly, the estimates of resource saving are based on presumptions that something would have happened and any empirical evidence of the resource utilisation of patients is not presented. Given the lack of empirical evidence, the investigators identified expert panels to estimate what might have happened if the intervention would not have occurred. Of course there is the potential for these panels to be biased in estimating the resource utilisation. The interventions identified in these studies are often based upon self reports by the pharmacists, which may lead to other sources of bias.

Inpatient Services

In a recent report from the St. Mary's Medical Centre in Evansville, Indiana hospital administrators indicated that the number of DVT cases was reduced, the average LOS for DVT patients shortened, and the overall incidence of adverse reactions to heparin and warfarin was decreased as a result of a clinical program to improve care for post operative patients.[49] The program utilised protocols for anticoagulation, a clinical pathway for post operative patients to reduce the number of cases of DVT and an intensive educational effort for nursing, pharmacy, physicians and patients. Staff were educated through grand rounds seminars, presentations, in-service training, pharmacists rounding with physicians and in house articles in the hospital newsletter. Patients were targeted with oral, written and video instructions on the proper use of warfarin. The program resulted in a 33 percent decrease in DVT, a decrease in average LOS of 0.52 days and adverse reactions to heparin and warfarin decreased by approximately 80 percent.

While clearly beneficial to patients' clinical outcomes, we cannot clearly judge if the dollars spent on the program were spent most effectively since the study did not measure cost data. However, there were pharmacoeconomic considerations inherent in the above study. For example the clinical pathway for post operative patients and the anticoagulation protocols were, by definition, developed based on standards of care, practice guidelines and economic information. These tools, used together allow clinicians to differentiate between competing alternatives and decide in advance what care (products or services) a patient should receive and which are most cost effective. Because of the important role that medications play in medical care, pharmacoeconomic analyses are vital to pathway development since they allow clinical decision-makers to assess the true value of a drug therapy. This allows practitioners and administrators to consider the clinical as well as economic and humanistic outcomes that result from drug therapy.

In another study of 3,081 patients admitted to the Walter Reed Army Medical Centre[50] it was demonstrated that adding a clinical pharmacist to medical and surgical teams improved patient outcomes. Clinical pharmacy interventions included primarily adding or changing prescription orders, as well as educational efforts and providing information to physicians. To evaluate the effect of the clinical pharmacy interventions the study examined drug cost per admission, length of stay (LOS) and mortality. The quasi-experimental design compared patient outcomes between two groups of patients. The experimental group was composed of patients from two general medicine and one general surgical team. This group was assigned clinical pharmacists as part of the patient care team. The non-equivalent control group was composed of patients from three general medicine teams and two general surgical teams and no clinical pharmacist on the patient care team. Data on drug cost per admission, LOS and mortality were obtained from hospital records over the one year study period

The results revealed that the clinical pharmacists interventions were effective in improving patient outcomes effectively decreasing the average length of stay from 8.2 to 7.6 days. The average drug cost for patients in the clinical pharmacists groups was $140 compared to $168 for patients in the control groups. Drug cost and LOS showed significant differences between the clinical pharmacist group and the control group. Mortality was not significantly different, even though there were fewer deaths in the pharmacist intervention group than in the control group (1,201 or 1.75% in the pharmacist group versus 1,880 or 2.45% in the control group).

Based on the study results the researchers calculated that the clinical pharmacist interventions saved $377 per hospital admission, or a total savings of approximately $150,000 per clinical pharmacist per year. The cost/ benefit of implementing this service was assessed by comparing the total saving generated per pharmacist ($150,000) to the cost of the pharmacist interventions, based solely on the pharmacists' salaries. The pharmacist salaries were costed out at 50 percent, or $25,000 for the one year study. This provided a cost/benefit ratio of 1:6. A sensitivity analysis was performed varying the pharmacists' salaries and the cost of the hospital stay providing a range of cost/benefit ratios ranging from 1:1.5 to 1:13.

Due to the quasi experimental design, the number of patients enrolled, and the collection of economically relevant data, this study provides strong evidence that pharmacist services may be cost saving. A point worth noting is the method by which patients where admitted to teams with clinical pharmacy services and controls. The patients were admitted to teams on an alternating daily basis, where all patients admitted to general medicine were cared for by one team and other teams took patients on a rotating basis. This method of rotating medical teams and patient admits should provide equivalent patient mixes on teams, unless there is some cyclical pattern of patient admits at that institution. This reduces selection bias, a common source of potential bias in other studies examining the impact of various health professionals. Other points worth noting were the relatively large sample patients affording enough statistical power to detect changes in resource utilisation (LOS), and that the evidence was empirically based with thorough data collection techniques of economically relevant data.

Each of the studies cited above are limited in the amount and type of cost data collected. While some provided some insights into costs avoided through pharmacist interventions few provide a clear estimate of the costs of these programs and interventions. Yet, it seems that there is a clear association between clinical services and cost savings. From these studies we learn that documentation of services and accurate assignment of costs are crucial to an evaluation of clinical service.

CONCLUSION

The above cases illustrate the need for a variety of methods when assessing outcomes across diseases states. Most often, researchers utilised an approach that might best be described as a determination of cost savings or cost identification. In cost saving analyses, direct medical costs and specified indirect costs are summed for two or more technologies (e.g. medicines) and compared. Some may be tempted to classify this style of analysis as a cost benefit approach, as these analyses include the enumeration of cost beyond the initial expense of the health input (e.g. technology), and accordingly the cost offsets (e.g. reduction in hospital utilisation) may be classified as benefits. However, in a robust CBA total benefits must be enumerated, inclusive of some measure of *willingness to pay*, either on the part of the patient, payer, or society for a stated level of reduction in disease related morbidity. Thus, future research efforts will need to encompass an assessment of global direct and indirect cost structures so as to arrive at robust findings for the purpose of crafting rational health policy.

References

1. Melton LJ, Chrischilles EA, Cooper C, Lane AW, Riggs, L. (1992) Perspective: How Many Women Have Osteoporosis. *Bone Miner Res.* **7,** 1005–1010.
2. Cummings, SR, Kelsey, JL, Nevitt, MC, O'Dowd KJ. (1985) Epidemiology of Osteoporosis and Osteoporotic Fractures. *Epidemiology Reviews.* **7,** 178–199.
3. Nguyen T, Sambrook P, Kelly P, Jones G, Lort S, Freund J, Eisman. (1993) Prediction of Osteoporotic Fractures by Postural Instability and Bone Density. *BMJ.* **307**
4. Gardsell P, Johnell O, Nilsso BE, Gullberg B. (1993) Predicting Various Fragility Fractures in Women by Forearm Bone Densitometry: A Follow-Up Study. *Calcif Tissue Int.* **52,** 348–353.
5. Gardsell P, Johnell O, Nilsson GE. (1989) Predicting Fractures in Women by Using Forearm Bone Densitometry. *Calcif Tissue Int.* **44,** 235-242.
6. Melton LJ, Atkinson EJ, O'Fallon WM, Wahner HW, Riggs BL. (1993) Long-Term Fracture Prediction by Bone Mineral Assessed at Different Skeletal Sites. *J Bone Miner Res.* 1227–1233.
7. Jacobsen SJ, Goldberg J, Miles TP, Brody JA, Stiers W, Rimm AA. (1990) Hip Fracture Incidence among the Old and Very Old: A Population-Based Study of 745,435 Cases. *AJPH.* **80,** 871–873.
8. Farmer, ME, White, LR, Brody JA, Bailey K. (1984) Race and Sex Differences in Hip Fracture Incidence. *AJPH.* **74,** 1374–1380.
9. Hinton RY, Smith GS. (1993) The Association of Age, Race, and Sex with the Location of Proximal Femoral Fractures in the Elderly. *J Bone Joint Surg.* **75-A,** 752–759.
10. Rodrigues JG, Sattin RW, Waxweiler RJ. (1989) Incidence of Hip Fractures, United States, 1970-83. *Am J Prev Med.* **5,** 175–181.

11. White BL, Fisher WD, Laurin CA. (1987) Rate of Mortality for Elderly Patients after Fracture of the Hip in the 1980's. *J Bone Joint Surg.* **69A**, 1335–1340.
12. Kotzan JA, Martin BC, Reeves J. (1997) A Three Year Study of Osteoporosis in Post Menopausal Medicaid Patients. University of Georgia, Athens, GA.
13. Phillips S, Fox N, Jacobs J, Wright WE. (1988) The Direct Medical Costs of Osteoporosis for American Women Aged 45 and Older, 1986. *Bone.* **9**, 271–279.
14. Norris RJ. (1992) Medical Costs of Osteoporosis. Bone. **13**, S11–S16.
15. Aitken JM, Hart DM, Lindsay R. (1973) Oestrogen Replacement Therapy for Prevention of Osteoporosis after Oophorectomy. *BMJ.* **3**, 515–518.
16. Meema S. Bunker ML, Meema HE. (1975) Preventive Effect of Estrogen on Post Menopausal Bone Loss: A Follow Up Study. *Arch Int Med.* **135**, 1436–1440.
17. Hammond CB. Woman's Concerns with Hormone Replacement Therapy-Compliance Issues. *Fertility Sterility.* 1994; **62**(suppl 2):157s–160s.
18. Ravnikar VA. (1992) Compliance with Hormone Replacement Therapy: Are Women Receiving the full Impact of Hormone Replacement Therapy Preventative Health Benefits? *Woman's Health Issues.* **2**, 75–82.
19. Berman RS. (1997) Patient Compliance of Women Taking Oestrogen Replacement Therapy. *Drug Info J.* **31**, 71–83.
20. Regier DA, Narrow WE, Rae DS, *et al.* (1993) The *de facto* US mental and addictive disorders service system: Epidemiologic catchment area prospective 1-year prevalence rates of disorders and services. *Arch Gen Psychiatry.* **50**, 85–94.
21. Rupp A, Keith SJ. (1993) The Costs of Schizophrenia: Assessing the Burden. *Psychiatric Clinics of North America.* **16**, 413–23.
22. Andreasen NC, Flaum M. (1991) Schizophrenia: The Characteristic Symptoms. *Schiz Bull.* **17**, 27–49.
23. Rice DP, and Miller LS. (1993) The economic burden of schizophrenia. Paper presented at the Sixth Biennial Research Conference on the economics of mental health, Bethesda, MD. 1992; 1-17. Cited in: Rupp, A. and Keith, S.J. The costs of schizophrenia: Assessing the burden. *Psychiatric Clinics of North America.* **16**, 413–423.
24. Davies LM, Drummond MF. (1994) Economics and Schizophrenia: The Real Cost. *Br J Psychiatry.* **165** (suppl. 25): 18–21.
25. Evers S, Ament A. (1995) Costs of schizophrenia in The Netherlands. *Schizophrenia Bulletin.* **21**, 141–153.
26. Hall W, Goldstein G, Andrews G, Lapsley H., Bartels R, Silove, D. (1985) Estimating the economic costs of schizophrenia. *Schizophrenia Bulletin.* **11**, 598–611.
27. Rice DP, and Miller LS. (1996) The economic burden of schizophrenia: Conceptual and methodological issues and cost estimates. In Schizophrenia: Handbook of Mental Health Economics and Health Policy. Volume I. Eds. M. Moscarelli, A. Rupp, and N. Sartorius, John Wiley and Sons. 321–334.
28. Soumerai SB, McLaughlin TJ, Ross-Degnan D, *et al.* (1994) Effects of Limiting Medicaid Drug Reimbursement Benefits on the Use of Psychotropic Agents and Acute Mental Health Services by Patients with Schizophrenia. *New England J Med.* **331**, 650–655.
29. Lehman AF, Thompson JW, Dixon LB, Scott JE. (1995) Schizophrenia: Treatment Outcomes Research - Editors' Introduction. *Schizophrenia Bulletin* **21**, 561–6.
30. Lehman AF, Burns BJ. (1996) Severe Mental Illness in the Community. In: Spilker B, ed. Quality of Life and Pharmacoeconomics in Clinical Trials, 2nd ed. Philadelphia, PA, USA: Lippincott-Raven. 919-24.
31. Revicki DA, Lucy BR, Weschler JM, *et al.* (1990) Cost-Effectivenss of Clozapine for Treatment-Resistant Schizophrenic Patients. *Hosp and Comm Psychiatry.* **41**, 850–854.
32. Meltzer HY, Cola P, Way L, *et al.* (1993) Cost Effectiveness of Clozapine in Neuroleptic-Resistant Schizophrenia. *Am J Psychiatry.* **150**, 1630–38.
33. Davies LM, Drummond MF. (1993) Assessment of Costs and Benefits of Drug Therapy of Treatment-Resistant Schizophrenia in the United Kingdom. *Br J Psychiatry.* **162**, 38–42.
34. Berardi, RR. (1996) Peptic ulcer disease and Zollinger-Ellison syndrome. In: DiPiro, J.T., Talbert R.L., Hayes P.E., *et.al.,* eds. Pharmacotherapy: A Pathophysiologic Approach. 3rd ed. New York, N.Y.: Elsevier.
35. Veldhuyzen van Zanten SJ, Sherman PM. (1994) Helicobacter pylori infection as a cause of gastritis, duodenal ulcer, gastric cancer and nonulcer dyspepsia: a systematic overview. *Canadian Medical Association Journal.* **150**, 177–85.

36. Parsonnet J, Friedman GD, Vandersteen DP, *et al.* (1991) Helicobacter pylori infection and the risk of gastric carcinoma. *New England Journal of Medicine.* **325,** 1127–31.
37. Parsonnet J, Hansen S, Rodriguez L, *et al.* (1994) Helicobacter pylori infection and gastric lymphoma. *New England Journal of Medicine.* **330,** 1267–71.
38. Sonnenberg, A. (1994) Peptic Ulcer. In: Everhart, J.E., ed. Digestive Diseases in the United States: Epidemiology and Impact, Washington D.C.: US Department of Health and Human Services, Public Health Service, National Institutes of Health (NIH), National Institute of Diabetes and Digestive and Kidney Diseases. *NIH publication* 94–1447.
39. Walsh, JH, *et al.* (1995) The Treatment of Helicobacter Pylori Infection In The Management of Peptic Ulcer Disease. *New England Journal of Medicine.* Oct. 12, **333**
40. Imperiale TF, Speroff T, Cebul RD, McCullough AJ. A Cost Analysis of Alternative Treatments for Duodenal Ulcer. *Annals of Internal Medicine.* 1995; 123:665–672.
41 NIH Consensus Development Panel. Helicobacter Pylori In Peptic Ulcer Disease. *Journal of the American Medical Association.* July 6, 1994; vol.**272**.
42. Cerda, JJ, Mae, F., *et al.* (1994) A Revolution in Peptic Ulcer Disease. *Patient Care.* May 15.
43. Berardi, RR, *et al.* (1995) Helicobacter pylori: A Breakthrough in Peptic Ulcer Disease Management. APHA Special Report, March.
44. Hirth, RA, Fendrick, AM, *et al.* (1996) Specialist and General Physicians' Adoption of Antibiotic Therapy to Eradicate Helicobacter pylori Infection. *Medical Care.* **34:** 1199–1204.
45. Soll, AH. (1996) Medical Treatment of Peptic Ulcer Disease. *Journal of the American Medical Association.* February 28, vol. **275,** no.8.
46. Taylor, JL, Zagari, M., *et al.* (1997) Pharmacoeconomic Comparison of Treatments for the Eradication of Helicobacter pylori. *Archives of Internal Medicine.* January 13, vol.**157.**
47. Rupp MT. (1988) Evaluation of Prescribing Errors and Pharmacist Interventions in Community Practice: An Estimate of Value Added. *American Pharmacy.* December Vol. NS28, No.**12,** 22–26.
48. Fincham J, Hunter J. (1996) Documenting the Worth of Pharmacist Care. *NARD Journal.* April, 29–32.
49. Gold RS, Murphy R. (1996) How my hospital worked to improve disease management in deep vein thrombosis. *Hospital Pharmacist Report.* July **67** XX
50. Bjornson DC, Hiner WO, Potyk RP, Nelson BA *et al.* (1993) Effect of clinical pharmacists on healthcare outcomes in hospitalized patients. *American J Hosp Pharm.* **50,** 1875–84.

6

The use of interactive computer models to present pharmacoeconomic data

A Duggan

INTRODUCTION

For the purposes of this review, we will define a model as an interactive computer program that models a pharmacoeconomic analysis and allows users to change data for the parameters that influence the final result(s). Generally this will mean that costs, disease event data, treatment success rates and management interventions can be changed to consider the impact on cost and outcomes. Such models will usually be specially commissioned Windows programs, designed for use by sales personnel with customers. Some models may be sophisticated spreadsheet or database files.

PHARMACOECONOMICS IN THE SALES SITUATION

"High cost is usually a hurdle in the sales process, whilst low cost does not always help"

The idea of using economic arguments in a selling situation, though often necessary, is full of problems. If the product or service appears more expensive than a competitor at first consideration, then the sales process is uphill from there on. It would be unwise to think that there is any panacea for this challenge, and certainly pharmacoeconomics should only be seen as an aid to the process rather than a solution. It may even be that the existence of a pharmacoeconomic report for a product, will only endorse the thought that a product is expensive. Certainly it is uncommon to see a pharmacoeconomic study carried out by the manufacturer of a product that is less expensive (to buy) than the major alternatives. Despite these challenges, the majority of medical decision-makers are beginning to see the value of looking beyond simple purchase price when selecting products or services. Their problems may start when they try to consider pharmacoeconomic reports. This is because pharmacoeconomic studies are usually based on mixtures of assumptions, clinical trial data, epidemiology and certain management processes. Sensitivity analysis is employed to present results based on varying ranges of data inputs, but it is almost impossible to write a report that all readers will relate to and agree with. The value of an interactive model is that individual customers can each carry out their own sensitivity analysis, using either local data or their own perceptions of reality. Most people find it easier to trust results based on their own numbers and thinking, so that a greater degree of buy in or ownership is generated.

THE VALUE OF MODELS

Judging by the significant increase in the use of interactive models, there is much to be gained by the sensible and planned use of a good model which represents a good sound case. Companies which have ventured into this new ground, having seen the benefit that can be realised, often proceed to develop models for other products. To date there appears to be little conclusive published evidence of the benefit gained by their use. However, an interview with sales or marketing managers, or representatives who have had experience with good models, will result in much anecdotal evidence that significant sales have been gained through their use. Certainly it seems to be a logical step, that if pharmacoeconomics can help sales, then interactive models which are the most effective way of presenting such data, must also be useful. Currently although the energetic protagonist can take a stance that the case is currently unproven, the number of advocates is growing in the UK, Europe and Northern America.

Main benefits of models

Representative confidence

Having an economic case that is sound in the majority of reasonable scenarios, can add significant confidence to the sales person who has to sell a product. Knowing that a customer can enter their own local data and opinions, and still find that your product saves money, simply makes reps feel better about using an argument.

Time with customers

The majority of customers find models interesting to use, and many are happy to book an extra separate appointment to spend time doing their local analysis. Customers are interested in what other people have entered and may be particularly influenced by a local specialist's opinion. Since customer data can be saved and retrieved, it is possible for sales persons to share local opinion.

May facilitate group decision-making meetings

Once a few key staff in a centre have been seen, it can be a very powerful approach to organise a meeting where local data are presented. Showing lowest and highest results with the average can have significant effects at a team meeting where all the key decision-makers are present. However, this requires good key account skills and may be beyond the skill level of average territory representatives.

Allows customers to investigate the impact of local / personal data sets

There are many aspects of medicine that are not black and white, and it is not difficult to find different opinions about success rates, relapse rates and management processes. Populations may differ from one centre to another, or different selection criteria may be used to choose patients for treatment. Different costs will apply from centre to centre, and budget holders may wish to define costs in various ways, eg actual total cost, cost without capital overheads included, incremental costs, opportunity costs. Allowing customers to investigate the impact of these can add considerable degrees of confidence in an economic case.

Can define action plans agreed with customers

Once a customer has been through a model and made changes to data, there will be a result. The customer may have chosen to use a treatment for a particular group of patients, at a certain dose or in conjunction with another therapy. The model can save these data and print a report that reflects the customer's agreed course of action. For a customer to receive such a printed reminder can be a strong element in any sales close.

Define the measurement of the impact of changes in action

The cycle of action can be completed by agreeing on a time scale for assessment of the impact of any changes. The model will forecast savings or other benefits which can be measured later. This can generate customer involvement in validation processes.

All marketing strategies can have a downside and it is worth noting the main negatives associated with the use of models. Careful planning can eliminate most of the impact of these possible negatives.

The downside

- Models can be perceived as loaded dice — a simple trick from the industry to prove that their product saves money. It is important that all models are transparent, and that if under certain circumstances a product is not cost effective or cost saving, then the model must allow that to be shown. Lack of transparency or fixed arithmetic will soon be highlighted. Under such circumstances the company is totally discredited, and their future claims likely to become incredible.
- Not all representatives will have the natural skills to understand the model. A badly presented model is of little value. It is important that a sales force is

trained, and in certain circumstances the model may be restricted to target groups of more senior or able individuals.

- The default settings in a model can be alien to customers. For certain diseases or treatments where there are wide geographical differences, it may be useful to have several startup options. In the UK for instance, there are significant differences between the south of England and Scotland with regard to cardiovascular disease.
- Sales personnel can be over enthusiastic with any new data, and this is particularly true with cost saving cases. They need to remember that there is more to closing a sales than just proving a point. Clever interactive models do not replace good sales skills.
- Results calculated on a model need to be presented as approximations to customers. It would be artificial and irritating to be told that if a particular course of action is taken, then that customer will save £23,456 per year. Results need to be presented as estimates only.

Fools rush in …

Before starting a project to use pharmacoeconomics in a marketing campaign, there are several key questions that should be asked, both of the study and any technique that will be used to communicate the data. Once you have established that cost is an issue for your product, there are seven questions that should be asked before any substantial commitment is made to a project.

Seven key questions to ask about any pharmacoeconomic study or interactive model before starting:

1. Is there a real commercial need or likely benefit?
2. Is there a case which is favourable to your product under a range of plausible scenarios?
3. Which customer group is it for and will they understand the case?
4. What action do you want that customer group to take?
5. What data are likely to facilitate that action?
6. How do you obtain, justify and present the data in a clear way?
7. How will the final argument be presented and communicated, do you have the resources to implement that communication?

These questions and the subsequent actions should be considered as early as possible in a product or campaign's life. Although our focus is on the use of interactive computer models in a marketing campaign, these check list questions can be asked of pharmacoeconomic projects in general.

1. *Is there a real need or likely benefit from an interactive model?*

The idea of an interactive model may be attractive for many reasons, not all of which are commercially valid. It would not be appropriate to have a model just because 'it worked last time or with a different product'. Each project should be evaluated on its own merits.

Minor products that will not be given much representative time, or which may not command much interest in customers, may not be well suited to a campaign supported by a model. Equally the (unusual) product that is cheaper and more effective than competitors, may not need support from a model. The validity of the pharmacoeconomic case that the model will be based on is foundational to the decision about developing a model to present the case. A poor argument is still a poor argument when it is creatively and dynamically presented in a model.

2. Is there a case which is favourable to your product under a range of plausible scenarios?

Although interactive models may not be any more expensive than similar audio/visual projects, it would be unwise to commission and pay for a project which you subsequently find shows that your product is more expensive than its competitor's. A first step must be to build a simple spreadsheet to allow for a full range of sensitivity analyses to be carried out, by identification of all reasonable ranges for each parameter, and then the unreasonable ones that key customers may be interested in seeing. There are often different definitions of data that need to be considered. Should dose be based on recommended, average actually used in real practice, or that used in clinical trials? Success can also be defined in a variety of ways, and each major one should be considered in the testing process. If the case holds, or is only marginally broken by the process, then one can be confident that the model will be useful. At this stage the spreadsheet model, if designed well enough, can be taken to some customers for their opinion. Only then can a bespoke model can be confidently commissioned.

Many pharmacoeconomic studies are based on calculations that use a cost for doctor time. This is one of the first parameters that GP's want to change when they interact with a model. The thinking is that "I'm here anyway, so how strong is your case if we cost my time at zero". Though this may not be very valid in pharmacoeconomic terms, it is a common human reaction that should be planned for. There may be other unreasonable scenarios that customers will want to investigate when exposed to your model. These must all be thought through at an early stage.

3. Which customer group is it for and will they understand the case?

This may sound like a simple question, but the complete range of target customers needs to be identified so that their individual perspectives (and budgets) can be accommodated. A strong case that is based on overall health service costs may not impress a budget holder who is only accountable for, say, staff and drug costs. Even a senior cross budget holder may want, or need to see results presented across a variety of budget headings. Different customers may take a different view of time scales, preferring one or five year analyses. Results may need to be presented differently for some customers, for instance someone in finance may be interested in payback periods or Net Present Values. During development and design it is useful to show outlines (or working spreadsheet versions) to customers.

Patient groups and journalists may be important groups for certain products or campaigns.

4. What action do you want that customer group to take?

The central question here is to do with product positioning. There may be a good economic case that is in conflict with your preferred positioning, because certain patient groups or levels of severity of disease benefit more markedly than others. Such data needs to be handled with care.

Different customer groups may be required to take a variety of actions. Traditionally doctors need to prescribe, pharmacists and supplies departments need to buy, a variety of people need to recommend or support, whilst others need to write about a product. It is a good step to identify the specific actions that one is aiming to encourage.

5. What data are likely to facilitate that action?

The answer to this question will usually involve a good study published in a peer reviewed journal, and it will usually be most appropriate to base a model on a published study. However, even the best of studies will be based on data that some customers will find alien. It is imperative that the model is flexible enough to accommodate the needs of different customer groups. Few studies will be based on patient numbers that a customer will readily relate to, so that it may be useful to front end the model with some introductory data and allow selection of an appropriate patient population. This population may be defined by numbers or type (age, disease state etc). The results must also be reported in ways that different customers will relate to. This is particularly relevant with regard to total patient populations, so that customers may see the impact on their own budget using local patient numbers.

6. How do you obtain, justify and present the data in a clear way?

From question 5 above, it is clear that most models will be based on a published study, so that the source of most data will be from the original paper. There are of course some excellent additional sources of data that may be appropriate to use. Published cost data, clinical and epidemiological reports as well as disease and treatment data from large GP databases like Mediplus, DIN Link and EPIC are all useful sources. Certainly, it may be valid to use cost data in the model that is different to that reported in a study, maybe reflecting more closely the local or latest costs available. Depending on the nature of the original study it may be valid to use the model to investigate the effect of using different patient groups, defined by age, severity or disease state. Such data need to be valid, referencable and acceptable to the target audience. A model can have completely different sets of data applied at the touch of a button, so that standard changes can be considered immediately.

A good model will have the ability to save customer data, so that one customer can see the opinion of others. It is also possible to use models to collect and report (to manufacturer or customers) the ranges of data entered by customers.

Much consideration needs to be given to the actual presentation of data, and the natural flow of a model. It may be necessary to have a few introductory pages for customers to be shown the basis of the case. It is useful to have a decision tree to describe the natural flow of patients and the scope of the study. If there is one, or only a few, major results that the model reports, it can often be useful to have these visible on every page, so that the immediate impact of data changes can be seen. In large models it is useful to have one central part where costs can be changed globally.

Throughout the model it should be easy to find the source of all data, using a standard referencing system of names or numbers.

7. How will the final argument be presented and communicated, do you have the resources to implement that communication?

The field force is the usual medium of communication. However it is possible to give simple well designed models direct to customers, although the amount of experience with this method is low, making an estimation of its value difficult. Exhibitions are excellent places to show such models. Using the right equipment, it is possible to attract large numbers of customers to a stand. Use of OHP palettes is not recommended as the ambient light needs to be so low that the overall stand can appear rather dull. Modern high output projectors or ultra large screens are more useful.

When a field force is to be used, it is worth considering what type of person is best suited to using models. Not everyone takes naturally to computers, and certain proportions of any population can struggle with numerical data. It will be necessary to train all users and may be appropriate to select a particular level or type of person to use interactive models. It is not unusual to use key account type sales persons. It may be wise to have two versions of any model. One can be a cut down version, with fewer fields that can be changed. This can allow most representatives to make a brief description of the case to customers, using higher skilled persons to visit those customers who want or need a more detailed presentation.

Training should include a full understanding of the basic economic argument deployed, and detailed explanation of how data are calculated. Users need to trust the model themselves and feel confident that they can answer questions.

EXAMPLE

The development and production of a model to compare an SSRI type anti-depressant to standard TCA anti-depressants

This is an example of a model that the client wanted to be based on a published economic evaluation. The published report demonstrated a saving in favour of the newer SSRI agent, as did the sensitivity analysis. However, before providing an interactive model to a field force, it was important for central marketing to understand the circumstances in which the case became negative. A good base case that falls over as soon as a customer enters some reasonable or semi-reasonable data, is not the sort of model that most companies would want to supply to field force.

First Steps

1. Develop a simple spreadsheet of the case so that we can gain an insight into the relative strengths and weaknesses of the economic case.
2. Research the likely ranges of data that users might be expected to enter.
3. Run the ranges of data through the spreadsheet to see how often the case is still in favour of the new SSRI agent.

Second phase

1. Consider related and alternative data sources to those used in the main published study.
2. Plan the proposed layout of the model, taking account of the opinion of intended users of the model. The results must be presented in ways that are meaningful to customers.
3. Build the model, write user manual and train company users.

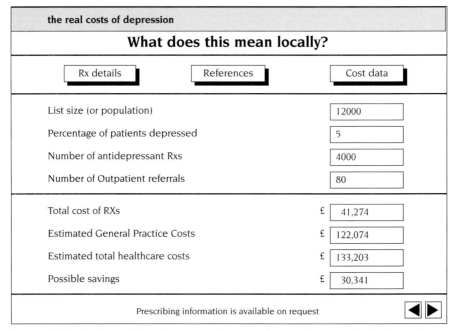

Screen 1. Relating the model to the local population, and generating some simple first estimates of the savings that may be possible. *Users obtain a first estimate of savings on this screen, and can alter population, patients and use of hospital referral services. From here further data can be accessed to allow further interaction.*

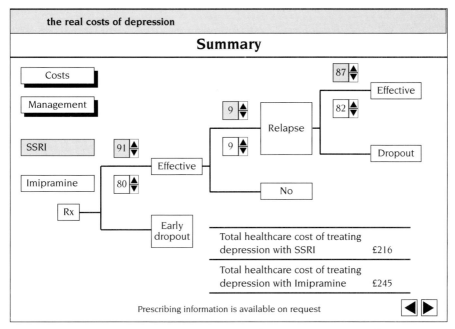

Screen 2. Describing the main decision tree tool used in the evaluation and allowing users to change major clinical data. *In addition to showing the decision tree format of the evaluation, users can alter key clinical data on this screen. By allowing users to enter local prescribing data, they can see the effect of default data on prescribing patterns and alter them to suit their own locality. On further screens, this can be done at drug and dose level.*

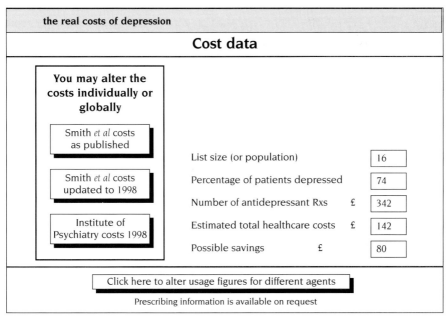

Screen 3. Allowing users to alter all relevant cost data. *Users can alter data to suit their locality.*

the real costs of depression

Clinical management

Number of surgery visits in one year

First time presenters	6 ⬍	Failures to respond	10 ⬍

Failures

% referred to hospital (O/P)	100 ⬍	Number of O/P visits per patient	5 ⬍

Hospital activity

% non responders referred to psychotherapy	4 ⬍	Average Psychotherapy sessions	6 ⬍
% referrals who become inpatients	5 ⬍	Average Inpatient stay (days)	14 ⬍
% referred who receive ECT	1 ⬍	Ave No of ECT sessions	6 ⬍

Total costs of treating depression with SSRI   £216

Total costs of treating depression with Imipramine   £245

Prescribing information is available on request

Screen 4. Allowing users to alter data relating to clinical management processes. *Users can change basic decisions about clinical management; for instance, how often would patients be seen in the surgery, what % of product treatment failures would be referred to a specialist.*

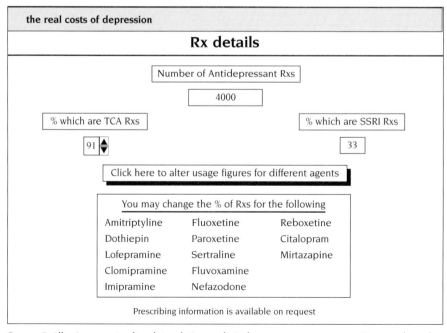

the real costs of depression

Rx details

Number of Antidepressant Rxs

4000

% which are TCA Rxs		% which are SSRI Rxs
91 ⬍		33

Click here to alter usage figures for different agents

You may change the % of Rxs for the following		
Amitriptyline	Fluoxetine	Reboxetine
Dothiepin	Paroxetine	Citalopram
Lofepramine	Sertraline	Mirtazapine
Clomipramine	Fluvoxamine	
Imipramine	Nefazodone	

Prescribing information is available on request

Screen 5. Allowing users to alter data relating to clinical management processes. *Users can change data about local prescribing patterns.*

SUMMARY

Interactive models can be a significant contributor to a sales and marketing campaign, but are a long way from being a panacea for all cost objections. Good quality data on good quality products, delivered by well trained sales personnel, using clearly defined marketing objectives are still the key to success. Models must fit with your overall campaign. There are many situations where a model is not the right answer and careful thought is needed before a project is started.

The right model must reflect the target audience and their needs for data. Different budgets should be respected and reported appropriately. Models must be transparent and the temptation to load a model in your favour must be avoided.

Sales personnel need to be trained in both the pharmacoeconomic data upon which the model is based, and in use of the model itself. It may be sensible to restrict access to the model to more senior or able individuals, or a short cut down version of the model may be developed for general field force use.

7

Pharmacoeconomics and clinical drug research

JT Lee, JT Osterhaus and RJ Townsend

INTRODUCTION

The increasingly competitive marketplace along with the need to find new ways to offset the growing costs associated with bringing a new drug to market have led many pharmaceutical companies to invest considerable amounts of resource (human and capital) into developing pharmacoeconomic research programs for new and existing compounds.[1] This investment reflects a fundamental shift in the development targets for the industry, from faster time to regulatory approval to faster time to optimal commercialization. This shift recognizes that in the current environment it is not sufficient to concentrate efforts solely towards approval, but significant efforts must be expended early in the development process to better ensure that new compounds will be accepted and reimbursed in the marketplace. Demonstrating the value of new compounds has become an important strategy in achieving development targets.

The most appropriate time to begin gathering data regarding the value which a pharmaceutical product will bring to the healthcare setting is during clinical drug development. Pharmaceutical companies are increasingly being called on to document the value of their products, not only clinically, but also in terms of economic and humanistic value. This value can be measured via appropriate data collection and analysis techniques. Information collected early in clinical trials regarding the impact of a new product on the healthcare system can help to determine its price and provide initial information to prospective purchasers regarding the value this new product will have versus current alternatives. Once a product is on the market, its value must be continually reassessed relative to its role in providing comprehensive pharmaceutical care.

PHARMACOECONOMIC RESEARCH: A BURGEONING FIELD

Pharmacoeconomic research methods can be used to assess the economic and humanistic value of therapies by identifying and measuring relevant variables that are expected to be affected by healthcare interventions. Such research asks what happened to the patient after an intervention and what impact did it have on the use of other healthcare resources. What were the outcomes? Was the patient relieved of symptoms, was a condition cured, an illness prevented, or functional status restored? Until recently, such outcomes of medical care received little research attention. There is a paucity of data regarding the outcomes of medical care, surgical procedures and behavioral interventions. In fact, drugs are considered to be the best paradigm for clinical outcomes in the U.S. because of the rigorous testing required for approval of new drugs in the U.S. marketplace.[2]

In order for a drug to be approved for marketing, safety and efficacy must be demonstrated, usually by presenting evidence from two adequate and well-controlled studies. This experimental model is well established; safety and efficacy are critical factors to address, but that model, in outcomes terms, is incomplete. To obtain a complete assessment of the outcomes of healthcare procedures and treatments requires scientific evaluation in three dimensions: clinical, economic, and humanistic. Although economic and humanistic measures are not currently required for the approval of a drug by the Food and Drug Administration (FDA), because of their mandate to regulate the promotion of pharmaceutical products, recently they have stated their intention to develop guidelines for standards of research to support pharmacoeconomic promotional claims.[3] Additionally, decision-makers in large healthcare institutions, governmental agencies, and other healthcare payers are gaining an appreciation for the importance of evaluating all three dimensions. Increasingly, these decision-makers are expecting pharmacoeconomic issues to be addressed in a standard fashion prior to approval or inclusion on a formulary. Outside the U.S., these data are critical to inform pricing and reimbursement decisions, which can greatly affect the early market success of new compounds.

How are the three dimensions (clinical, economic, and humanistic) of outcomes from pharmacotherapy measured? Within the clinical dimensions, safety and efficacy, are evaluated during the drug development process in clinical trials. The economic and humanistic dimensions of outcomes are measured using emerging pharmacoeconomic research methodologies and data collection techniques employed within and alongside of the traditional drug development process. Although the process of drug development has been described elsewhere,[4] a brief overview of the process will provide a better understanding of how and where pharmacoeconomic research fits into the process.

THE DRUG DEVELOPMENT PROCESS

After basic animal research has been conducted and the preclinical studies have shown that a compound warrants further testing, a pharmaceutical candidate is then tested in humans. This process is divided into three study phases. Phase I studies employing small samples of normal, healthy *volunteers* evaluate the safety of the drug. If the drug appears safe, Phase II studies begin in *subjects* who have the disease for which the drug is expected to be indicated. Phase II studies are designed to define initial efficacy parameters and optimal dosing of the drug, employing a small number of subjects in various controlled clinical trials. After the demonstration of safety and initial efficacy, Phase III studies begin in large numbers of subjects in controlled trials. Phase III studies are conducted to gather additional evidence for specific indications and usually are considered to be the pivotal safety and efficacy studies that support a new drug application.

The results of these three phases of studies, along with pre-clinical results, are compiled into a New Drug Application (NDA) or Marketing Authorization Application (MAA) and submitted to the FDA and other regulatory agencies worldwide with requests for approval to market the drug. During the time regulatory agencies are reviewing the data contained in the submission, most companies will initiate Phase IIIB studies in order to provide additional knowledge regarding use of the drug. These studies usually involve large numbers of subjects, with safety and efficacy as major endpoints. They also address practical questions regarding the drug's use in more realistic situations. Many times, pharmacoeconomic parameters are included in these studies which provide additional experience regarding the use of the drug.

Although this traditional method of evaluating drugs via safety and efficacy studies is well-established, from an outcomes measurement perspective, it is incomplete. Because of the controlled nature of clinical trials, the safety and efficacy data obtained are likely to only approximate the effectiveness of the drug under 'real world,' or less controlled conditions. When conducting and interpreting clinical trials, it must be kept in mind that efficacy information indicates whether a drug can work under controlled conditions, whereas the effectiveness of a product is a measure of how the drug works in the real world, under average conditions created by, for example non-compliance, use of concomitant therapy, or lack of access to care. Results obtained early in controlled trials may be compared and contrasted to results from Phase IV studies which may have fewer controls, to determine the consistency of outcomes results . Pharmacoeconomic researchers and evaluators must keep in mind that data collected within any controlled study may not be representative of all subjects who take the drug. Study design and the pharmacoeconomic methods used will help to determine the degree to which data gathered will approximate what might be observed in the healthcare setting.

The shifts which are now occurring in the basic foundation of the medical care system necessitate incorporating pharmacoeconomic research within the context of clinical trial research. However, there are advantages and disadvantages with conducting this research. This chapter will identify issues and discuss considerations surrounding the incorporation of pharmacoeconomics into clinical trials. Baseline factors, design issues, instrument selection and administration, data management, analysis and interpretation, and reporting of results will be discussed.

DETERMINING THE BASELINE

It is difficult to know whether or not a treatment has been successful if the natural course (condition without treatment) of the disease is unknown. The absence of baseline information markedly reduces the value of any information generated by the incorporation of pharmacoeconomics into an isolated clinical study since there is no benchmark with which to compare the results. It is therefore critical to document these baseline effects early in the research program in order to more confidently interpret subsequent results from ongoing trials. Incorporating epidemiological research and methods into the drug development and pharmacoeconomic research plans early on will aid in the interpretation of later study results. Epidemiological research methods can be used to establish the natural history of the disease and document current treatment options as well as to provide information that will be useful in understanding the burden of the disease from multiple perspectives.

Before developing the pharmacoeconomic research plan, a thorough review of the literature should be conducted. The literature search can be generated via MedLine® using typical clinical search terms. Literature sources such as Social Science Abstracts, International Pharmaceutical Abstracts, government documents, and other data bases should be considered as well. Literature searches are valuable not only in determining what relevant information exists, but moreover by identifying where the research gaps lie. A comprehensive research plan will be tailored based on this information.

Identifying what is known about the condition and its current treatments helps focus the research effort. Questions of interest typically include "Who does the condition most affect? In what ways? Who bears the burden of the illness?" For example, asthma may affect a child clinically, and in terms of lost school days, but in an economic sense it may also affect a working mother or her employer. Likewise, Alzheimer's disease has tremendous economic and humanistic consequences on the caregivers. Additionally, some diseases have no effective treatment and the healthcare system can provide only minimal care for the patient. However, these conditions may incur costs outside of the healthcare system. Depending on the perspective taken, those costs may be as important as the costs incurred within the system. For example, the cost of AIDS is great in terms of the morbidity costs incurred outside of the healthcare system.

It is important to assess the humanistic factors affected by the disease in order to capture the total burden of the illness and establish baseline information. Health-related quality of life (HRQOL) effects and patient satisfaction, with specific aspects of current treatments or interventions, should be considered and appropriately assessed. These baseline humanistic assessments may indicate the degree to which there is "room for improvement" from the patient's perspective. If baseline scores indicate minimal dissatisfaction or impairment, it is unlikely that an intervention will result in significant improvement in satisfaction or HRQOL, assuming valid, reliable, precise instruments are used. Examples of such research includes a comparison of migraine subjects to age and sex adjusted controls which demonstrated that even between migraine headaches, the condition had a significant impact on patient health related quality of life.[5] Lindley *et al.* measured the quality of life of subjects before and after highly emetogenic chemotherapy and demonstrated the impact of nausea and vomiting on patient perceptions.[6] Lee and colleagues assessed the effects of generalized anxiety disorder on functioning and well-being relative to age-based norms.[7]

Baseline HRQOL assessment may involve cross-sectional data collection or longitudinal collection. Cross-sectional data collection provides a fingerprint of HRQOL at one point, with subjects reporting their health status during the past week or month. Following a group of subjects over time to collect longitudinal data can provide information about changes in health status during the measurement period.

It is also valuable to establish baseline levels of resource use. The basis for economic evaluation is an appropriate and complete assessment of the resources being used as opposed to dollars being spent. This is particularly true when collecting data from multiple locations and within environments where costs are subject to change. Resources used also represent, in part, the processes of care involved in patient diagnoses and treatment. Until recently, there have been only minimal attempts to link such processes of care to patient outcomes. If resources are limited, it is important for decision-makers and policy makers to ensure that providers are using resources efficiently and effectively. If it is not known what or how much is being used to achieve an endpoint, it is impossible to know whether or not efficiencies are being attained. As resource use comes under greater scrutiny, it becomes more important to know what resources are involved in treating a condition in order to make proper use of the existing resources and ensure that new treatments are properly framed.

Although prospective studies may be required to capture the baseline data there are other sources to consider. Some of these sources include patient diaries, government surveys, and medical charts. These sources can be used to capture resource use over time. Various databases exist that can provide some information regarding resources used to treat conditions. These databases exist because many healthcare providers have been paid based on the resources they use, so there is an incentive to provide such data. However, administrative databases do have shortcomings since they were not designed to provide complete outcomes information; they were designed to pay claims. If the condition is clearly and easily defined by a disease or treatment computer code, claims databases may provide information regarding the processes of care. Appropriate validation techniques are essential to demonstrate the accuracy of the claims.

The importance of establishing appropriate and rigorous baselines for pharmacoeconomic assessment cannot be overstated. The management of outcomes is dependent on the ability to measure them, and measurement must have a frame of reference.

DEVELOPING A PHARMACOECONOMIC RESEARCH PLAN

Determining the baseline effects of a disease on economic and humanistic parameters is a key step in initiating a pharmacoeconomic research plan for a new development program. The research plan should document the key activities that will be required to provide pharmacoeconomic support based on the likely clinical effects of the compound and should be closely tied to the commercial objectives for a program. Typically, a pharmacoeconomic research plan will provide background information that has been gathered from literature reviews. This background information may include burden of illness information, but additionally may assess key issues in the treatment of the disease as well as provide information regarding current (and future) competitors and their ongoing research activities.

Based on this background information, the specific pharmacoeconomic research activities which are planned for the compound should be detailed. This includes clinical trial-based assessments which will be incorporated into the clinical development program as well as non-clinical trial projects (e.g. burden of disease, instrument development, functional status). For each project, the plan should describe the core activities as well as outline project responsibilities and resource requirements. Most importantly, key projects should be explicitly linked with the commercial objectives of the program. An additional component which may be useful is an initial communications plan. The communications plan should outline key manuscripts and presentations and should include target journals and important national and international meetings.

In designing global pharmacoeconomic research strategies, the industry researcher must balance many competing considerations. Early pharmacoeconomic work for a new drug is often coordinated centrally, and must be conducted such that study results are as broadly applicable across multiple markets as possible. A key step in designing a multinational research programme begins by communicating to contacts within the various markets to fully determine the critical pharmaco-economic data needs for a given market. Ideally, there will be a considerable amount of overlap in terms of the core pharmacoeconomic data needs, though often this is not the case. Different healthcare systems may desire different types of data, against different comparators, over different periods of time. Ultimately, central research groups must weight their activities based on research priorities for key markets. The best balance between overall corporate objectives and local market need results from consistent interaction with the markets and appropriate division of activities between central and local researchers.

For the research plan to be appropriately focused, the plan should be reviewed and input should be solicited from key clinical and commercial team members. In addition, pharmacoeconomists from critical markets should have that opportunity to review and contribute to the plan. This review phase can be time-consuming, but is critical to ensuring a comprehensive, accepted plan. Once the initial plan is agreed, it should be updated at lease annually or as new information becomes available.

One centrally-organised research plan is unlikely to satisfy all local needs of the various markets participating in the development programme. In this case, it is best to be pragmatic and gather data that is useful to most markets but allows for a market-specific focus in subsequent postmarketing studies.

INCORPORATING PHARMACOECONOMIC PARAMETERS IN CLINICAL TRIALS

Rationale

Much has been written about conducting pharmacoeconomic studies within the clinical trial framework.[8-13] Typically, early clinical trials provide the first opportunity to explore the potential economic and humanistic effects of a new drug[8, 11] In addition, they provide the primary opportunity to document and support potential economic and humanistic claims that are targeted for promotion at the time of launch of a new product. Thus, for timing, convenience, and preliminary research needs, the clinical trial setting provides a suitable laboratory for health outcomes researchers.

However, using clinical trials as a primary setting to collect health outcomes data is not without limitations. Potential drawbacks to this approach include at least the following:[9, 13]

- studies may not be powered to detect significance in health outcomes parameters
- protocol-induced resource use
- inadequate subject follow-up
- lack of relevant comparators

Thus, while clinical trial-based efforts may be extremely useful in supporting promotional claims, product labeling, and identifying potential pharmacoeconomic effects of a new compound, it may not address the types of questions that are most pressing to decision-makers. This last fact has been the basis of criticism by many who suggest that pharmacoeconomic data collected in clinical trials is of little use to "real world" decisionmakers.[10, 14] On the contrary, these data may be very useful to decisionmakers who need early information to determine whether a new drug will be included on a formulary, particularly when augmented with additional data that may help bridge these clinical data to a more realistic framework. Using this approach allows decisionmakers to consider clinical trials-based data as providing an important piece of the puzzle (not the whole puzzle) as it relates to the pharmacoeconomic impact of a new drug.[15]

Ideally, pharmacoeconomic and clinical study plans should be developed in tandem. The degree of pharmacoeconomic involvement will most likely be a function of the phase of research in which the study is being conducted, the clinical study design, the condition of interest, and the information gathered at baseline regarding the condition and its impact. Key questions to address include "What is the primary purpose of the study? Are economic and quality of life measures of primary or secondary importance? Why does this study need to be conducted?" The process defined to address these questions should be clear and transparent so that any potential issues surrounding study design or bias are easily addressed.

Objectives

The pharmacoeconomic research question(s) should be defined in consideration of the clinical research question(s) raised. The questions should be clearly stated so that the study can be designed to answer the question. Pharmacoeconomic research may be incorporated into a clinical trial as a secondary objective or as a primary objective. For example, if the study is a pivotal, Phase III study in which the primary goal is to measure safety and efficacy for an NDA/MAA submission, pharmacoeconomics may be considered as an "add on," and it is unlikely that the study will be (or should be) modified in order to make it more "appropriate" for a pharmacoeconomics study.[16, 23] On the other hand, a Phase IIIB or Phase IV study, with the primary intent of measuring HRQOL or resource use in a general population with the condition under study, should be designed with the objective of answering the pharmacoeconomic question.[17, 23] Having a study designed primarily to collect pharmacoeconomic parameters does not mean that safety and efficacy are ignored; clinical data must be collected in order to assess the relationship between resource use and HRQOL changes with the clinical response.

Design Issues

The pharmacoeconomic endpoints should be clearly identified in the protocol. The protocol should be closely adhered to and standard precautions should be taken to minimize any potential biases or systematic error that may lead to erroneous conclusions. If the major purpose for conducting the study is to assess pharmacoeconomic changes with treatment, then the completion of baseline evaluations should also be part of the inclusion criteria in the protocol.

When designing pharmacoeconomic studies, it is critical to adhere to sound scientific principles. Randomized controlled trials (RCT) are generally considered to provide the strongest level of evidence of efficacy. Hence, clinical trials, especially those intended to be part of a regulatory submission, are typically randomized, double-blind, and placebo-controlled. However, other study designs (observational, pre-test/post-test, modeling) may be better suited to evaluating a pharmacoeconomic question, where blinding may mask the actual use of resources or the impact of a means of drug administration on health related quality of life. Observational studies are sometimes used by health services researchers if the goal is to evaluate resource use in a realistic setting for various populations using one intervention or another. The results must be interpreted cautiously and should not be reviewed in isolation.

If resource use assessments are incorporated into the study, the perspective, (e.g. patient, society, employer) must be identified as well. Several perspectives may be of interest, given the current healthcare system. As the system undergoes further shifts, some perspectives will no doubt be of greater interest than others. Clearly, society and patient perspectives are of interest, because as a society, certain types of healthcare resources, such as vaccinations, are highly valued in part because of their external benefits. Third party payer perspectives are of interest because of the decision-making power which they have in the current healthcare system.

It is difficult to collect resource use and other economic data that is representative of realistic situations in a clinical study designed primarily to assess safety and efficacy. This is more true for chronic conditions such as hypertension or studies designed to prevent conditions that use intermediate outcomes as endpoints, (cholesterol reducing studies designed to reduce coronary artery disease, or studies to prevent sequelae of osteoporosis). On the other hand, some clinical trials of acute conditions may very closely mimic reality (treatment of sepsis for example). The researcher must be aware of the extent of the limits imposed by the clinical trial design and document them in subsequent publications or presentations.

Likewise, the extent to which humanistic data collected in controlled clinical trials is representative of the true population of patients, is a function of the type of subjects enrolled in the trial and whether the study design reflects a realistic use of the drug. For example, an antihypertensive clinical trial may include only individuals with mild to moderate hypertension and exclude individuals with other pre-existing conditions. On the other hand, a study of migraine subjects, with strict enrollment criteria, may enroll only the most severe sufferers. The subjects participating in a clinical trial may serve as a proxy or may provide an indication of what to expect to observe in future use outside of trial conditions. If mild patients show some improvement, one might expect to see larger improvements in more severe patients. If the intervention is linked with the improvement, results will indicate what dimensions (economic or humanistic) changed, which can predict expected results for future studies. The results of pharmacoeconomic evaluations in early clinical trials will allow for more focused research in later studies.

Rigour vs. Relevance

For health outcomes researchers working in the pharmaceutical industry, no balancing act is more difficult or more important than the balance between scientific rigour and commercial relevance when designing health outcomes studies. This balance is often described in the medical literature as a conflict between internal validity (confidence that the results are valid within a study) and external validity (the generalizability of study results beyond the study population).[9, 14] The appropriate balance between internal and external validity is typically dictated by the primary objective of the study. Clearly, studies conducted to measure the efficacy of a new compound in a given disease state must be designed with an emphasis on internal validity. For example, Phase II and III studies are typically, randomized, blinded, and placebo-controlled, with strict adherence to study protocol, scheduled visits, and fixed dosing regimens. These types of studies are essential to obtaining FDA approval for a new drug. Alternatively, a study to observe the effects of a new drug on health resource utilization in an uncontrolled setting would typically be designed to achieve higher levels of external validity.

In an ideal setting, every study would be designed to target only one primary objective, allowing the design, conduct, and analyses to focus solely on answering one question, such as: "Is this drug effective in treating this condition?", "Does this drug improve health-related quality of life?", or "Is this drug cost-effective relative to a viable alternative?" Unfortunately, resource and timing constraints limit the ability to design a separate study for every research question, and most of the time multiple questions are addressed within a given study. For example, a Phase III trial may have a primary clinical objective which dictates much of the study design, however secondary objectives of this trial may include safety, economic and/or humanistic parameters as well. It is within this framework where the balance of rigor and relevance becomes most critical.

Sample Size

In planning the design of the study, it is essential to determine the appropriate sample size. Sample size may be a function of efficacy parameters, specific HRQOL parameters, or economic parameters. If pharmacoeconomics is the primary objective of the study, the sample size should be estimated based on changes expected in those parameters. Currently there is little information about sample size based on pharmacoeconomic parameters. Norms for the SF-36 Health Survey scales in the general U.S. population have been published by age and gender.[18] However, until more information becomes available, pilot studies with pharmacoeconomic parameters, or previous trials, may also provide useful data. As an alternative, clinical parameters may be used to generate sample sizes; however, such an approach does not guarantee an appropriate estimate. For example, the number of subjects needed to show a clinical difference in asthma treatment might be 40 based on FEV_1, however a cost-effectiveness study might require 140 subjects if the power calculation is based on the expected difference in emergency room visits. Post hoc power calculation will provide support for future studies. Additionally, in cases where pharmacoeconomic measures were not used to estimate sample size, sensitivity analysis should be conducted to place the results obtained from a study in proper perspective.

Instrument Selection

Selection and design of the data collection instrument is another important aspect of this research plan. Recognizing the symptomatology of the condition, and how the population is affected, will enable the researcher to select or create an instrument to measure how an intervention might lessen the economic and humanistic burden of the specific condition in question. The decision of instrument selection is critical; if HRQOL measures are to be included, the condition in question will be the determinant of whether or not a disease-specific instrument is required. If no appropriate instrument exists, an existing instrument may have to be modified,

94

or a new instrument may have to be designed. If it is unclear whether a disease-specific HRQOL instrument is needed, it is better to err on the conservative side and use one. A feasible approach is to use a standardized, validated core instrument to collect HRQOL measures, with customized additions to address the specific considerations warranted by the condition under study.

The issues of validity, reliability, and instrument sensitivity should be considered before an instrument is selected for use in baseline measurement and for use in a clinical trial. It is certainly possible to use a new instrument in a clinical trial without previous knowledge of its validity or reliability, however the risk the researcher takes is that after the fact, the instrument may be shown to lack those desired properties. Before using an instrument in a controlled trial, if possible, one should consider conducting a pilot test to verify that it is valid, reliable, and sensitive. If time does not permit it, one needs to consider the risks involved in ending up with data that is not usable.[19] Resource utilization questionnaires too, should also be carefully developed and tested prior to use within a clinical trial. Data to be collected directly from subjects by use of these instruments requires special considerations. Some points to consider before the instrument is selected are literacy and translation of clinical terms into language that the patients will understand. The number of items one intends to include will be a function of the disease of interest.

Proper administration of the data collection instruments is also important. The protocol should specify how data will be collected, who will collect it, the specific time(s) during the study data will be collected, and who will provide the information. Investigators need to be informed of their responsibilities in providing and/or collecting data. Anticipating these questions and addressing them before data collection starts is important to the success of the data collection and therefore the study results.

Selection of investigators is an important consideration to the success of the study. The number of sites involved in a study may vary. Increasing the number of sites increases the potential complications, from a management perspective. However multiple sites are often needed in order to enroll patients within a reasonable time frame.

If the patient is the main source of pharmacoeconomic information, the burden placed on the patient needs to be considered. Most subjects will not object to providing information. However, if the subjects are going to be asked to provide information, they must be notified via informed consent. Patients should be told how much is expected of them, what they are to do, who will answer their questions, and other facts about the study and its effect on them. These issues must be clearly stated in the patient consent form.

Translations

A critical issue in conducting multinational pharmacoeconomic studies involves the necessary translation of economic and. particularly, humanistic instruments which are to be incorporated into a study. In order to be certain that an instrument is measuring similar parameters across any number of cultures and languages, a formal translation process must be pursued.[20] Three common methods for instrument adaptation and translation are typically considered. The *sequential model* involves an established set of procedures for translation of instruments from an original source instrument into the intended language. The *parallel model* is used to establish a basis for cross-national comparability in the original development and validation stages of an instrument. Finally, the *simultaneous approach* allows researchers to agree up front regarding the domains to be included in the instrument, so that each country will develop its own items using a standard approach.

The general approach of translating an instrument includes four basic steps. The process begins with a *forward step*, where the instrument is translated from the language of origin to the intended language. Many times, this step will be undertaken independently by multiple translators. Secondly, a *quality control* step helps to ensure the translation is conceptually equivalent to the original version. This step can be addressed through expert quality ratings or backward translations. A third step is a *pretest*, where the translated version will be tested by a small group of people in the intended population. Many times, a fourth step, *international harmonization*, will be undertaken by bilingual translators to ensure multiple translations are conceptually equivalent.[21]

This process is time-consuming, so it is important to embark on this process as early as possible. In order to accomplish this, it is important to work with clinical research colleagues to obtain early information on which countries will be participating in a given trial, and the expected number of subject who will be participating within that country. Sometimes it will not be feasible to translate an instrument into every possible language. For example, it may not be worthwhile to go to the trouble and expense of translating an instrument into a particular language if that country is not enrolling a suitable number of subjects. Generally, efforts should be focused on countries where sufficient numbers of subjects are enrolled so that by-country analyses can be conducted meaningfully should data be unsuitable for pooling across countries.

DATA MANAGEMENT

Data Collection

In most traditional clinical trials, data is collected in the practitioner's office, the hospital or the clinic. Since the physician is usually the investigator and may be making decisions about clinical efficacy, this method is appropriate. Pharmacoeconomic data are frequently, but not always, collected from the patient. Knowledge of the disease helps indicate who can provide the most reliable information about its burden. The patient and the physician are often respondents of choice. However, if the trial involves paediatric patients, or the elderly with cognitive dysfunction, or patients with other mental impairment, the patient may not be the most ideal source of information. Rather, care givers or parents may be more appropriate respondents.

There are trade-offs between asking subjects to provide information at the healthcare provider's site (office, pharmacy, etc.) versus collecting it at home. Collecting data at the provider's office means that pharmacoeconomic data is collected at the same time that clinical data are collected. If subjects complete questionnaires at home, the ability to link their response with a clinical response may be a bit more difficult. On the other hand, subjects may feel more rushed at the site, especially if they are asked to provide additional information during their visit. The likelihood of obtaining complete responses is higher if subjects complete data collection forms before they leave the site, and the completeness can be checked by the investigator or one of the staff. Also, if questions arise, subjects have someone close by to ask for help.

Another potential concern of asking subjects questions at the provider's site is that the patient may respond in the manner that they think will please the provider as opposed to how they really feel. The issue of social response bias should not be ignored, but also should be kept in perspective. It is, in part, a function of what questions are being posed. If patient satisfaction with the provider is the issue, a social response is of concern. But if the questions focus on the patient's ability to work or attend school, response bias may not be as significant. Response bias is not limited to a physician's office, it could also occur in a home where a spouse may coach a patient as to the "right" responses. Social response bias may be reduced via the data collection medium. A personal interview in a waiting room is not likely to generate any information that the patient considers confidential. Patient self-report via a paper and pencil format or computer may provide a better sense of security. There is no generally agreed upon means to collect such data, each method has its pros and cons, but whatever means is used, it is important to be consistent across all patients, and throughout the study. For example, the SF-36 Health Survey, a commonly used, validated instrument, consistently generates higher scores when collected over the telephone as opposed to a paper-pencil completion.[22] If change over time is of interest, consistent use of one approach is most appropriate.

Frequency of Data Collection

How often should pharmacoeconomic data be collected? If change is to be measured, a baseline and final assessment are required, at a minimum. Additional data collection points will be a function of the trial design and the condition being evaluated. When making the frequency decision, one should consider the pattern of intervention, and whether measures can be concentrated on where the maximum response to treatment is expected. Distinguishing between early and late effects of an intervention may be useful. The frequency with which data is to be collected should be stated in the protocol. Conservative estimates are recommended as data can always be aggregated, but it cannot be disgregated any finer than the original data collection points. Patient burden should also be considered when making these decisions. For an acute treatment, a baseline and final assessment may be appropriate, for a long term trial, more frequent measures may be necessary in order to reduce the subject's recall period.[23]

Data Entry

Proper procedures must be in place to assure that data being analyzed are of acceptable quality. As with most studies, expected problems in the analysis of such data will surround missing data, multiple responses to single item questions, illegible items, and stray marks. As the data proceeds through data entry, quality assurance and quality control, procedures such as how missing data are to be handled should be identified and adhered to scrupulously. A code book should be developed addressing each variable to be entered, and decisions made beforehand of how to deal with likely problems. When new problems arise with data entry, (and they will), decide the response, be consistent, and note it in the code book. In the case of HRQOL analysis, where several items may comprise a scale, it will be important to state at what point missing items will negate the use of an observation. In the case of economic data, missing items may reduce the usable sample size. Lack of critical demographic information may mean that work status cannot be identified. Missing data can be minimized by using appropriate questionnaires that are easy to complete with minimal burden on the patient.[23]

ANALYSIS AND INTERPRETATION

An analysis plan also should be developed and either stated in the protocol or maintained as a separate document. The data analysis methods included in the statistical section of the protocol will be dictated by the types of data collected. Variables should be identified that are hypothesized to change over time. As is the case for the clinical component of many studies, a single variable may not suffice as "the answer" for a pharmacoeconomic study. Therefore, primary and secondary measures should be identified. The more measures identified to be of primary importance, the larger the sample size needed and the greater the likelihood of having one measure reach statistical significance due to chance. In the case of resource utilization variables of interest may include length of hospital stay, or intensity of resource use. For HRQOL measures, an index, a profile, or a battery of measures may be primary variables. If HRQOL is evaluated via a standard instrument, the instrument should be scored according to the developer's instructions. Data "dredging" is inappropriate, unless it is a pilot study intended to generate hypotheses as opposed to testing hypotheses.

The subjects to be included in the analysis need to be identified. In some cases, the "intent to treat" sample is the appropriate choice — this includes all subjects enrolled in the study — whether or not they actually followed the protocol. The intent to treat analysis is considered to more closely reflect actual use of a drug. Not everyone is compliant, not every patient provides data for all collection points. Another option is to analyze only those subjects who completed the study "per protocol". This subgroup may be of interest if the HRQOL effects of an intervention is of concern, (for example, there may be interest in evaluating only subjects who took the drug properly). Analysis of both "intent to treat" and "per protocol" groups and a comment on the similarities and differences is also an option, but it is more time consuming.

There are a variety of methods by which pharmacoeconomic data may be analyzed. Clearly, the analytical methods to use will be a function of what data is collected (e.g. nominal, ordinal, interval, etc.), its distributional properties and the number of time points at which data is collected (cross-sectional or longitudinal data). Direct comparisons, trends, percent successes, survival analysis, repeated measures, and multivariate analyses have all been used. Whichever method is chosen, it should be stated and justified in the protocol. In general, it is best to keep the analysis as simple as possible. Results should be reported in unweighted averages, in standard form. If HRQOL is measured using a profile, each dimension should be reported separately. Treatment groups should be separated and analyzed by treatment.

Potential confounders of data also need to be considered. Before one can attribute an effect to a specific intervention, it is important to minimize the likelihood of that effect being due to other variables. Randomization into groups, control groups, adequate sample sizes, and appropriate control of baseline parameters helps to minimize confounding, although one can never be entirely sure. Uncertainty can be addressed in two ways. Statistical methods can be used to address uncertainty that may be due to sampling techniques. Sensitivity analysis can be used to address uncertainty due to lack of knowledge. Sensitivity analysis ask 'what if?' and tests the robustness of the data. When assumptions are made about certain parameters, sensitivity analysis quantifies how comfortable one can be with those assumptions.

For example, there is no general agreement on the precise discount rate that should be used to discount future health benefits or future health costs. Since the precise rate is unknown, it is reasonable to test study results with a low, high, and middle value. If study results vary widely, one can have less confidence in any single set of results. Sensitivity analysis can demonstrate the dependence of a conclusion on a certain assumption, or that an assumption does not affect results significantly. It can also be used to establish a minimum or maximum value that a variable must possess for study results to be positive.

If the study is multinational, cross-cultural differences must be considered. Before clinical data such as blood pressure and laboratory values can be pooled for analysis, the data must be evaluated for homogeneity. In the same vein, neither HRQOL nor economic data should be pooled without cultural and homogeneity issues being taken into consideration. There may be substantial differences in HRQOL responses across cultures.[17] Thus, instruments need to be translated to assure linguistic and conceptual equivalence. From an economic perspective, different countries may have different pricing policies and the decision as to what monetary value to use is not always clear. It may be more simple to express economic evaluations in terms of resources used rather than in monetary increments. Despite attempts to control for various parameters, differences may still exist, and in those cases, data should not be aggregated.[23]

REPORTING OF RESULTS

When reporting pharmacoeconomic data that were collected in clinical trials it is useful to keep the presentation simple. If the initial questions asked were clearly stated, such an approach is realistic. One should avoid discussions of individual subjects; rather, summary measures should be used to discuss the differences between treatments over time. One should be aware of potential censoring of HRQOL or economic results by death and/or early drop outs. For example, if subjects in a duodenal ulcer prevention trial are followed and subjects who have more than two relapses are dropped from the study as treatment failures, these subjects may be using up significantly more resources than subjects who are doing well and still in the study. If the treatment failures are lost to follow-up, it will be very difficult to trace the real impact of treatment due to limited knowledge of what happens to people in whom the treatment does not work. The value of treatment may be underestimated if the subjects in the placebo group are dropping out. The components of variance should be discussed and sensitivity analyses should be conducted so the reader can have an idea of the robustness of the data.[23]

SUMMARY/CONCLUSIONS

Incorporating pharmacoeconomic parameters into clinical trials is becoming a major strategic component in assessing the value of new compounds. As additional regulatory agencies require and others consider requiring economic information as a component to the drug approval and/or reimbursement process, the needs for having dedicated resource to evaluating the pharmacoeconomic potential of new compounds should be considered. However, just as resource availability may limit a pharmaceutical company's ability to develop all of the potential drugs it has in its pipeline, resources may also limit the extent to which pharmacoeconomics will be incorporated into specific drug development programs. Realistically, some pharmaceutical products and healthcare interventions will be in greater need of pharmacoeconomic support than others. For example, drugs that are expected to be used for chronic conditions, to palliate symptoms, or slow the spread of an illness, but not cure it, are more likely to generate queries regarding their pharmacoeconomic benefit than a drug that cures an acute condition. Marketplace competition and demands also play roles in the decision. If a company plans to enter a market in which a number of similar drugs already exist it may be sufficient to compete only on the basis of price, as long as equal efficacy and safety can be demonstrated. HRQOL studies may only be of interest if there is a reason to suggest a difference in the side effects or functional status due to the intervention.

Pharmacoeconomics is a valuable tool used for making rational choices about pharmaceutical care interventions. Data can be collected in controlled trials before a drug has been approved and such data can be very useful as long as certain caveats are acknowledged. Whatever pharmacoeconomic assessment is chosen, it is imperative that all aspects of the study be transparent and able to stand the tests of reproducibility and reasonable challenge.

References

1. Andersson F: (1995) Why is the Pharmaceutical Industry Investing Increasing Amounts in Health Economic Evaluations? *International Journal of Technology Assessment in Healthcare*, **11**(4): 750–761.
2. Wennberg JE. (1988) Improving the medical decision-making process. *Health Affairs* **7**(1): 99–106.
3. Wechsler J. (1993) Re-evaluating clinical trials: devices, outcomes and efficacy. *Applied Clinical Trials* **2**: 12–16.
4. Spilker B. (1987) Designing the Overall Project. In: Guide to Planning and Managing Multiple Clinical Studies, New York, Raven Press: 36–62.
5. Osterhaus JT, Townsend RJ, Gandek B, Ware JE Jr. (1994) Measuring the functional status and well-being of patients with migraine headache. *Headache* **34**: 337–343.
6. Lindley CM, Hirsch JD, O'Neill CV, *et al.* (1992) Quality of life consequences of chemotherapy-induced emesis. *Quality of Life Research* **1**: 331–340.
7. Lee JT, Nielsen KE, Hirsch JD, Michael LW. (1994) Assessing the quality of life of patients with generalized anxiety disorder using the SF-36: a comparison with chronic physical conditions. Association of European Psychiatrists Seventh European Symposium, Quality of Life and Disabilities in Mental Disorders, Vienna.
8. Mauskopf J, Schulman K, Bell L, Glick H. (1996) A Strategy for Collecting Pharmacoeconomic Data During Phase II/III Clinical Trials. *Pharmacoeconomics* Mar **9**(3): 264–277.
9. Rittenhouse BE, O'Brien BJ. (1996) Threats to the Validity of Pharmacoeconomic Analyses Based on Clinical Trial Data. In: Quality of Life and Pharmacoeconomics in Clinical Trials, edn. 2. Edited by Bert Spilker. Philadelphia, PA: Lippincott-Raven Publishers, 1215–1222.
10. Rittenhouse BE. (1995) The Relevance of Searching for Effects Under a Clinical-trial Lamppost: A Key Issue. *Medical Decision-making* **15**: 348–357.
11. Data JL, Willke RJ, Barnes JR, DiRoma PJ. (1995) Re-Engineering Drug Development: Integrating Pharmacoeconomic Research Into the Drug Development Process. *Psychopharmacology Bulletin* **31**: 67–73.
12. Gray AM, Marshall M, Lockwood A, Morris J. (1997) Problems in Conducting Economic Evaluations Alongside Clinical Trials. *British Journal of Psychiatry*. **170**: 47–52.
13. O'Brien B. (1996) Economic Evaluation of Pharmaceuticals – Frankenstein's Monster or Vampire of Trials? *Medical Care* **34**(12): DS99–DS108.
14. Rittenhouse BE. (1996) Another deficit problem: the deficit of relevant information when clinical trials are the basis for pharmacoeconomic research. *Journal of Research in Pharmaceutical Economics* **7**(3): 3–15.
15. Lee JT. (1997) Friend or foe?: the industry as a source of pharmacoeconomic data. *New Medicine* **1**: 293–298.
16. Cady RK, Dexter J, Sargent JD, *et al.* (1993) Efficacy of subcutaneous sumatriptan in repeated episodes of migraine. *Neurology* **43**: 1363–1368.
17. Hurny C, Bernhard J, Gelberg RD *et al.* (1992) Quality of Life Measures for Patients Receiving Adjuvant Therapy for Breast Cancer: An International Trial. *Eur. J Cancer* **28**(1): 118–124.
18. Ware JE Jr., Snow KK, Kosinski M, Gandek B. (1993) SF-36 Health Survey Manual and Interpretation Guide. The Health Institute, New England Medical Center, Boston.
19. Young TL, Kirchdoerfer LJ, Osterhaus JT. A development and validation process for a disease specific quality of life instrument. *DIA Journal* (under review).
20. Approaches to instrument translation: issues to consider.(1997) *Medical Outcomes Trust Bulletin* **5**(4): 2.
21. Acquardo C, Jambon B, Ellis D, Marquis P. (1996) Language and translation issues. In: Quality of life and pharmacoeconomics in clinical trials, 2nd edition. B Spilker, ed. Lippincott-Raven Publishers, 575–585.
22. McHorney CA, Kosinski M, Ware JE. (1994) Comparisons of the costs and quality of norms for the SF-36 Health Survey by mail vs. telephone interview. *Medical Care*. **32**(6): 551–67.
23. Osterhaus JT, Townsend RJ. (1996) Incorporating pharmacoeconomic research into clinical trials. In: Principles of pharmacoeconomics, Bootman JL, Townsend RJ, McGhan WF, eds. Harvey Whitney Books, 196–211.

8

The potential and limitations of pharmacoeconomic research in the pharmaceutical industry

RJ Churnside and PK Hopkinson

INTRODUCTION

In recent years, the increasingly pressing requirement to contain costs in the healthcare sector has motivated clinicians, budget holders and other decision-makers to consider 'value for money' in addition to safety and efficacy when assessing the overall impact of medical technologies, of which pharmaceuticals form an important component. For drugs used in the hospital setting, formulary committees are becoming increasingly cost conscious. Value for money is rapidly becoming an additional criterion for market access. In some countries this has been publicly recognised in formal requirements for pharmacoeconomic data to support applications for pricing and/or reimbursement.[1] In others, central authorities have sought to improve the quality of healthcare decision-making by publishing guidelines for the conduct of economic evaluations of medicines and cost effectiveness 'league tables' for healthcare technologies including drug therapies.[2]

This increasing pressure for cost containment in healthcare has led to a growing interest in identifying, measuring and evaluating the balance between the benefits of new medical technologies and their costs. This trend applies to the use of pharmaceuticals as to other healthcare interventions. Although healthcare professionals and institutions are primarily concerned with the safety, efficacy and quality of pharmaceuticals, they are also concerned with costs, since medicines form an important component of the total expenditure of both primary healthcare providers and healthcare institutions. As the use and cost of pharmaceuticals are readily identifiable, they present a well - defined area for cost containment initiatives.

However, it is also recognised that sole or excessive concentration on only one side of the economic equation (ie. costs) to the exclusion of associated consequences, can lead to sub optimal solutions to health policy issues. Therefore, the search now is for 'value for money', the optimal balance of outlays and outcomes, rather than for cost containment *per se*.

THE OBJECTIVES OF PHARAMACOECONOMIC RESEARCH

From the point of view of pharmaceutical companies, pharmacoeconomic research is used within the clinical trial setting primarily to demonstrate the economic and humanistic value of alternative drug therapies in the same way as these trials are used to demonstrate clinical efficacy and safety.

Outside of the clinical trials process, where the research interest is the therapy area rather than investigational drugs, pharmacoeconomic research can be used to raise customer and decision-maker awareness of the existing economic and humanistic burdens associated with the therapy area and to provide a link between results gained from clinical trials settings and real world practice, ie between the efficacy of a pharmaceutical and its effectiveness.

Pharmacoeconomic research attempts to demonstrate the value for money of individual pharmaceutical products by establishing, for alternative therapies, the direct and indirect costs of their acquisition and use and, where appropriate, the benefits conferred on recipients in terms of additions to the quantity and/or quality of life.

THE RELATIONSHIP BETWEEN PHARMACOECONOMICS AND VALUE

The above discussion of the increasing importance of economic consideration in healthcare decision-making presupposes a common understanding of the terms 'value' and 'value for money' in the pharmacoeconomic context. In terms of pharmaceuticals, the concept of 'value' can be considered to be multidimensional, comprising three principal and distinct components:

- Clinical value: the extent to which medicines relieve the physical symptoms of disease, or cure the disease itself.
- Economic value: the extent to which the use of medicines impacts resource use both directly, in terms of drug acquisition prices and medical resource use, and indirectly, in terms of effects on human productivity in work and non-waged settings.
- Humanistic value: the extent to which pharmaceutical therapies impact the actual and perceived well - being of patients beyond the clinical symptoms and effects of disease.

The relationship between these three dimensions of value is depicted in **Figure 1**.

Within the clinical trials process

Within the clinical trials setting, clinical parameters identify and measure medical value, whilst the role of pharmacoeconomic research is to identify and measure the

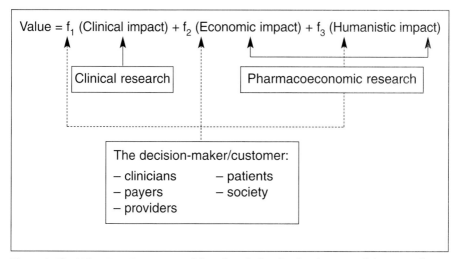

$$\text{Value} = f_1 \text{ (Clinical impact)} + f_2 \text{ (Economic impact)} + f_3 \text{ (Humanistic impact)}$$

Clinical research

Pharmacoeconomic research

The decision-maker/customer:
- clinicians   - patients
- payers   - society
- providers

Figure 1: The Value Equation. We gratefully acknowledge the development of this Figure by Dr. Raymond J. Townsend

economic and humanistic components of value, such as resource use and patient quality of life. Although the identification and measurement of these individual parameters may provide the data on the three principal dimensions of value, exactly how these individual dimensions are weighted and summed to produce an aggregate measure of 'value' in any given case depends on the preferences and perspectives of particular decision-makers and customers, principally healthcare providers, healthcare purchasers, patients and society as a whole. These views and perspectives, in turn, are likely to be conditioned by the positive and negative incentives, explicit or implied, which exist in specific healthcare systems, such as those generated by departmental budget boundaries in healthcare institutions. It is a primary function of pharmacoeconomics to make the non-clinical components of value transparent to the decision-maker/customer.

However, the design of clinical trials can impose obstacles to demonstrating value in terms of pharmacoeconomic measures and endpoints. By definition, clinical trials are primarily designed to demonstrate safety and efficacy rather than pharmacoeconomic outcomes. They are also usually designed to test a single, or a limited number of, specific clinical hypotheses, and, as such, they need to be tightly pre -specified terms of clinical processes and homogeneity of patient population which limit the sources of variation in pharmacoeconomic parameters.

This tends to impact pharmacoeconomic assessments within clinical trials in two ways:

- Comparator agents and regimens often do not adequately reflect actual practice. The use of realistic comparators in real world practice within market - relevant clinical procedures are required to illustrate pharmacoeconomic value.
- Populations which are homogeneous in terms of clinical criteria can be

expected to be less homogeneous in terms of their resource use and heterogeneous in terms of their expectations, experiences and demography— all factors which may affect patient assessments and which can be expected to increase individual variability in both humanistic and economic assessments. The result usually is that trials in Phases II and III are statistically powered to demonstrate clinical safety and efficacy alone. Clinical trials tend to have relatively small sample sizes and are under powered in terms of their ability to detect differences in pharmacoeconomic endpoints in general and in humanistic endpoints in particular.

In addition, clinical trials programmes, and their pharmacoeconomic components, are often affected by the challenges of international development. Cultural diversity of clinical practice may particularly impact the measurement of pharmacoeconomic parameters in specific therapeutic areas, such as the practice of anaesthesia, which tend to differ widely both within and between countries. This may result in some clinical trial sites having to make adjustments in practice to accommodate a clinical trial protocol, thereby compromising the potential for demonstrating pharmacoeconomic value.

In some cases clinical trial designs are modified in the course of the trials programme, thereby allowing various biases into studies. Such mid - study modifications could be expected to introduce more variability into a trials programme, thus making assessment of pharmacoeconomic value more difficult.

Outside of the clinical trials process

Outside of the clinical trials process, which necessarily focuses on specific investigational drugs, pharmacoeconomic research can be instrumental in setting the pharmacoeconomic scene for the drug development process and in interpreting measures of pharmacoeconomic value collected in clinical trials in the context of the real world environment. For example, in order to estimate the effect of a new compound on resource use in a particular therapy area and healthcare setting, it is often necessary to gather data on the level of baseline resource use in actual practice conditions. In many cases such data will be novel both to the pharmacoeconomic researcher and to healthcare practitioners themselves. Such data can, therefore, be of use in two ways. Firstly, it can add to the level of understanding of the resource impacts, both positive and negative, of healthcare interventions on healthcare institutions themselves, on patients and on society. Secondly, they can be of use in extrapolating pharmacoeconomic impacts from the efficacy endpoints used in the clinical trials setting to the measurement of therapeutic effectiveness in actual practice settings.

For example, in recent years numerous articles have been written on resource use in general anaesthesia.[3,4,5] The majority of these, however, have focused on resource use within formulary and theatre management operating systems and have not addressed the effects of general anaesthesia on resource use outside of these functional boundaries, such as effects on recovery room time and length of hospital stay. Because anaesthetics and adjunct drugs tend to be relatively expensive, the proportion of formulary and operating theatre running costs which they comprise is relatively large, about 20%. However, it has been shown that, in terms of total surgical procedure costs, which encompass overhead costs, recovery room time and staffing costs and length of hospital stay, the cost of anaesthetic agents and adjunct drugs is very small, typically less than 1%.[6] The implication is that new, short - acting anaesthetic agents which can reduce the time spent by patients in high resource - intensity areas, such as recovery rooms, could lead to significant cost savings to healthcare institutions, even after their acquisition costs to formulary budgets are taken into account.

Pharmacoeconomics can also be applied to the costing of adverse events actually associated with a therapy area (eg. from clinical trial results), to provide a link between the clinical assessment of the efficacy of study drugs and the associated economic costs of their use. In this way, such studies can create a bridge from clinical outcomes to economic outcomes.

Baseline resource use data can also be used to calibrate models, both simple and sophisticated, of the economic effects of drug use in real world settings, which then allows results from clinical trials to be extrapolated into actual practice. Numerous examples of this application of such data exist, such as a comparative assessment of a relatively simple and a relatively sophisticated modelling technique applied to the treatment of emesis following chemotherapy for the treatment of breast cancer.[7]

THE RELATIONSHIP BETWEEN PHARMACOECONOMICS AND VALUE FOR MONEY

Figure 1 above illustrates the relationship between the three principal dimensions of value in the pharmaceutical context. However, in order to analyse the concept value from an economic perspective, this equation needs to be expressed in monetary terms by incorporating the prices of drugs, the value placed on their associated healthcare outcomes and, finally, the notion of 'profit' (ie. the excess of value over cost) into the equation.

As a first step, **Figure 1** can be supplemented with the acquisition costs (ie. prices) of pharmaceuticals to arrive at the following relationship:

$$\text{Value for money} = f_1 \left\{ \frac{\text{Clinical impact}}{\text{Drug price}} \right\} + f_2 \left\{ \frac{\text{Economic impact}}{\text{Drug price}} \right\} + f_3 \left\{ \frac{\text{Humanistic impact}}{\text{Drug price}} \right\}$$

Figure 2: Value for Money and Drug Prices. We gratefully acknowledge the development of this Figure by Dr. Raymond J. Townsend.

It is clear from the second term in this equation that the full economic consequences of pharmaceutical therapies usually extend beyond the issue of drug acquisition costs alone to other areas, such as other forms of medical resource use and patient productivity. It is also helpful to consider this value for money relationship in terms of a more explicitly economic approach to the concept. For organisations which market their outputs, such as pharmaceutical companies, the concept of 'value for money' is readily grasped and measured: it is represented by the notion of profit which is used as a measure of corporate success. At its simplest, value for money can be expressed as:

$$\text{Value for money} = \frac{\text{Value of outputs, £}}{\text{Cost of inputs, £}}$$

This formulation of the profit equation differs from the more conventional method of defining profit as the difference between the value of outputs and the cost of inputs. However, this definition is useful in demonstrating the relationship between accounting identities and alternative methods of economic evaluation, as explained below.

In most healthcare systems, the outputs of the healthcare services are not marketed in any conventional sense of the word. Nevertheless, this concept of value for money is useful, and, indeed, necessary, if expenditure on pharmaceutical and other healthcare technologies are to be justified to purchasers and recipients of drug therapies on a rational basis. It is therefore useful to delve a little deeper into the concept of value for money.

In any organisation value for money has three components, customarily referred to as the "3Es":

1. Economy: the extent to which the cost of inputs is minimised.
2. Efficiency: The concept which relates the output of a system to the inputs used in creating that output.
3. Effectiveness: the attribution of 'value' to final outputs, or the extent to which programme objectives are met and a value placed on those objectives.

Figure 3 illustrates how the "3E's" can be related to the concept of value for money.

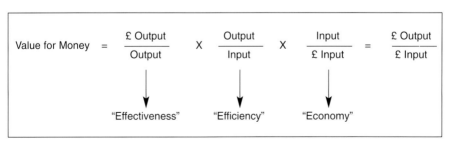

Figure 3: Value for Money – The "3E's".

Here, inputs and their costs (economy) are related to output and its value (effectiveness) via physical productivity (efficiency). This relationship may be clearer if considered in terms of the hierarchy analytical methods of economic evaluation used in pharmacoeconomic research. The calculation of the ratio of inputs to their costs (economy) equates to cost minimisation analysis (CMA), in which explicit consideration of outputs is not required. If the physical productivity component of value for money (efficiency) is added to, or, in this case, multiplied by, economy, the resulting equation resolves into a cost effectiveness analysis (CEA), i.e. cost per unit of physical output. However, if these two components are further supplemented with data on the ratio of final output to its value (effectiveness) the value for money equation can be resolved for both inputs and outputs in monetary units. The resulting relationship, therefore, equates to a full cost benefit analysis (CBA), as shown in **Figure 4.**

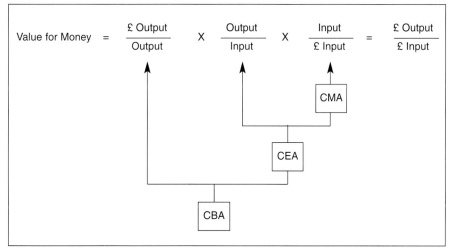

Figure 4: Value for Money - The "3E's" and Economic Evaluation Methods

Although a superior clinical profile of a new compound is neither a necessary nor sufficient condition to guarantee value for money in pharmacoeconomic terms, it is usual in the context of innovative pharmaceuticals (ie. not "me too" drugs) that superior clinical efficacy is accompanied by both greater healthcare benefits, whether economic, humanistic or both, and higher drug acquisition costs (prices).

In terms of both technical and allocative efficiency, the full array of possible value for money outcomes between alternatives is shown in **Figure 5.**

Outcomes which are either efficient or inefficient in the technical sense generally present decision-makers with few problems, since interventions will be either dominant over alternatives or inferior to them. It is the issue of allocative efficiency, in which a trade – off needs to be made either between higher costs and higher benefits or between lower costs and lower benefits, that calls for 'value for money' decisions to be made. It is a primary function of pharmacoeconomics to assess whether additional benefits outweigh the additional costs of pharmaceutical interventions.

	COSTS		
	Higher	**Same**	**Lower**
Higher	*Evaluate*	Accept	Accept
Same	Reject	*Indifferent*	Accept
Lower	Reject	Reject	*Evaluate*

In comparison to the next best alternative intervention:

(BENEFITS — row labels)

Figure 5: Pharmacoeconomic Outcomes

PHARMACOECONOMIC VALUE AND CLINICAL VALUE

There remains the intriguing question of whether, for individual drugs, pharmacoeconomic value can exist in the absence of clinical value. Walker[8] strongly contends that the flow of causation is from clinical effectiveness to pharmacoeconomic benefits.

Whilst it is clear that the reverse flow is unrealistic, and setting aside the interesting, but ultimately distracting, phenomenon of the placebo effect, it is less clear that clinical effectiveness is either a necessary or a sufficient condition to guarantee pharmacoeconomic advantage. As shown in **Figure 5** above, a drug may be technically inferior to an alternative intervention in terms of clinical outcome, but it may be cost effective in terms of the balance between inferior outcome and lower cost. Although it is the case that the vast majority of new healthcare technologies, including pharmaceuticals, are brought to market because they are more rather than less effective than existing therapies, there is one measure of pharmacoeconomic outcome which addresses explicitly the issue of trading off inferior clinical outcomes against improved humanistic outcomes, and that is the Quality Adjusted Life Year (QALY).

The QALY seeks, for individual patients, to weight the number of life years gained by the effects of a medical intervention by the patient's preference for living in the health state afforded by the intervention. Here an improved aggregate outcome in terms of a higher QALY figure might well be comprised of the product of a shorter life expectancy and an improved quality of the expected remaining life compared with alternative therapies.

PHARMACOECONOMICS AND PRICING/ REIMBURSEMENT

As described in the discussion of allocative efficiency above, pharmacoeconomic research can help to provide rational justifications for drug prices which, in isolation, may otherwise be regarded as 'too high' in absolute terms. In this context, pharmacoeconomics data can be instrumental in gaining reimbursement status for drugs and in securing an agreed market price. Indeed, pharmacoeconomic data to support reimbursement are formally required by the relevant government agencies in Australia and in Ontario, Canada.

However, although the results of pharmaceconomic research may provide an important contribution to pricing considerations, it alone cannot constitute a metric for pricing, if only because final customers, which are most frequently reimbursement authorities or other government agencies, have at least equivalent market power to pharmaceutical companies in determining the prices at which drugs are marketed.

The issue of pharmaceutical pricing may be regarded as determining a point on a drug's cost — value continuum which is acceptable to all relevant parties, ie pharmaceutical companies, healthcare payers and healthcare providers.

At a minimum, drug prices may be set to cover only costs of production in terms of research and development (R&D) costs, and the costs of manufacturing and marketing. At the other end of the continuum, the price achieved for a breakthrough, or 'blockbuster', drug is more likely to reflect the value which customers place on its outcomes rather than on its (lower) costs of production. Between these two extremes prices may be set to reflect a 'break even' point at which the drug is cost neutral in net terms to the purchaser, or the need to provide additional R&D incentives to innovation, or the period of time for which the drug is protected by patent.

However, although pharmacoeconomic research may help to determine a price floor, in terms of a 'break even' price, and a price ceiling in terms of the monetary value placed on an individual pharmaceutical product by its purchasers, pharmacoeconomics alone cannot dictate at which point on this continuum the eventual price of the product will fall. In most healthcare systems drug prices will be determined by bilateral negotiation between drug purchasers and drug producers aimed at agreeing the balance between 'value for money' perceived by the purchaser and the 'money for value' desired by the supplier in terms of the eventual price set. However, as for all innovative drugs and new technologies, market prices will eventually fall as patents expire and competition grows.

PHARMACOECONOMICS AND MARKETING

Debate continues about whether pharmacoeconomics should be regarded as a science in its own right or used as an adjunct to the existing array of marketing tools. In reality, pharmacoeconomic research and marketing should be regarded as distinct disciplines, which, in any specific instance, may or may not compliment one another. Pharmacoeconomic data may be used in marketing activities to:

- Differentiate products from competitors.
- Gain access to formularies and restricted lists

- Gain incorporation into treatment guidelines and disease management programmes

However, there remains concern about the extent to which pharmacoeconomic data and results can be regarded rigorous and robust. As Drummond,[9] has pointed out, 'Although clinical trial data are used in the marketing of [pharmaceutical] products, they are usually perceived as scientific data in support of licensed indications. It is not clear whether the same is true of economic evaluation data, which may be more open to interpretation.'

The main issue in this context is the credibility of pharamacoeconomic studies and their results. Concern has been expressed about the greater potential for bias in economic studies than in clinical studies, the extent to which the use of pharmacoeconomic data in marketing and price setting raises ethical concerns and the robustness of pharmacoeconomic endpoints compared with clinical endpoints.

Bias in pharmacoeconomic studies may arise from the choice of question selected for study; from the analytical methods used and from the reporting of results. Although the risk of bias exists, pharmacoeconomic studies will only command general confidence if they employ robust methodological standards and approaches and use assumptions which are clearly articulated and transparent to their audience. Moreover, these are exactly the characteristics that define high quality scientific research, whether it is pharmacoeconomic or not, and whether it is used for marketing purposes or not.

Ethical concerns about the use of pharmacoeconomic studies in the marketing of drugs also centre to the issue of bias in pharmacoeconomic studies and, as such, the solutions identified above also are of relevance in this case. However, as Drummond[9] states, individual prescribers are unlikely to accept pharmacoeconomic-based marketing arguments which clearly contradict the prescriber's clinical experience. Nevertheless, improved prescriber education and training in pharmacoeconomics would help to guard against this type of potential ethical problem.

Finally, the results of pharmacoeconomic studies, both in terms of resource use and quality of life, are often regarded as being based on 'softer' data than are clinical results. Whilst it is the case that many economic variables are not as amenable to conventional statistical testing as are clinical parameters, this is not always the case. Moreover, in terms of measures of quality of life, it is by no means clear that pharmacoeconomic indicators are any less hard than clinical measures of patient improvement, which are frequently included in clinical trials, or the measurement of self reported perceptions, such as those of pain.

PHARMACOECONOMICS AND THE RESEARCH AND DEVELOPMENT PROGRAMME

As stated above, the changing demands of the healthcare market now require pharmaceutical companies to demonstrate not only the safety and efficacy of their products but also their economic benefit. Traditionally this has been achieved by "piggy backing" onto late development (ie, Phase IIIb-IV) clinical trials or by performing retrospective economic analyses, sometimes with inadequate or inappropriate data. It is becoming clearer that this is often too late in the R&D process and that to fully support a product in registration and reimbursement negotiations, the economic component of the products package must be available earlier. Incorporating pharmacoeconomics into the programme sooner, rather than later, can help to ensure that comprehensive and relevant pharmacoeconomic data, which meet the requirements of the decision-makers who comprise the customer base of the pharmaceutical industry (eg, patients, physicians, pharmacists, formulary committees, commissioning agencies and governments), are available in a timely manner.

In addition to meeting the external demands of decision-makers/customers, early inclusion of pharmacoeconomics in the R&D programme can offer significant internal benefit for companies. The cost of R&D is astronomical, with pharmaceutical companies spending billions on it yearly. It has been estimated that it costs $300 million to bring a single product to market, and there is growing evidence that these R&D costs are rising in real terms.[10] Pharmacoeconomics can contribute significant efficiencies to this process by helping senior management within companies prioritise, terminate products early if necessary, and make key "go/no go" decisions. It can also help internally by contributing to pricing decisions and their justification.

Pharmacoeconomic strategy and assessments can begin when a product emerges from research and enters the first clinical trial, Phase I, when the drug is tested in human volunteers. In Phase II studies (ie, small dose ranging and safety studies in patients), the pharmacoeconomic strategy can be refined, instruments (eg, questionnaires) can be developed and piloted. During Phase III trials (ie, efficacy studies in large numbers of patients), the required pharmacoeconomic data can then be collected in an efficient and targeted manner. This process ensures that each product has an iterative pharmacoeconomic strategy incorporated throughout the entire drug development process (**Figure 6**).

Pharmacoeconomics' rightful place is as an integral component of a product's development strategy and it should be considered as fundamental to the overall strategy as toxicology, clinical, commercial, etc. This position has been achieved successfully in some companies who have undergone a change of mind-set and incorporated early in development an iterative pharmacoeconomic R&D strategy for each therapeutic area and individual product.

Development of an Initial Pharmacoeconomic Strategy: Late Research/Phase I

Once there is a picture of a likely clinical profile and a therapeutic target area, an initial pharmacoeconomic strategy can be formed. This process essentially consists of two stages, a descriptive stage and a decision analytic model stage. The descriptive stage involves a comprehensive literature review and the abstraction of essential data, which is then inputted into a decision model developed to describe

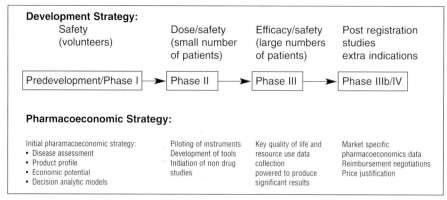

Development Strategy:

Safety (volunteers)	Dose/safety (small number of patients)	Efficacy/safety (large numbers of patients)	Post registration studies extra indications

| Predevelopment/Phase I | → | Phase II | → | Phase III | → | Phase IIIb/IV |

Pharmacoeconomic Strategy:

Initial pharamacoeconomic strategy: • Disease assessment • Product profile • Economic potential • Decision analytic models	Piloting of instruments Development of tools Initiation of non drug studies	Key quality of life and resource use data collection powered to produce significant results	Market specific pharmacoeconomics data Reimbursement negotiations Price justification

Figure 6: Incorporating Pharmacoeconomics early into the Drug Development Process

the disease and to present in a systematic fashion the pharmacoeconomic features of the product.

Pharmacoeconomics in late research/Phase I begins with a descriptive stage, during which the disease is characterised and the potential product impact is assessed. Clinical, epidemiological and economic literature is reviewed. Disease aetiology and progression are defined, current treatment regimens are identified, and the current "gold standard" treatment is assessed (eg, dosage, mode of administration, side effects and costs). Epidemiological information provides prevalence and incidence data, country-specific variations and an indication of the overall burden of disease. Pooling of data can be achieved using meta-analytic techniques. Such data are increasingly available through the development of evidence-based medicine and groups such as the Cochrane Collaboration.[11] At this stage the key patient-derived outcome measures (eg, quality of life instruments) are also identified.

Even during Phase I, the pharmacoeconomic potential of a product can be analysed using the product's clinical profile (ie, potential efficacy, side effects and improvement over current therapy). These clinical benefits can then be translated into pharmacoeconomic benefits, in other words, assessed in terms of their impact on costs and humanistic/patient outcomes. The key audience (eg, type of patient) for the product can also be identified and an initial needs assessment of the audience can be conducted to ascertain the potential impact of pharmacoeconomic messages.

Having completed the descriptive stage, the pharmacoeconomist should have the required data to develop initial decision analytic models. Decision analysis is a systematic approach to decision-making under conditions of uncertainty. It has been used widely as a technique to aid decisions in areas as diverse as military planning, economics, marketing and, increasingly, medicine. It allows decision-makers to identify the component parts of a problem, structure them into a logical format, quantify them in terms of probabilities and values placed on outcomes and analyse the decision to identify the most appropriate option.

Models can be developed which describe the disease and treatment pattern using the current gold standard therapy. This can be used as a template to identify the key cost drivers and potential benefits of the new product. Scenario testing can establish parameters which the new product must achieve in order to establish incremental cost effectiveness compared with current therapy. Conclusions can be analysed to test the sensitivity of the product's cost-effectiveness to changes in variables such as efficacy, incidence of side effects, costs, formulations, and treatment of various indications or patient sub-groups (eg, the elderly). Initial pricing data can be obtained using threshold analysis, in which the cost of the product is varied and compared to the base case cost estimate until a threshold value for cost-effectiveness is determined.

During the descriptive and decision analytic stages, the pharmacoeconomist should have identified the key resource use and patient outcomes (ie, efficacy criteria that must be met for the product to be viable). Data which will need to be collected outside of the clinical trial process will have been identified (eg, burden of illness data). These studies can now be initiated so as to run in parallel with the clinical trials. Work on positioning and pricing can begin. All this information can be fed into the prioritisation and "go/no go" process, the early commercial assessment of the product and can form the foundation of the pharmacoeconomic data collection during the clinical trial process. This strategy must be updated constantly and developed in an iterative fashion throughout the product life cycle.

Pharmacoeconomic Strategy During Phase II/III

Phase II trials involve small numbers of patients and are used to confirm efficacy and to determine the dose of the drug. Although limited by their size for use as economic evaluations, they do provide an excellent resource to pilot economic data collection instruments. Various quality of life questionnaires can be piloted and compared in order to establish which ones are most appropriate for the Phase III studies. If the initial pharmacoeconomic assessment has recommended that a new quality of life instrument be developed, Phase II studies are used for initial validity and reliability tests, which are required to establish whether the instrument is assessing what it is supposed to assess (validity) and whether the results can be repeated under similar conditions (reliability). As Phase II studies are often international they also provide an opportunity to evaluate translations of the instrument into different languages and to assess the performance of the instrument within different countries.

Data from the Phase II trials can be fed into the initial decision analytic models. Greater knowledge will have been obtained about the drug's clinical efficacy and the occurrence and nature of side effects. The models, therefore, become more robust. Scenario testing comparing this data with values from standard therapy give a clearer indication of the product's pharmacoeconomic potential. This data can then be used in decisions of whether to move into large expensive Phase III studies.

Phase III studies consist usually of large multicentre, randomised, controlled trials that are statistically powered to demonstrate clinical efficacy of the drug. They are very costly to conduct and any unnecessary data collection must be kept to a minimum. Having already developed the pharmacoeconomic strategy, the pharmacoeconomist should be clear at this point as to what instruments need to be included in the Phase III studies. The instruments will have been translated, if necessary, and validated, and inappropriate instruments will have been excluded. The pharmacoeconomic component of the study should be focused on collection of only essential data, so as to minimise the burden on both the data collectors and on the patients.

Unlike Phase I and II trials, the size of Phase III trials better allow full prospective economic evaluations to be completed (eg, cost effectiveness or cost utility analysis). These can be powered to produce statistically significant results. The design of the studies can be adjusted to obtain the pharmacoeconomic data required for reimbursement, as well as the clinical data required for registration.

The Phase III data can again be inputted into the models, which as a result should be much more robust. As this data should be statistically significant, any error around the model estimates and conclusions should be reduced.

Pharmacoeconomics in Phase IIIb/IV Studies (Post-Registration)

The core data set from the Phase III studies can be tailored for various countries and indications. Phase IIIb studies can be initiated to collect data for specific indications. Phase IV studies can collect country-specific data or naturalistic data which more reflects routine medical practice. The model can be used for reimbursement, pricing and formulary negotiations. Values for local practice and costs can be inputted. Conclusions can be tested further for the impact of using different healthcare systems and different healthcare decision-maker perspectives. The model can and should be constantly updated as new competitor and product information is produced during the full marketing life cycle of the product.

Limitations

Early inclusion of pharmacoeconomics in R&D programmes has been criticised by some. The very nature of drug research, with its high failure rate, means that involvement too early could be regarded as a waste of resources. This criticism can be countered by developing generic pharmacoeconomic strategies and models which are applicable to a disease state rather than to an individual product. Therefore, the investment of time is appropriate if the information can be applied to a series of products in a disease portfolio. As the drug progresses, the strategy and models can be increasingly customised to its specific profile.

Early termination of a product may be inappropriate when the clinical profile is not clearly defined and where there is considerable uncertainty in the data. Often products introduced for one indication find use for others not at first realised. To avoid inappropriate termination of products, pharmacoeconomics should be used as a component of "go/no go" decisions, but alongside others such as efficacy, safety and traditional return on investment analyses, rather than the definitive criterion.

Use of pharmacoeconomics in randomised controlled trials has also received criticism. Although the trials achieve high levels of internal validity in terms of the results relating to the study patients, they do not automatically reflect routine clinical practise and, therefore, resource use. They have been accused of producing artificial environments. As a result, it has been suggested that it may be more accurate to determine the economic impact of a product in observational or naturalistic studies.

Economic modelling has been severely criticised. The limitations include the potential to produce "black box" effects, where they are so complex that they cannot be understood or where they are manipulated to emphasise a certain perspective. On the other hand, they have been thought of by some as too simplistic, reducing complex medical situations to a few outcomes. Sheldon[12] critically reviewed the use of models in economic evaluation, in which he highlighted areas of concern, inappropriate application and common errors. He recommended three areas for which models could be used: hypothesis testing, comparison of treatment strategies and identification and assessment of information gaps.

Incorporation of pharmacoeconomics early into the R&D programme of a novel pharmaceutical product has immense potential to benefit the company internally, in terms of aiding key development decisions, improving efficiency in the R&D programme, reducing costs, terminating products sooner, as well as externally, in terms of addressing the increasingly stringent economic data requirements of the pharmaceutical market. However, it should not be seen as a panacea for future success for the pharmaceutical industry by providing a prescriptive automated decision process, but rather pharmacoeconomics should be viewed realistically as an important component of the overall drug development strategy and an aid to rational decision-making by practitioners and payers alike.

SUMMARY AND CONCLUSIONS

In this chapter, we identified the potential of pharmacoeconomic research to:

- Identify and measure pharmaceutical value as perceived from the different perspectives of healthcare providers, healthcare purchasers, patients and of society.
- Provide indictors of value which help to differentiate between new drugs that may provide only marginal clinical improvements over existing therapies.
- Widen the focus of decision-makers to encompass not only clinical value but also value in terms of economic and humanistic benefits.
- Help to establish the broad boundaries in which pricing decisions can be made.
- Provide data in support of pricing and reimbursement submissions.
- Support marketing objectives by helping to differentiate products from competitors, to gain access to formularies and restricted lists and to disease management programmes.

- Set the therapeutic area scene in terms of non- drug studies by providing data on baseline resource use to enable results from the clinical trials to be extrapolated to real world practice.
- Contribute to the R&D process in terms of product prioritisation, product continuation or termination decisions and improving efficiency.

We have also identified some of the main limitations of the science in that it cannot:

- Act as a 'magic bullet' to demonstrate PE value where it does not exist.
- Overcome the inherent methodological difficulties associated with working in clinical trials which are designed specifically to demonstrate clinical efficacy and safety rather than pharmacoeconomic value.
- Prove value for money outside of the study context.
- Alone determine drug prices.
- Guarantee that resources used by pharmacoeconomic research at an early stage of in the R&D process will be wasted.
- Act as a metric for decision-making in the R&D process.

REFERENCES

1. Drummond MF. (1992) Cost Effectiveness Guidelines for Reimbursement of Pharmaceuticals: Is Economic Evaluation ready for Its Enhanced Status? *Health Economics* **1**, 85–92.
2. The Department of Health Register of Cost effectiveness Studies. (1994) Department of Health, London.
3. Broadway, PJ and Jones JG. (1995) A Method of Costing Anaesthesia Practice. *Anaesthesia* **50**, 56–63.
4. Jones, RE and Martinec, CL. (1993) Costs of Anaesthesia. *Anesthesia and Analgesia* **76**, 840–848.
5. Rhodes SP and Ridley S. (1993) Economic Aspects of General Anaesthesia. *Pharmacoeconomics* **3**(2), 124–130.
6. Churnside RJ, Glendenning GA, Thwaites RMA, Watts, NWR. (1996) Resource Use in Operative Surgery: UK General Anaesthesia Costs in Perspective. *British Journal of Medical Economics* **10**, 83–98.
7. Wolstenholme EF, Clifford K. A (1996) Comparison of Decision Analysis and Systems Dynamics as Pharmacoeconomic Tools. Abstract presented at the 18th Annual Meeting of the Society for Medical decision-making, Toronto, October.
8. Walker A. (1994) Why Pharmacoeconomics Should Not be Part of R&D decision-making. Proceedings of 'Successfully Using Pharmacoeconomics', AIC Conferences, London, 13 - 14 July.
9. Drummond M. Economic Evaluation of Pharmaceuticals: Science or Marketing? Discussion Paper 91, Centre for Health Economics, University of York, 1991.
10. Grabowski H. (1997) The effect of pharmacoeconomics on company research and development decisions. *Pharmacoeconomics* **11**(5), 389–97.
11. Chalmer I, Dickersin K, Chalmers TC. (1992) Getting to Grips with Archie Cochrane's Agenda. *British Medical Journal* **305**, 786–8.
12. Sheldon T. (1996) Problems of using modelling in the economic evaluation of healthcare. *Health Economics.* **5**, 1–11.

9

The role of pharmacoeconomics in response to globalization and increased competition in the pharmaceutical industry

GP Hess, ML Watrous, DR Strutton and AG Bower

INTRODUCTION

Within the past two decades, pharmaceutical companies have faced increasing competition and have increased global reach, and simultaneously the use of pharmacoeconomics (PE) has grown. These are not coincidental events, but in part reflect the need for pharmaceutical companies to gain global competitive advantage, and the realisation that pharmacoeconomics contributes to meeting that need.

A global competitive capability can place a company in an advantaged position against competitors and market forces. By competing in and coordinating activities across multiple markets, a variety of competitive advantages can be gained, including economies of scale, reduced learning curves, and enhanced product positioning or differentiation. Pharmacoeconomic analyses contribute to providing these competitive capabilities and are being increasingly used to help create these advantages. Specifically, at early stages of development, PE is being used to improve internal decisionmaking. At later stages, as customers' purchasing decisions have moved beyond traditional considerations of safety and efficacy, PE is being used during launch and commercialisation to help demonstrate the value of products, and to obtain price, reimbursement and formulary listing. The pharmaceutical industry has realised that economic evaluations of their products, as well as related disease areas and targets, can create strategic and tactical advantages critical to a competitive capability. Translating this potential advantage to a concrete advantage (increased reimbursement, access, or price) in today's market place is a key issue facing PE departments within the industry at this time.

In the above context, the following discussion examines the role of pharmacoeconomics in responding to the increased competition and globalization of the pharmaceutical industry. Specifically, the discussion addresses the following points:

- Evidence that competition and globalization of the industry has increased
- Factors that have driven increased competition in the industry
- Factors that have driven globalization in the industry
- Evidence that pharmacoeconomic activities have increased
- How pharmacoeconomics contributes to a company's success in an increasingly global and competitive environment

EVIDENCE THAT COMPETITION AND GLOBALIZATION IN THE INDUSTRY HAS INCREASED

A number of indicators can be cited that demonstrate that global competition has increased in the pharmaceutical industry. Four of those indicators are

1. the increase in the number of pharmaceutical mergers and acquisitions — especially international mergers and acquisitions which increase global reach — as strong firms purchased their competitors;
2. the increase in consolidation as fewer firms controlled more of the market;
3. the increase in the number of alliances, as firms selectively joined forces to gain advantage over other competitors; and
4. buyer power has continued to grow, adding to the competitive pressures which contributed to smaller annual price increases by manufacturers.

Mergers and Acquisitions Increased

The table on Major Mergers and Acquisitions (M&A) in the Pharmaceutical Industry (**Table 1**) demonstrates the indirect pressure and effects of competition. Of the twenty three mergers and acquisitions identified from 1980 onward, seventeen (74%) occurred since 1992 immediately following major healthcare reform debate in the US and the acceleration of market-based competition, as discussed below. Thus, the rate of M&A activity increased over 800% after 1992. A substantial number of these mergers involved a European and American firm, which strongly suggests that many mergers occurred partly to increase global capabilities.

Consolidation occurred, with a smaller number of companies dominating more of the market

Consolidation over the last dozen years has led to a smaller number of companies taking control of a larger per company share of the pharmaceutical market (**Table 2** & **Figure 1**).[1] Competitive advantages may be gained when a company has a greater market share, due to economies of scale in production and marketing. The competitive advantages, in turn, may theoretically be leveraged to gain more market share and drive competitors from the marketplace. In that context, it should be noted that the majority of firms listed in **Table 2** compete globally.

Table 1: Major Mergers and Acquisitions (M&A) in the Pharmaceutical Industry (1980-1996)[2]
Data Source: Wood Mackenzie Pharmaceutical Company Reviews, July 1997.

Company	Acquiring Co.	Acquired Co.	Deal Type	Year
Monsanto	Monsanto	Searle	Acquisition	1985
American Home Products	American Home Products	A.H. Robbins	Acquisition	1989
Bristol-Myers Squibb	Bristol-Myers	Squibb	Acquisition	1989
SmithKline Beecham	Merged: SmithKline Beckman and Beecham		Merger	1989
Rhone-Poulenc Rorer	Merge of: Rhone-Poulenc and Rorer		Merger	1990
Roche	Roche	Genentech	60% Stake	1990
Hoechst	Hoechst	Copley	51% Stake	1993
Merck	Merck	Medco	Acquisition	1993
Zeneca	Demerger: Zeneca and ICI		Demerger	1993
American Home Products	American Home Products	American Cyanamid	Acquisition	1994
Eli Lilly	Eli Lilly	PCS Health Systems	Acquisition	1994
Roche	Roche	Syntex	Acquisition	1994
Sanofi	Sanofi	Sterling Rx Business	Acquisition	1994
SmithKline Beecham	SmithKline Beecham	DPS	Acquisition	1994
SmithKline Beecham	SmithKline Beecham	Sterling OTC Business	Acquisition	1994
SmithKline Beecham	SmithKline Beecham	Bayer	Divestiture	1994
Glaxo Wellcome	Glaxo	Wellcome	Acquisition	1995
Hoechst	Hoechst	Marion Merrell Dow	Acquisition	1995
Rhone-Poulenc Rorer	Rhone-Polenc Rorer	Fisons	Acquisition	1995
Upjohn	Merged: Upjohn and Pharmacia		Merger	1995
Warner Lambert	Warner Lambert	Warner Wellcome	Acquisition	1995
Hoechst	Hoechst	Roussel Uclaf	Remaining Stock buy	1996
Novartis	Merged: Ciba and Sandoz		Merger	1996

Alliances increased as firms sought additional means to gain competitive advantage

As a further reflection of the intensification of global competition in the marketplace, **Figure 2**[3] graphically demonstrates the increased number of alliances that occurred in the industry from 1980 through 1996. Alliances are defined as a variety of formalised relationships, where two or more companies combine their resources to create greater competitive advantage and profitability than if they had acted alone. Examples of alliances of pharmaceutical companies include co-development, co-promotion, and co-marketing of products, as well as licensing arrangements. Recent reports[4] in 1997 included:

Table 2: Leading Pharmaceutical Corporations Cumulative Market Share

1996 Rank	Corporations	% Market Share 1985	% Market Share 1996
1	Glaxo Wellcome	2.5%	4.6%
2	Novartis	5.2%	4.5%
3	Merck	2.6%	4.2%
4	Bristol-Myers Squibb	3.0%	3.6%
5	Johnson & Johnson	2.2%	3.4%
6	American Home Products	4.2%	3.3%
7	Hoechst Marion Roussel	3.9%	3.2%
8	Pfizer	2.4%	3.2%
9	SmithKline Beecham	3.5%	2.8%
10	Roche	2.7%	2.7%
	Top 10 Corporations	32.2%	35.5%
11	Abbott	1.2%	2.3%
12	Eli Lilly	1.9%	2.2%
13	Bayer	2.0%	2.1%
14	Astra	0.8%	2.1%
15	Rhone-Poulenc Rorer	2.2%	2.1%
16	Schering Plough	1.4%	2.1%
17	Pharmacia Upjohn	2.4%	1.9%
18	Boehringer Ingelheim	1.9%	1.4%
19	Takeda	2.0%	1.4%
20	Warner-Lambert	1.7%	1.4%
	Top 20 Corporations	49.7%	54.5%
21	Zeneca	1.1%	1.3%
22	Sankyo	1.5%	1.2%
23	Sanofi	1.3%	1.0%
24	Schering AG	1.0%	1.0%
25	Yamanouchi	1.1%	0.8%
26	Eisai	1.1%	0.8%
27	Otsuka	1.0%	0.8%
28	Monsanto (Searle)	0.8%	0.8%
29	Amgen	0.0%	0.7%
30	BASF	0.9%	0.7%
	Top 30 Corporations	59.5%	63.5%

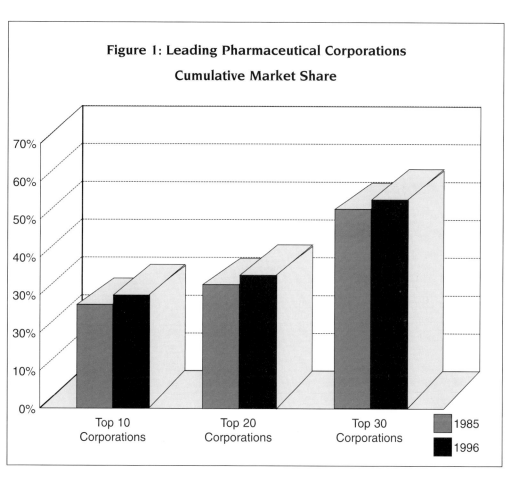

Figure 1: Leading Pharmaceutical Corporations Cumulative Market Share

- Proctor & Gamble and Regeneron Pharmaceuticals reaching a 10 year agreement to jointly develop and market new drugs for arthritis, cancer and cardiovascular disease.
- Eli Lilly agreeing to invest $70 million in Millenium Pharmaceuticals to further research in genome mapping.
- Schering-Plough working with a biotechnology firm to co-develop a product for the treatment of Hepatitis C.
- SmithKline Beecham and Texas Biotechnology forming an alliance to develop and market Novastan®, an anti-coagulant therapy, in North America.

Continued pressure from competition and the marketplace has led to smaller price increases

Ultimately, the opportunity for manufacturers to increase prices is often curtailed as surviving firms come under pressure from their buyers and increased competition in the marketplace. As demonstrated by **Figure 3**,[5] this effect can be seen in the US

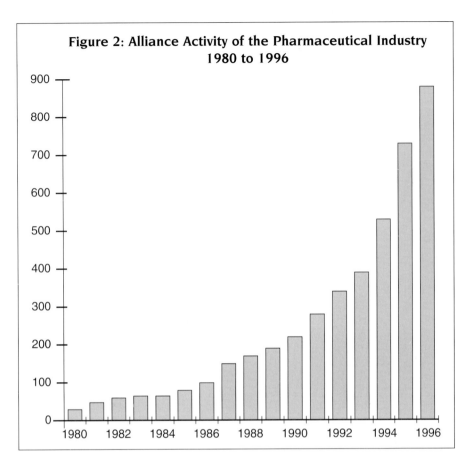

Figure 2: Alliance Activity of the Pharmaceutical Industry 1980 to 1996

pharmaceutical industry, with the Producer Price Index rate of growth decreasing from 1988 through 1997. Most of the decrease in the rate of growth has occurred since 1991, when inflation in the overall economy has remained close to 3%. Another factor contributing to this decline was the pressure from Congress to limit price increases.

In the European environment, price pressures have been more severe, as governments have employed a variety of mechanisms to directly or indirectly constrain pharmaceutical prices. In France, Italy, and Spain, for example, prices are negotiated between the government and the respective companies. Budget constraints and overruns have led these governments to ask for financial concessions from companies. Price increases, occasionally granted by governments in the 1980s, have become rarer in the mid 1990s. In Germany, while companies are technically free to set their own prices, in the mid 1990s the government introduced a reference pricing system as well as controls on physician expenditures, which also constrain pricing. In this context, economic and outcomes evaluations are becoming increasingly important means of demonstrating value to help meet pricing, reimbursement, and formulary requirements.

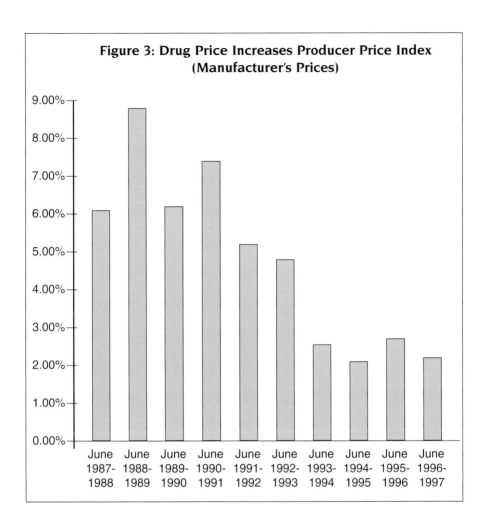

Figure 3: Drug Price Increases Producer Price Index (Manufacturer's Prices)

FACTORS THAT HAVE DRIVEN INCREASED COMPETITION IN THE INDUSTRY

The consolidation of healthcare purchasing power, typified by the rise of managed care in the US, has dramatically and visibly changed the traditional relationships pharmaceutical companies have had with providers, patients, and payers. However, other less visible factors have also significantly contributed to those changes, and the surrounding increase in competition in the pharmaceutical environment. In Porter's (1980) framework, there are four key competitive forces that affect a firm:

- Bargaining power of suppliers
- Threat of substitute products or services
- Bargaining power of buyers
- Threat of new entrants

In the last decade, each competitive force has increased within the pharmaceutical industry.

Increased Bargaining Power of Suppliers

In essence, this element refers to the cost of raw materials, labour, and a wide variety of inputs that a firm uses as a starting point for producing its goods or services. In the case of pharmaceuticals, the inputs include, for example, the cost of specialised technology, access to key opinion leaders and external investigators, and privately held databases, as well as key segments of the labour force, including pharmacoeconomists. As a barometer of the increasing demand for key personnel, the MSL index, which monitors advertised demand for executives, in 1997 rose to its highest second quarter level since 1989; high technology demand was 41% higher vs. 1996.[6] As a reflection of this high demand and subsequent power as individual suppliers, 1997 salaries in these areas were recently noted by the US Federal Reserve Board to be growing faster than the rate of inflation.

Increased Threat of Substitute Products or Services

In the pharmaceutical industry, an increased threat of the past dozen years has been more rapid generic entry. The 1984 Drug Price Competition and Patent Term Restoration Act and additional pieces of legislation have fostered the entrance of generics into the US market. While this act extended the period of patent protection, it simultaneously decreased the testing requirements for approval of new generic brands of existing chemical entities (Frank and Salkever, 1992). In addition, the speed of generic penetration — and thus the rapidity with which innovating firms lose profits on the brand — has increased substantially. Generic penetration 18 months after entry increased from an average of 47% of molecule prescriptions in 1989-1990 to 72% of molecule prescriptions in 1991-1992 (Grabowski and Vernon, 1995), and is probably higher today.

Other nations have passed similar legislation to encourage generic entrants and stimulate competition:

- The Netherlands has encouraged generic substitution by compensating the community pharmacists and dispensing general practitioners 1/3 of the price difference between the branded and the generic drug when they prescribe the generic.
- Denmark has recently passed new provisions to encourage generic and therapeutic substitution. Substitution will occur by default, unless the patient or physician refuses.
- In Germany, the Statutory Sickfund Drug Guidelines have been updated to include a recommendation to further promote generic prescribing.
- Italy's Health Minister has announced reforms directed at the pharmaceutical sector. A main feature of the revised pharmaceutical policies would target an increase in generics, with simultaneously greater controls on physician's prescribing.

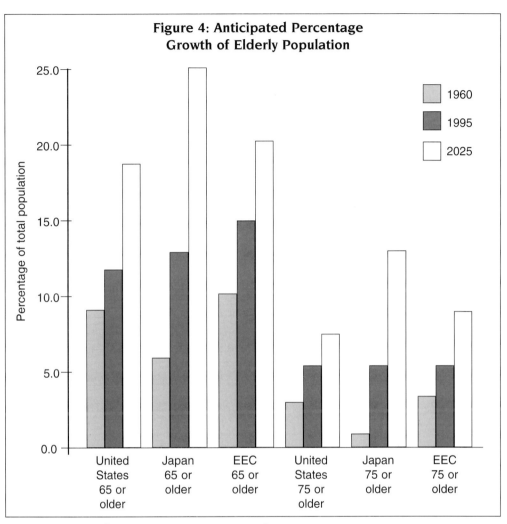

Figure 4: Anticipated Percentage Growth of Elderly Population

Increased Bargaining Power of Buyers

As healthcare costs have increased, healthcare buyers have taken increasingly aggressive steps to hold constant or reduce these costs. Governments, as payers, have enacted legislation to indirectly and directly reduce costs. Indirect measures include increasing competition in the marketplace by fostering new entrants, such as generic manufacturers, as previously mentioned. Direct measures include, for example, the US Omnibus Reconciliation Act that in essence stipulates that the government must be given the same, best price from manufacturers that private purchasers have negotiated. Private purchasers have also exerted increased pressure, through the use of prescriptive guidelines, restrictive formularies, pharmaceutical benefit management companies, consolidated buying groups, and/or a variety of "managed care" structures (Reeder et al, 1993; Kozma et al, 1993). Societal and governmental healthcare costs will be pressured to continue to rise[7] based on the steady increase in the elderly population[8] (**Figure 4**)[9] (with proportionally higher per capita healthcare consumption) and the increasing cost of new, albeit valuable, healthcare technologies. Subsequently, the pressure buyers will exert on their suppliers, including pharmaceutical companies, can also be predicted to remain intense and/or increase.

Threat of New Entrants

The rise of the biotechnology industry is well documented. Biotechnology products are a threat as new entrants, potentially replacing the need for a variety of traditional pharmaceutical products. As an example, Parkinson's disease studies have been conducted using injected, undifferentiated stem cells to recreate the natural production of dopamine and replacing the need for L-dopa therapy. Those cells could potentially be produced via biotechnology in the future. Subsequently, the threat exists for those firms unable or unwilling to invest in this new area that a number of future therapies and drugs could come from a new source. As an analogous threat, genetic therapies present the potential to be actual cures and replace traditional products in situations where signs and symptoms of a disease are only temporarily controlled.

It should be noted that these small biotech firms frequently partner with larger, fully integrated firms for late stage development and marketing. These arrangements can be profitable for the pharmaceutical firm, but only if its development and marketing expertise is sufficient to earn an economic rent on its services. Significant profits from the innovation itself will accrue to the biotech firm, as competing firms bid up the price for the rights to develop and/or market the innovative product. In any case, an increased number of quality products from the biotech industry could reduce via competition the traditional profit opportunities from innovation historically available to large, fully vertically integrated firms.

FACTORS THAT HAVE DRIVEN GLOBALIZATION

Porter identifies a dozen factors that can lead to globalization. Of those, the pharmaceutical industry has three key factors that have most significantly led to its globalization.

Increased Globalization of the Customer (Medical Community)

Conferences and journals are increasingly global in attendance and scope. Over time, there has been increased emphasis on sharing best practices within the medical community across national lines. This has decreased the advantage that local pharmaceutical firms have historically had in sales and marketing, and allowed global firms to identify and work with key customers on a worldwide scale. Marketing to a global community will be done more effectively by a company that is itself global, and able to relate its products to global and local needs simultaneously. Similar trends toward globalization can be seen developing in the areas of patient advocacy groups (e.g, AIDS), disease management programs, and payer needs.

Increased Integration of Governmental Regulation

The European Union, for example, has created a centralised Technical Approval procedure, which allows firms to file for technical approval just once for the EU. Approval then allows firms to proceed to market in all free-price countries, or to price and reimbursement negotiations in price-controlled markets.[10] The ability of the EU to create a centralised procedure partly reflects a convergence in thinking of the European medical and patient community. If medical standards were completely different, then centralised approval would never be implemented. This increase in the homogeneity of medical practices (and hopefully, convergence to best demonstrated global practice) reduces the barriers for global firms to compete in individual markets, since increasingly a single medical message for approval and marketing will be effective globally.

Less well documented, but still seemingly a trend, is an increased willingness of national regulatory bodies to consider foreign clinical trial data. Again, this decreases the barriers for global firms to operate effectively.

Increased Recognition of Global Markets

The pharmaceutical industry is characterised by very high fixed costs of development, often low variable costs of production, and a series of focused markets (e.g., no company sells "drug," they sell a specific product for a specific disease). These factors would naturally lead to a global industry, as a company must invest huge amounts up front to produce a patented product for a single focused disease area. It is increasingly imperative that a company can successfully market to all the available customers in that area to reap maximum profits (and maximum consumer benefit) in an increasingly competitive global market.[11]

The above discussion has shown that competition and globalization has increased, and has outlined some of the forces that have contributed to those trends. The next section documents the rise of pharmacoeconomic activities, and the following section discusses why PE is particularly well suited to help firms compete globally.

EVIDENCE THAT PHARMACOECONOMIC ACTIVITIES HAVE INCREASED:

- PE staff in companies has increased and additional recruiting continues
- The number of clinical trials incorporating pharmacoeconomics is increasing
- Authorities are increasingly requesting/mandating pharmacoeconomic evaluations
- The number of published PE studies, clinical and non-clinical trials, is increasing

PE staff in companies has increased and additional recruiting continues

Expenditure levels and the number of personnel employed in pharmacoeconomics are indices of the growing importance of economic evaluations and outcomes research. In a private survey of 12 major pharmaceutical companies conducted by Deloitte and Touche,[12] 75% reported that they are hiring new staff to meet the demands of expanding departments. The Zitter Group and Technology Assessment Group, Inc. previously found similar results with companies reporting increases in the number of internal outcomes researchers and the size of their departments (**Figure 5**).

The number of clinical trials incorporating PE is increasing

A survey conducted by the Boston Consulting Group in 1993 (**Figure 6**) indicates that the proportion of clinical studies incorporating health economics had increased from 2.6% in 1988 to 17.6% in 1992, with a projection to continue to increase through 1994. Based on direct observation, it is very likely that the upward trend has continued through 1997.

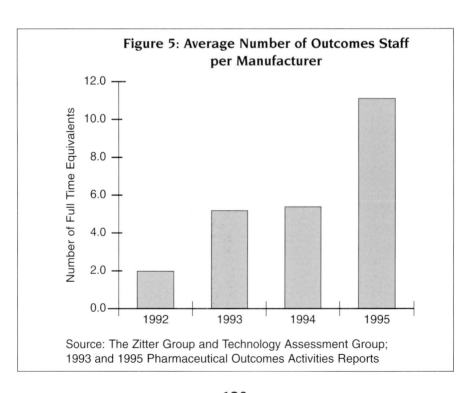

Figure 5: Average Number of Outcomes Staff per Manufacturer

Source: The Zitter Group and Technology Assessment Group; 1993 and 1995 Pharmaceutical Outcomes Activities Reports

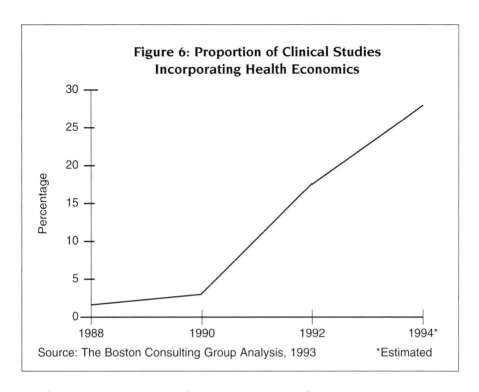

Figure 6: Proportion of Clinical Studies Incorporating Health Economics

Source: The Boston Consulting Group Analysis, 1993   *Estimated

Authorities Increasingly Request/Mandate Pharmacoeconomic Evaluations

Australia was the first country to implement the mandatory inclusion of an economic evaluation for reimbursement of pharmaceuticals, with guidelines first drafted in 1990 and fully implemented in 1993. Canada was the second country to include such a regulation, implemented in 1994. Both of these countries have published explicit guidelines addressing the characteristics and criteria necessary for economic evaluation.

The desire of authorities to control healthcare and/or pharmaceutical costs is probably a significant driver in the increasing importance of pharmacoeconomics and health economics in many developed countries. Countries are increasingly mandating (or strongly requesting) that economic submissions be supplied by pharmaceutical companies to obtain pricing, reimbursement, and/or formulary listing (**Table 3**; Drummond M.F *et al*, 1993). A number of concerned parties have emphasized that economic evaluation should be used to assess the value for money, in effect the costs *and* consequences of a pharmaceutical product, and ultimately be used as *one* criteria to improve prescribing decisions. Unfortunately, in a number of cases economic evaluation appears to have been used to simply assess the cost side of the equation and curtail access to "expensive" therapies.

The development and proliferation of pharmacoeconomic guidelines and principles has intensified and will likely continue in the future. This trend raises the

Table 3: Range of Potential Uses of Economic Evaluation of Pharmaceuticals in Europe

Country	Undertaking National Price Negotiations	Deciding on Reimbursement Status or Copayment Level	Deciding on Inclusion in Local Formularies or in Treatment Guidelines	Improving Prescribing Decisions
Belgium	?	+	?	?
Finland	+	+	?	?
France	+	?	+	?
Germany	-	-	+	?
Italy	?	+	+	?
Netherlands	-	+	+	?
Portugal	-	+	?	?
Spain	-	?	?	?
Sweden	+	+	+	?
Switzerland	-	+	+	?
United Kingdom	-	-	+	+

(+) Economic data could be, or have been used (-)Economic data are not required
(?) Uncertainty regarding the role of economic data

question of possible consolidation to one global standard, much in the same spirit of "harmonized" global standards for traditional clinical and manufacturing practices in pharmaceuticals. Given the emerging nature of the discipline, and disparate character of countries, perspectives, and customer's needs, the principles must remain broadly specified and provide a range of methodologic options that ultimately keep in mind the "cost/benefit" of any analysis undertaken. Conceivably, mandatory economic evaluations could become a "fourth hurdle" and serve only to limit the diffusion of valuable and useful, new therapies. The recent status of PE guidelines in nine countries with large pharmaceutical expenditures are surveyed below:

Canada

Revisions to the 1994 Canadian guidelines are under consideration. Ontario has developed its own guidelines, with other provinces considering and/or following a similar route. The Canadian guidelines outline steps to be considered "good pharmacoeconomic practice." Health economic justification is an important consideration for formulary acceptance of new therapies.

United Kingdom

In 1994 the National Health Service (NHS) published guidelines for the economic evaluation of pharmaceuticals. In the past, the House of Commons Health Committee has supported two policies which if implemented could lead to an increase in the use of economic evaluations: a prescribing list partly dependent on economic criteria and increased funding for cost-effectiveness analyses of pharmaceutical products.

Germany

Joint committees of Sick Funds (a significant market power covering 90% of medical expenses of the total population) and ambulatory physician syndicates are increasingly developing guidelines for pharmaceutical prescribing which include health economic considerations. Health economic evaluations are also increasingly being used for product differentiation and promotional purposes.

France

Pricing guidelines, consideration of healthcare budgetary impacts, and bi-annual pricing reviews have increased the importance of manufacturers providing epidemiologic and economic assessments. The number of PE studies submitted to the Transparency Commission rose from 10 in 1994 to over 20 in 1995, and is reportedly continuing to increase.[13]

Spain

Assessments have been considered mainly in regard to formulary decision-making.

Italy

This year (1997), Ministry of Health guidelines have been revised, stating that, for the first time, PE arguments should be provided to support pricing and reimbursement decisions.

Netherlands

Authorities met in 1997 and held hearings with academics and industry to discuss the development of formal guidelines and potential implementation as an element for reimbursement decision-making. An approach similar to the Canadian guidelines appears likely.

Japan

Officials encourage economic submissions to support pricing requests. The government-sponsored Institute for Health Economics and Policy was created in 1993.

United States

Guidelines have been proposed by PhRMA, the Public Health Service, and others. The Food & Drug Administration has held two public meetings on PE promotional guidelines. Fee-for-service is transitioning to managed care, with a growing demand for economic evaluation and justification pertinent to their membership.

The number of published studies, clinical and non-clinical trials is increasing

In order to assess the growth rate of research in health economics and pharmacoeconomics over the past decade, a count was conducted of the number of health economic and cost-effectiveness articles (which is of course a conservative estimate of the total amount of research being conducted) published in the literature in 1980, 1985, 1990, and 1995.[14] To do this, the Medline, Healthstar, and Embase databases were accessed. In an effort to be broadly inclusive and comprehensive, the following key search terms were included: pharmacoeconomics, health economics, cost-of-illness, cost analysis, cost/benefit, cost-effectiveness, healthcare costs, indirect costs, and treatment costs. As these search terms capture quite a large area of research, the most common type of analyses, "cost-effectiveness," was then used as a proxy for pharmacoeconomics research and the database assessment was repeated using only that search term (**Figure 7**).

The greatest growth in research has been in the period from 1990 to 1995. The

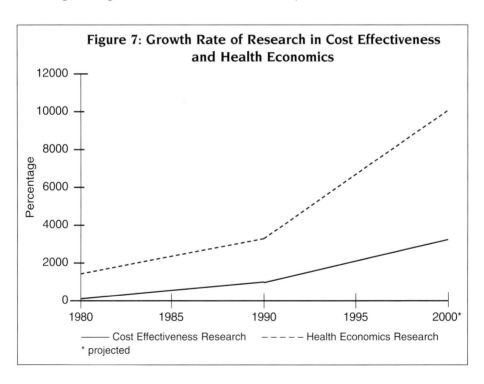

Figure 7: Growth Rate of Research in Cost Effectiveness and Health Economics

——— Cost Effectiveness Research   − − − − Health Economics Research
* projected

ageing population, the continued expansion of healthcare technology, and the increasingly competitive healthcare market will likely create continued growth of such studies and publications in the near term. Ultimately, the amount of research in this field is linked to the market-driven demand for these types of analyses and subsequently, is also tied to the amount of industry and government funding available. These influences will function as the contributing or constraining factors for the growth rate of this research.

In an analogous assessment of the amount of research being done using cost-effectiveness and cost-benefit analyses, (Elixhauser *et al*, 1991) also demonstrated a steadily increasing rate of pharmacoeconomic research, with the largest number of studies at that time being conducted in the United States. Subsequently, we assume that the majority of the research depicted in our graph was also done in the US.

HOW PHARMACOECONOMICS CONTRIBUTES TO A COMPANY'S GLOBAL COMPETITIVENESS

The trend to a more competitive and more global industry has been documented and the reasons for this trend discussed. Pharmacoeconomics contributes to a company's attempts to achieve global competitive advantage. This section discusses three economic factors that have driven the increase in PE, and several barriers to expanded and effective use of PE within the industry. The three factors contributing to increased use of PE that drive global competitive advantage, in order of importance, are:

- Product differentiation among increasingly economically sophisticated customers
- Economies of scale in marketing
- Pursuit of comparative advantage

Product differentiation among increasingly economically sophisticated customers

Increased competition leads to increased efforts to differentiate products (Porter, 1980). Product differentiation creates a defensible position for coping with competitive forces by providing insulation against other companies' competitive strategies, developing brand loyalty and decreasing price sensitivity. The alternative to differentiation is to compete in a commodity-type environment, which in the pharmaceutical industry with its large fixed costs leads to very low prices and greatly hampered profitability.

Product differentiation is perhaps the most important contribution that pharmacoeconomics makes to global competitiveness. Pharmaceutical companies have traditionally marketed their products on the basis of superior efficacy and safety. While these remain important selling points, in many cases, pharmaceutical companies are now being asked — or are proactively attempting — to differentiate their products based on their value for money and effects on patient well-being.

The application of pharmacoeconomics early in clinical development can help identify which products are likely to meet this demand or provide insight into what data might be required for the demonstration of economic differentiation (Clemens *et al*, 1993). Some are quite optimistic regarding its use in phase I or phase II development. For example, Freiman (Marketletter, 11/9/92) states "Pharmacoeconomics will be the fastest growing discipline in the world of pharmaceuticals, determining whether a drug should be developed early on in the development process." In phase III, Genentech expanded the estimated market value of one of their products from $78 million to $350 million by incorporating an economic/quality of life component to a clinical trial and by consulting healthcare payers about what they wanted.[15]

Pharmaceutical manufacturers are developing PE data and models to make three types of differentiation arguments. First, to illustrate to a buyer the cost associated with a selected disease for which drug therapy is an important component of treatment. Second, to demonstrate the superiority of a particular product over another and, third, to justify a value-based price that may be higher than existing competitors or alternative therapies.

Pharmacoeconomic evaluations that demonstrate cost savings or offsets to other parts of the healthcare system may provide an entry barrier for newly developed alternative products and delay adoption of competitor products. PE can similarly create a price and reimbursement hurdle to new entrants by cost-conscious payers that will require demonstration of similar data and cost effectiveness.

Providing global customers with the necessary tools to evaluate the economic costs and benefits of new pharmaceutical therapies can push customers to evaluate new technology at a more sophisticated level. If a company is proficient in its application of pharmacoeconomics, educating the customer on the requirements of a sound economic evaluation can provide a potential hurdle to less capable competitors. It can also provide the customer with a tool which will allow them to make a variety of healthcare evaluations. Agencies such as the Joint Commission on Accreditation of Healthcare Organisations, and surveys such as the Healthcare Employer Data Information Survey (HEDIS) are beginning to formally integrate performance measurement into their accreditation processes, and healthcare providers will need to apply the concepts of health economics and outcomes assessment to meet new requirements. With pharmaceutical firms providing pharmacoeconomic analysis and familiarity to these customers, it could provide the customer with a tool to evaluate their standards of care and meet these additional requirements.

PE analyses have also been driven by an increased desire and willingness of key customers to listen to PE arguments and data. Large buyers — increasingly prevalent in today's market — increasingly have the expertise and resources to analyse PE arguments. A 2 million-life HMO can spread the fixed costs of making a rational drug purchase decision based on PE over many units of the drug to be purchased. Small buyers (e.g., individual physicians in a classic fee for service environment) do not have the time and often do not have the expertise to utilise PE as a decision tool. The existence of PE articles and arguments also has a self-reinforcing trend as the decision analysis technology diffuses throughout the industry. Buyers are growing more capable of assessing the economic information provided to them and are beginning to develop the expertise necessary to make informed decisions based on these data. Once they see the value, they demand more of the same type of arguments. (Of course, poorly formed or biased arguments can lessen the demand for PE, as discussed in the next section). In a survey of over 200 health plans, 70% cited lack of sufficient and timely cost effectiveness data as reasons for not covering a new drug, second only to lack of sufficient effectiveness (Arthur D Little, 1993).

At present, economic evaluations and other outcomes evaluations have widely differing levels of importance for regulatory approval, reimbursement, and marketing throughout the world. The US is, arguably, the most advanced in the development and application of these studies and pharmaceutical companies are increasingly using them to influence reimbursement decisions, justify pricing and enhance the marketing of their products. The combination of outcomes data with traditional measures of safety and efficacy are providing governments, insurers, and other healthcare decision-makers with new information to make approval, reimbursement, and adoption decisions. While the FDA does not require economic data for approval of a product, cost-effectiveness claims (like any other claim in a label or advertisement) must be supported by submitted data. As such claims can provide competitive advantages in markets, and there is a growing incentive to have these data available and used in promotion.

Economies of scale in marketing

Central pharmacoeconomic departments identify and implement strategies that demonstrate the economic value of new products on a global basis. The costs of producing the central strategies, analyses and models to support pricing and market adoption are moderately significant, but are incurred only once. In relative terms, the cost of the adaptation and application of the deliverables to individual markets is much less. An example of these economies of scale is the inclusion by a central team of economic appraisals alongside multinational clinical trials. The clinical trial offers a vehicle for collecting data on health outcomes and resource utilisation associated with the disease and therapy under study. Relative to the costs of the trial, there are minimal incremental costs associated with adding an economic analysis. Further, this offers the ability to collect data in a standard fashion that will allow for development of individualised country-specific analyses where required.

Economies can also be realised when local affiliates share responsibilities for conducting pharmacoeconomic evaluations. Economic analysis for select payers or governments in one market can be applied to similar types of payers in other markets, through either an adaptation of the economic analysis or simply sharing the findings and publication resulting from the analysis. Through the local adaptation process many lessons can be learned and shared.

Pursuit of comparative advantage

Increased global competition leads to increased efforts of firms to exploit comparative economic advantages; i.e., firms will increase their efforts to utilise the basic economic endowments — land, labour, and capital — of their home countries. A significant portion of the labour pool for PE is in the United States and the United Kingdom. Thus, US and UK-based firms have had a head start in recruiting capable personnel to formulate PE arguments. This reflects the advanced stages of the discipline in these countries, but European companies are moving fast to narrow this advantage (Malek, 1995).

BARRIERS TO THE USE OF PE

Persistent differences in systems and populations

While trends suggest that healthcare delivery and issues are converging across markets, there will always be limitations due to the inherent differences among markets. These differences include: culture, state of economic development, income, practice patterns, access to care, population demographics, healthcare seeking behaviour, and customer expectations. These differences will influence demand for different types of economic evaluations on differing populations. In developing economic analyses for worldwide applications, companies must carefully examine the extent to which additional costs will be incurred in adapting analyses across multiple markets. If the cost of producing additional varieties of evaluations is large (and it is likely that they are at least not trivial), then the value of purely centralised PE, and PE in general, is of course less. Global firms with a combination of central groups and capable local affiliates with experience in conducting pharmacoeconomic evaluations will be better suited to overcome this barrier.

Differing Standards for PE Increases Costs and Creates Confusion and Disenchantment

The problem of differing standards is a global one, but may be most acute in Europe. If each country adopts different economic requirements, the pathway to market approval and launch will become hindered with new obstacles just as the EU is attempting to harmonize approval. This is a serious threat to most global pharmaceutical firms, as onerous PE guidelines could result in increased developmental spending, delays and increased burden for marketing products. From the industry's perspective; mandatory guidelines might constitute an additional hurdle to be negotiated after demonstrating efficacy and safety.

Another factor currently limiting the usefulness of pharmacoeconomic analyses is the lack of consensus regarding methodology (Luce, 1993). Related to this is the fact that there are no agreed criteria or threshold articulated by payers for judging what is cost-effective and what payers are willing to pay for.[16] With multiple customers of pharmaceuticals with different perspectives and standards, one strategy or approach is often not sufficient. As such, efficiencies can be lost, if multiple products must be developed on an individual customer by customer basis.

Related to the standards issue is a credibility issue. Since PE has been mostly visibly used to differentiate products, many consider it a marketing tool. As such, it has been greeted with some skepticism by payers. As a result, standards have been a topic of increased interest to the industry and academics. An inability to develop and adhere to objective, clear, and professional PE arguments will lead to a decrease in the credibility of the discipline as practiced by the industry. The methodology for PE is fact-based decision analysis, and we believe that it is a key decision tool to help frame resource allocation decisions such as drug purchasing. If methodology is clearly delineated, the fact-based and rigorous nature of the analysis should allow all parties to conduct and interpret research that is credible.

Organisational impediments within pharmaceutical firms

Classic organisational theory states that large complex organisations evolve as hundreds of differentiated units that can produce highly specialised sub-products. As an organisation gets larger, it becomes more differentiated. As this happens it becomes increasingly important, yet difficult, to integrate these differentiated units (Lawrence and Lorsch, 1969). The problem is compounded when these units — such as PE — are functional in nature; that is, organised around similar skills rather than around customers or strategic geography. Integration and coordination across these functional units is especially difficult.

Further, PE is a relatively new discipline in the industry, and can be seen as not only a tool to help but also as a threat to traditional pharmaceutical, R&D and marketing activities. This perception of threat can be exacerbated by the technical nature of the analysis, which can seem strange or artificial to those who are not familiar with it. Successful integration of a PE function requires communication, education, and a willingness on the part of PE researchers to work hard to integrate their results into the overall drug development and marketing plan. Organisationally, success requires significant commitment from senior management to fully leverage this new competitive capability, including integration in key decision-making groups, clearly defined and supported roles and responsibilities, and sufficient levels of resourcing as an emerging key competency.

Differentiation offered by PE not relevant to payers sitting in budgetary silos

PE quantifies the "costs and benefits" of various therapies and products. At its heart is a recognition that drugs have an effect on the underlying disease, which has ramifications for other costs in treating the patient. If the decision-maker does not bear the responsibility of paying for those costs, then the PE argument may fall on deaf ears. For example, reimbursement for nicotine patches — which are often highly cost effective — has been denied in some instances simply because the agency does not directly bear the costs and consequences of smoking in its budget, and cannot "afford" to reimburse for it. Further, there is no strong organised constituency at this time for paying for smoking cessation. Thus, in a narrow and short term sense, one could argue that PE has failed to adequately create reimbursement for this product. However, the arguments may help form the political constituency, and then the funds, to pay for nicotine patches in the future.

CONCLUSION

Intensified global competition has led large integrated companies to focus on new ways of achieving competitive advantage. In today's global market, companies are initiating efforts (or being asked) to justify drug prices and reimbursement with information on cost-effectiveness, patient well-being, and long-term outcomes. Global success will partly depend on a company's ability to learn, adopt and apply pharmacoeconomic research faster than its competitors.

Over the next decade, globalization will continue. Mergers, acquisitions, and expansions to new markets will predominate. As healthcare expenditures continue to rise, particularly in developing nations, and put pressure on payer budgets, there will be continued pressures to maintain economic assessments. Economic evaluations and other outcomes assessments will play an increasingly important role in the US, Europe, Japan, and evolving markets, as patients, healthcare organisations, governments, and other third party payers demand greater demonstrations of the value they are receiving from pharmaceutical products.

As the discipline continues to evolve, it will become increasingly important to document how these new approaches of applying economic evaluations to pharmaceuticals will translate into added value for the investing firm. To the extent that pharmacoeconomic data can play a role in strategic targeting, development decision-making, regulatory approval, reimbursement, and pricing negotiations, companies will continue to see value in this function and will provide support to carry out the necessary studies. More intense competition means that companies that know how to use these data and capabilities effectively will have a distinct advantage over those who do not.

The precise means of how to use PE to form effective and customer focused arguments is a key part of the current work of the industry. Such work will require a melding of the social science discipline of pharmacoeconomics and the applied discipline of global pharmaceutical development and marketing.

REFERENCES

1. Andersson F. Why is the Pharmaceutical Industry Investing Increasing Amounts in Health Economic Evaluations? *International Journal of Technology Assessment in Healthcare*, **11:** 4: 750–761, 1995.
2. Bootman JL, Townsend RJ, McGhan WF, Principles of Pharmacoeconomics, Second Edition. Harvey Whitney Books Company. Cincinnati, Ohio, 1996.
3. Clemens K, Garrison LP, Jones A, and MacDonald F, Strategic Use of Pharmacoeconomic Research in Early Drug Development and Global Pricing. *Pharmacoeconomics* **4:** 5: 315–322, 1993.
4. Drummond M.F., Ruben, Brenna, *et al*, Economic Evaluation of Pharmaceuticals: A European Perspective. *Pharmacoeconomics* **4:** 3, 1993.
5. Drummond, M, Evaluation of Health Technology Economic Issues for Health Policy and Policy Issues for Economic Appraisal. *Soc Sci Med,* **38:** 12: 1593–1600, 1994.

6. Drummond MF, Bloom BS, Carrin G *et al.* Issues in the Cross National Assessment of Health Technology. *International Journal of Technology Assessment in Healthcare,* **8:**4 671–682, 1992.
7. Elixhauser A, Luce BR, Taylor WR, Reblando J. Healthcare CBA/CEA: an Update on the Growth and Composition of the Literature. *Med Care,* **31:**7 suppl: JS1–11, JS18–149, 1993.
8. Flannery EJ, Hutt PB. Balancing Competition and Patent Protection in the Drug Industry: The Drug Price Competition and Patent Term Restoration Act of 1984. *Food Drug Cosmetic Law Journal* **40:** 269–309, 1985.
9. Frank R, Salkever D. Pricing, Patent Loss and the Market for Pharmaceuticals. *Southern Economic Journal,* **59:** 165–179, 1992.
10. Grabowski H, Vernon J. Longer Patents for Increased Generic Competition: The Waxman-Hatch Act After One Decade. working paper, June 1995.
11. Kozma CM, Schulz RM, Dickson WM *et al.* Economic Impact of Cost-Containment Strategies in Third Party Programmes in the US (Part 2). *Pharmacoeconomics,* **4:** 3: 187–202, 1993.
12. Little, Arthur Inc, Current Health Economics Practices Among Pharmaceutical Companies, 1993.
13. Luce BR. Cost-Effectiveness Analysis, Obstacle to Standardisation and its Use in Regulating Pharmaceuticals. *Pharmacoeconomics,* **3:** 1–9, 1993.
14. Malek M. Pharmaco-economics; The New Discipline of Pharmaco-economics and its Impact on R&D Strategy. *Pharmaceutical Forum Issue* **4:** 17–19, Spring 1995.
15. Menzin J, Oster G, Davies L, *et al.* A Multinational Economic Evaluation of rhDNase in the Treatment of Cystic Fibrosis. *International Journal of Technology Assessment in Healthcare,* **12:** 152–61, 1996.
16. O'Chi H, Kuwayama T, Tanaka N, Hess G, Kozma C, Grogg A. Japanese Pharmacoeconomic Survey. *Japanese Journal of Health Economics & Policy,* published by the Institute for Health Economics & Policy. **2:** 95, 83–92.
17. Porter M, Competitive Strategy; Techniques for Analyzing Industries and Competitors, The Free Press, 1980.
18. Reeder CE, Lingle EW, Schulz RM *et al.* Economic Impact of Cost-Containment Strategies in Third Party Programmes in the US (Part 1). *Pharmacoeconomics,* **4:** 2: 92–103, 1993.
19. Sims J. Europe Looks to U.S. for Disease Management Pointers. *Medical Marketing & Media,* **31:** 6:36(6).

FIGURE REFERENCES

1. Data Source: IMS, 1997.
2. In regard to pharmaceutical companies, Wood Mackenzie defines major strategic moves as: mergers, acquisitions, divestments, joint ventures, public placements, major R&D collabourations (judged as having a large impact on a companies' strategies).
3. Source: Recombinant Capital (www.recap.com), July 1997. Based on SEC filings, press releases, and other searches to capture deals/alliances among the following: biotechnology companies with pharmaceutical companies, inter-company biotechnology alliances, biotechnology companies with universities and non-profit organisations, and major mergers and acquisition between pharmaceutical companies.
4. PR Newswire, EDS Pointcast, 1997 reports.
5. Source: Bureau of Labour Statistics, Producer Price Index, August 1997.
6. MSL, *The London Sunday Times,* July 27, 1997.
7. For example, "in the Netherlands, costs are forecast to rise by 1% per year until 2030, of which 70% will be due to aging, the rest to population growth." (Sims). Other industrialised nations are experiencing similar trends.
8. WHO, 1996 Fact Sheet N 131 indicates that the global population is aging. The average life expectancy has increased from approximately 40 years at birth in the 1950s to 62 years in 1990, with a projection to rise to 70 years by 2020.
9. Data Source: OHE Compendium of Health Statistics, 9th Ediition, 1995.

10. While there have been discussions regarding more centralised pricing procedures in Europe, not surprisingly, no country has been willing to cede control over its pricing (and thus its budget) to a third party. It is likely that centralised pricing is at least 10 years away in Europe.

11. First is the realisation that there are no borders for disease; for example, the pandemic of AIDS. Just as disease has no boundaries, neither does scientific information or knowledge. Freiman, *Marketletter*, Nov. 9, 1992.

12. The Evolving Structure of Health Economics. *Scrip Magazine*, March 1997.

13. "In France," said Transparency Commission chairman Bernard Avouac, "such [PE] studies are a particularly good approach for drug listing and pricing..." Report on PharmEcon Europe 95 meeting, organised by ICBI, EU: Pluses and Minuses of Pharmacoeconomics. *Marketletter* July 17, 1995.

14. The projection of the number of health economics and cost-effectiveness studies published for the year 2000 was based on the assumption that the growth in the 1990 to 1995 period would continue to the year 2000, which seems reasonably conservative.

15. Quote from Senior Manager Health Economics at Genentech, Pat Barnett; *Regulatory & Healthcare News.*

16. For example, in Japan, according to a recent survey, no consensus on methodology or objectives exists (O'Chi *et al*, 1995).

10

Pharmacoeconomics and the future of the pharmaceutical industry. Should they be encouraged to establish a pharmacoeconomic team?*

D Jones

INTRODUCTION

Pharmacoeconomics has only recently arrived on the industry scene. Even now, there is still little agreement amongst industry practitioners as to the appropriate title for their profession, being variously called health economists, pharmacoeconomists, socio-economists, or outcomes researchers. Ultimately, the choice of title seems to be largely determined by the perceived nature of their role within the company.

Many industry practitioners prefer to call themselves pharmacoeconomists in order to emphasise that their primary focus is on the application of the principles and techniques of economics to pharmaceutical products and services. On the other hand, there are equally as many who prefer to call themselves health economists on the grounds that they have skills that can be applied to broader healthcare issues such as providing healthcare solutions to funding constraints or the evaluation of disease management practices. This definition would also fit in with the belief that pharmacoeconomics is essentially a sub-speciality of health economics, or a specific application of health economics.

On the other hand, some companies prefer to use the alternative title of socio-economist in order to emphasise that in evaluating the economic value of pharmaceutical interventions, they need to consider not only the direct costs of the intervention but also the intangible benefits of treatment such as the impact on quality of life or the impact on the broader societal benefits such as productivity. On the other hand, some companies have dropped the word economics from their title altogether, preferring instead to call themselves outcomes researchers. This is designed to emphasise that their primary responsibility is the identification, measurement, and communication of the outcomes of new interventions. These outcomes may be economic, clinical, quality of life, or measures of patient satisfaction. The results of the outcomes research would then be used in order to demonstrate the added-value of the new therapeutic intervention.

*The views expressed in this paper are entirely those of the author and do not necessarily represent the views of SmithKline Beecham Pharmaceuticals

In order to reflect the differences in the definitions described above, some pharmaceutical companies have established one or more departments, variously called outcomes research, pharmacoeconomics, socioeconomics or health economics, with the first three titles usually reserved for departments located in the corporate clinical/medical division and the latter title (or variations of) usually reserved for functions located in the corporate marketing division and/or in the operating units. The former departments tend to see their role as largely economic research, capturing data to support the economic value of their products, usually alongside clinical trials, whilst the health economic departments tend to see their responsibility as largely one of strategy and co-ordination (if in a central role) and communication and dissemination (if in an operating role). In other words, health economic departments, primarily see their role as one of guiding pharmacoeconomics/outcomes research in order to ensure that it meets the needs of the target external customers. Of course, this over-simplifies the situation since some companies have combined the central functions into one department. Furthermore, the location of this single central department can also vary, but is usually located either within the medical or marketing divisions. One of the benefits of a single central function is to ensure a more seamless process of pharmacoeconomic input throughout the product lifecycle.

The health economist based in the operating unit usually provides the interface between the central functions and the end-user. It is largely his/her role to ensure that the end user perspectives are reflected in the economic research carried out by the central team and that the results of this research can be transformed into meaningful and relevant messages for the customer. However, in response to the need for more customer-focused studies, more primary economic research is being carried out by the operating companies. Furthermore, some companies have also created specialist groups that focus specifically on disease management and/or the development of quality of life instruments.

Many of the larger companies have now employed pharmacoeconomists of varying numbers, with varying backgrounds, with varying roles and responsibilities, with varying titles depending on their precise function, and with varying locations and reporting structures within the overall company organisation. There is at present little uniformity in approach. This probably reflects the lack of clarity that still surrounds the role and responsibilities of a pharmacoeconomics function and the uncertainty surrounding the level of investment that would be appropriate for such a function.

There is now a universal recognition that the environment for pharmaceuticals has changed, probably irreversibly. In many countries, we have seen a shift of decision-making away from the traditional providers towards payers and patients. The shift in decision-making to the patient has arisen out of the emerging culture of patient empowerment and the growth in the availability of healthcare information to the patient. The shift in decision-making to the payers is largely a consequence of the increased concern over rising healthcare costs, the introduction of healthcare reforms focusing on cost-containment and the introduction of competitive practices into the healthcare market, although the latter policy is being reversed in the UK.

144

With costs now a perennial concern for payers, companies need to find ways to surmount the funding hurdles that could significantly limit the uptake of their products. Pharmacoeconomics is a discipline that carries out scientifically valid research into the economics of healthcare with the goal of optimising the delivery of healthcare to the patient. It would appear therefore that pharmacoeconomics would be a useful tool to identify and measure the cost-effectiveness of pharmaceutical products and services and to provide cost-effective healthcare solutions that could benefit both the payer, the pharmaceutical company and ultimately the patient population. If that supposition is accepted then pharmacoeconomics has a key role to play throughout the product development process. It follows therefore that some in-house expertise in pharmacoeconomics would seem appropriate.

However, for companies who wish to set up pharmacoeconomic teams then a number of issues need to be considered before committing themselves to a global investment that is likely to be substantial. These issues relate to roles and responsibilities, the nature of the deliverables, the size of the function(s), the appropriate people to recruit, and where they should be located within the organisation. These areas will be briefly explored in the following sections.

For the remainder of this chapter, and to avoid confusion, I shall refer to all of these groups as pharmacoeconomists, in line with the terminology used in this book. However, this is not to suggest that the title 'pharmacoeconomist' is necessarily ideal, or that such a notion as an ideal title actually exists. As suggested above, the choice of title seems to ultimately depend on the perceived nature of the role and responsibilities of the practitioner working within a pharmaceutical company.

BACKGROUND

It is universally recognised that every country in the world has a healthcare cash crisis with costs outstripping inflation in many cases. A number of reasons have been put forward to explain the situation, notably the slowing down of economic growth, the aging population, raised consumer expectations, and the introduction of expensive new technologies. These factors, together with the underlying dynamic of infinite demand for healthcare and the finite supply of healthcare resources, has led to a scarcity of healthcare resources. Consequently, one has to make rational choices in the allocation of the scarce healthcare resources in order to achieve maximum efficiency from the resources available.

The government reaction to the cash crisis has been to identify and adopt strategies for containing costs. These have varied across the globe from reference pricing, to profit capping, to direct price controls, to generic substitution, parallel importing, patient co-payments, to managed care and the creation of an internal market. However, in nearly all cases, drugs have been the primary target for containing costs because they are an easy target both politically and economically. Furthermore, the drugs bill is a variable cost item that tends to increase in line with the amount of healthcare activity. This makes them easier to control than fixed or semi-variable costs (like hospital staffing levels) and would not require major restructuring of the healthcare system. This has led to fears amongst the pharmaceutical industry that too much cost-containment in this sector would seriously harm industry profitability, leading to job losses, reduced R&D investment, fewer innovative new drugs and ultimate ruination of the industry.

With the drive for efficiency in healthcare, and with its focus on cost-containment in pharmaceuticals, there has arisen a recognition, principally within the industry, that economic evaluations would be useful tools to demonstrate the true economic value of pharmaceutical products. During this time, there has been an upsurge in the use of pharmacoeconomics by industry in order to demonstrate, through scientifically conducted studies, that their products are 'cost-effective' and justify the price. The number of publications which were either full economic evaluations or partial evaluations doubled in the 10 years during the '80s. Most of these evaluations were carried out or sponsored by industry. The industry has certainly been the most vociferous in claiming that its products are good value for money because of the economic benefits that arise from their improved efficacy and safety. However, while it was largely recognised, at least in theory, that such evaluations could be useful tools for managing the healthcare system in a rational way, economic evaluations were perceived as being of dubious quality, methodologically flawed, lacking transparency, irrelevant, impractical and in many cases highly misleading, and probably biased.

In order to improve the value and credibility of such evaluations, government and academic bodies, as well as industry, have been instrumental in putting together guidelines for carrying out economic evaluations in order to ensure that such evaluations meet acceptable scientific standards. In addition, recommendations have been made for such evaluations to be carried out by independent researchers and that the sponsors should be named and their relationship with the researchers acknowledged.

The increase in economic evaluation activity in recent years has not just been confined to a small number of countries. Most major countries now have some economic evaluation activity and one would expect that the growing localisation of decision-making would increase the need for and use of economic evaluations. However, despite this growth, very little is known about the impact of such evaluations on decision-making. In Australia and Canada, the reforms have led to a mandatory requirement for economic data for pricing and reimbursement. In Australia, for instance, cost-effectiveness analysis is used routinely by the PBAC to make policy decisions about the reimbursement of new healthcare interventions. The guidelines for such evaluations are still being discussed between industry, researchers and the government. The commercial impact of this process has been to delay launches and restrict indications. In Canada, a large number of cost-effectiveness studies are carried out by the CCOHTA in order to inform reimbursement decisions with significant commercial implicaitons for the industry.

In some European countries, the reforms have led to an environment where the provision of economic data to support pricing and reimbursement, whilst not mandatory, is considered advisable. For instance, in France it is recommended that economic data should be made available for pricing negotiation, in Italy it is advisable that economic data should be made available for reimbursement/

copayment status, and in the UK it is recommended that data should be made available for local formularies/treatment guidelines. In Sweden, in the last few years, health economics has become a common part of healthcare policy and in the Netherlands, there is growing attention to health economics but as with many countries there is a gap between actual and potential use. In Germany, economic evaluations are carried out to influence the decisions of various institutions such as the sickness funds. It is anticipated that economic evaluations will play a bigger role in Germany in the future as competition increases between the insurers.

Many countries in Europe now have guidelines for economic evaluation or at least proposals for such guidelines. In Spain, the use of economic evaluations is still in its infancy although a project was completed in 1995 on the methodological standardisation of economic evaluations of healthcare technologies in Spain that was commissioned by the General Directorate of Planning of the Spanish Ministry of Health. Economic evaluations are being used in Spain to influence prescribing practices and, to a lesser extent, to influence pricing and reimbursement. In fact, the environment in Europe has become one where superior economic performance of a drug is often a pre-requisite for superior commercial performance. However, overall, it is not clear to what extent these economic evaluations have had an impact on decision-making. The suspicion is that the impact is not very great. However, with the growing prevalence of disease management activity, this situation may change and provide new opportunities for health economics and for industry.

Pharmacoeconomics is increasingly being discussed in formulary and drug use decisions in US HMO's. Decision-makers typically use assessments of clinical effectiveness, safety, cost of treatment, cost-effectiveness, and, less commonly, quality of life in their decision-making. It is likely that socioeconomic assessments will be used increasingly to determine optimal healthcare programmes by managed care insurance plans. These developments are providing opportunities to influence prescribing practices.

The use of cost-effectiveness studies by US pharmacy benefit managers is also likely to increase with the implementation of disease management programs particularly as these organisations have got access to large quantities of claims data as well as the availability of internal expertise to use the data effectively for making decisions about effectiveness and cost-effectiveness of specific pharmaceutical interventions. Furthermore, the pharmacy benefit managers and HMO's seem happy to collaborate with pharmaceutical companies as well as academic groups in carrying out outcomes research and economic evaluations.

Increasing interest is also being shown in economic evaluations in Japan, primarily as an aid to pricing and reimbursement decisions. However, as yet, there are no clear requirements nor specifications for submission of economic data to the government. Furthermore, since economic evaluations are still in their infancy in Japan, the development of guidelines will be a natural precursor to their growing use.

Alongside the global developments in the use of economic evaluations, pharmacoeconomics is still passing through a phase of major methodological change. Moreover, there are still considerable difficulties with capturing good quality economic data. Data is often not available or, where it is available, it is often of dubious quality and relevance and fails to meet the needs of the end-user. Sometimes the evaluations require a considerable amount of modelling to fill in the information gaps which leads to further suspicion of the reliability of the conclusions. What success stories there are would probably remain largely undisclosed since many of the decisions about drug prescribing are made behind closed doors and/or are based on a complex mix of factors where the impact of the individual factors cannot be distinguished.

However, it is clear from the discussion above, that the maturing of the healthcare industry worldwide is leading to an increase in the importance and influence of pharmacoeconomics on healthcare decision-making.

ROLE OF THE COMPANY PHARMACOECONOMIST

The role of pharmacoeconomics is to improve the efficiency of healthcare delivery by maximising the benefits from the available resources or conversely, maintaining the quality of care at the lowest cost. It is also important that these benefits should reflect real improvements in outcomes that go beyond mere changes in intermediary markers. Pharmacoeconomics has been instrumental in highlighting the need to identify and quantify the real outcomes of new healthcare interventions including the need to show significant benefits to the patient in terms of improvement in quality of life. It's only by measuring these benefits, many of which occur long-term, that pharmacoeconomics can be used to demonstrate the real economic value of healthcare interventions.

Pharmacoeconomics has also been a key driver in many countries for encouraging a culture of evidence-based decision-making in healthcare. The expression 'evidence-based medicine' seems to have crept into the medical language as if it was some fundamentally new and profound philosophy or concept when in fact it really means little more than what it actually says. Evidence-based medicine is a request or recommendation to base all clinical decision-making on quality scientific evidence, such as peer-reviewed randomised controlled trials. It suggests that basing decisions purely on judgement and hearsay, that could be biased, is no longer considered a satisfactory basis for making clinical decisions. This means that evidence concerning effectiveness and outcomes should be the primary basis for making clinical decisions. This is often used to mean the best clinical evidence, rather than a consideration of cost impact, although at the purchasing level, evidence relating to 'cost-effectiveness' would inevitably be an additional consideration in a resource-limited world. Pharmacoeconomists therefore have a role to play in influencing healthcare decision-making using the best available evidence in order to identify cost-effective solutions to funding issues.

The rise of managed care practices and disease management activities has also had its role in influencing the use of pharmacoeconomics. 'Disease management' like evidence-based medicine has been a buzz word for a number of years and like the latter it means little more than what it says. Disease management offers nothing less than the optimisation of the medical management of an entire disease state. The practice of disease management is likely to grow in Europe as companies realise the risk of not pursuing a disease management strategy. In the UK, for instance, curbs on disease management between the health service and industry are being lifted. This indicates a softening of attitude by the government. On the other hand, the US have led the way for a number of years in the application of disease management concepts. Pharmacoeconomics has a key role to play in identifying and evaluating disease management solutions to efficiency problems.

The response by industry to the new and evolving environment has been to establish a pharmacoeconomic infrastructure/capability. This capability has a number of key goals. It can be used, at the early business planning stage, to identify those drugs that are likely to achieve superior economic performance. It can be used to guide development of products with superior economic performance through the appropriate economic programme of activities/studies and to provide evidence of superior economic performance. The availability of sound economic data has the potential to strengthen approval submissions, to enhance product differentiation, to optimise pricing, to maximise reimbursement coverage and to optimise market penetration through the inclusion of medicines on formularies and their use by individual prescribers.

The primary goal of the company pharmacoeconomist is to demonstrate to the decision-makers how the company's drugs can lead to greater efficiencies in the healthcare system. Given that maximisation of efficiencies in healthcare is a key goal for most healthcare systems worldwide, it would be expected that pharmacoeconomics should be able to provide a valuable service to healthcare decision-makers. Economic evaluations of new investment opportunities can identify, through a cost-benefit analysis, where investments are worthwhile (allocative efficiency) and/or, through a cost-effectiveness analysis, the best investment opportunity available within a chosen economic sector (technical efficiency). This suggests that one of the most important roles of the pharmacoeconomist is to influence public health policy by demonstrating, firstly, that there is a high community need for specific healthcare interventions and, secondly, that such interventions can provide 'cost-effective' healthcare options.

In this context, one of the key roles of the company pharmacoeconomist is to educate both internal and external customers into the aims, uses, limitations and deliverables of pharmacoeconomics. This would require an on-going programme of educational activities that would culminate in an understanding of the principles of pharmacoeconomics and how they can be applied to areas such as public decision-making. Such a programme would also help to lift much of the suspicion and misunderstanding that is currently associated with the use of pharmacoeconomics.

Company pharmacoeconomists also have a particular responsibility to be the company experts on the local/international healthcare environment, particularly to the extent that it impacts on the application of pharmacoeconomics. It's critical for the pharmacoeconomist to understand the environment within which the drugs will be used if meaningful and relevant studies are to be carried out. This would involve a thorough research of the structure of the local healthcare system and its funding dynamics as well as the identification of the key stakeholders and their role in pricing, reimbursement and drug adoption. Market research, in conjunction with advisory panels, needs to be set in place in order to identify the interests and priorities of the customer and their need for economic studies. The pharmacoeconomist also needs to identify the stakeholders and decision-makers and to understand the criteria behind prescribing decisions. In particular, where economic evaluations form a part of the decision-making process (either explicit or implicit), the pharmacoeconomist needs to understand the data requirements and the perspectives of the decision-makers. On the other hand, where economic evaluations are not a part of the decision-making process, then it may be appropriate for the pharmacoeconomist to demonstrate their usefulness to the decision-makers through a process of education. This may mean targeting the key opinion leaders/influencers who may not be directly involved with the prescribing decision.

In many countries, where there is a decentralised healthcare system and price sensitivity, economic evaluations can have a great deal of influence over product uptake. Since the primary goal of the company pharmacoeconomist is to show that the company's drug is more cost-effective than competing healthcare options, then pharmacoeconomics should form an integral part of the marketing mix. It follows therefore that the integration of pharmacoeconomics into the strategic decision-making process, throughout the product lifecycle, is a critical factor in the successful commercialisation of the product.

Pharmacoeconomists need to get involved early in the drug development process in order to be able to assess the product's potential cost-effectiveness prior to major investment decisions. During this product development phase, data needs to be gathered in order to assess the product's potential for being a cost-effective treatment option both prior to and subsequent to the availability of pivotal phase III data.

Phase IIIb studies provide an opportunity to assess the economic value of the drug in a more real-life clinical setting. However, since the product is unlicensed at this stage, the trial has to be subjected to various protocol restrictions. Consequently, such studies are unlikely to completely reflect actual clinical practice (i.e. how the drugs would be used in real life) although they could be designed to approximate better to the real-life situation and be more compatible with customer needs than the pivotal phase IIIa trials. Phase IV 'naturalistic' studies may be essential for supporting the cost-effectiveness claims made at launch and showing that they apply in real-life practice. However, these studies require skillful designing in order to strike the right balance between ensuring the main design features are adhered to (particularly with regards to the capture of quality of life data) whilst, at the same time, reflecting actual clinical practice.

Economic arguments used to justify expenditure on a particular healthcare intervention are likely to have little impact on prescribing decisions unless they can be shown to provide real-life solutions to the real-life problems that confront customers. Lack of funding (and affordability) for new interventions by payers is a rising hurdle for the marketing of new products. It's also an aspect of the provision of healthcare area where pharmacoeconomics can help to provide a solution.

Economic studies should form the backbone of any business case presented to customers. On the basis of these business cases, deals can be struck up with customers that offer solutions to funding issues and the need to optimise healthcare. Studies can be set up to identify the optimum strategies for delivering healthcare but these may or may not lead to direct or immediate market expansion for the product. These studies need to be carried out in partnership with customers to ensure that they gain customer interest and acceptability. On the other hand, some of this credibility must be earned by the pharmacoeconomists themselves. For instance, pharmacoeconomists need to play, and be seen to play, an active role in developing the science and communicating the ideas. Such a role is vital, not only for the credibility of the pharmacoeconomist and the pharmacoeconomic study, but also to ensure that the tools are available that can address the healthcare issues and provide real-life business solutions.

SETTING UP AN IN-HOUSE PHARMACOECONOMICS FUNCTION

There are several options that a company can pursue. They can continue without dedicated in-house experts, and simply contract out the work wherever and whenever it is required. At the other extreme, they can create large teams of pharmacoeconomists with the view to carrying out all, or nearly all, the required pharmacoeconomics work in-house. Alternatively, they can recruit a small number of in-house experts, who would be responsible for determining the strategy for pharmacoeconomics within the company and planning the work that is required but, again, with much of that work being contracted out. This small team would effectively act as consultants to the company. However, in deciding on the best option for the company, there are a number of issues that need to be considered. These issues will be discussed below.

In-house expertise is important for a science which is still in the rapid development stage, where output is uncertain, and where the results can be high risk and controversial. In-house expertise would ensure that the research is appropriate, meets the target requirements, and is successfully communicated, thus reducing the risk of wasted resources. The benefit of in-house expertise is that additional analyses and consultancy advice would be available on call. On the other hand, in the absence of in-house expertise, dealing with agencies, perhaps different agencies with different areas of expertise and different levels of availability, would make it difficult to streamline studies and activities throughout the product lifecycle whilst ensuring a maximum return on the investment. On a per project basis, it is therefore likely to be cheaper and more effective to commission studies using in-house experts.

However, the size of the in-house pharmacoeconomics function is critical in determining what the function can or cannot achieve. If the plan is to carry out all, or nearly all, the economic evaluations in-house, then in the longterm, this is likely to be a very expensive option since, in the current environment, where for many countries pharmacoeconomics is optional, there are likely to be a large number of occasions where studies may not be required and surplus staff would then need to be re-directed to lower priority activities which are possibly not 'cost-effective' to pursue. In short, there would be a lack of flexibility that could be costly. Another drawback with in-house studies is the possible lack of credibility. This is a major issue for those countries where there is a widespread suspicion of bias in industry-performed studies or even in industry-sponsored studies. Although sponsoring may be unavoidable, it would still be an advantage in such an environment for industry to distance itself from the day to day conduct of the research. Maybe in time, with widely accepted guidelines, audits and peer-reviewed medical journals and proper understanding of the objectives and limitations of economic evaluations, more in-house work may be feasible. However, even then, for credibility purposes and to ensure that the study meets the needs of its customers, it is possibly beneficial to collaborate/partner with external customers in the development and implementation of such studies.

If all studies are to be done in their entirety in-house, then conceivably a large department would be required with a huge range of expertise across the fields of epidemiology, statistics, pharmacoeconomics, and clinical research whilst still having to rely on a lot of support from other functions within the company. This would be very costly.

Too much in-house activity can also lead to a rather staid and rather stagnant view of the theory and application of pharmacoeconomics. By collaborating with and working with external bodies, a much more dynamic approach to pharmacoeconomics would develop which would be more responsive to customers' needs, more pragmatic and more up-to-date with current thinking. Since pharmacoeconomics is a fast evolving science, in-house expertise, with the responsibility for conducting all studies in-house, would not only need to keep abreast of all the methodological developments but may also be required to do a lot of primary methodological research themselves. This wouldn't be the best use of company resources when there are a growing number of pharmacoeconomic departments in academia who are likely to be much better placed in terms of specialist knowledge and research facilities to do the required research.

The environment for healthcare is changing and, as with any evolving environment, there is a lot of uncertainty. In the case of pharmacoeconomics, there is no consensus on how such a function should be organised. The approach is therefore quite varied but there is clearly agreement amongst industry leaders that pharmacoeconomics is growing in importance and therefore investment in pharmacoeconomics is necessary and will continue to be necessary for the foreseeable future. On the other hand, there is some evidence that industry is currently going through a phase of reflection whereby it is reviewing its investment in pharmacoeconomics and re-evaluating the structure and role of its pharmacoeconomics function.

Three models for the organisation of pharmacoeconomics within the pharmaceutical industry, have been identified from a recent survey commissioned by Hoechst Marion Roussel and carried out by Deloitte & Touche Consulting Group (the results can be found in Scrip Magazine, March '97). The survey was based on the extent to which pharmacoeconomics effects strategic decision-making. One model represents companies where their pharmacoeconomists only involve themselves in product development and will carry out studies that support the product's value in the marketplace. Another model represents companies whose pharmacoeconomists get involved in both product development and portfolio management. This would include, in addition to the traditional pharmacoeconomic study, providing input into investment decisions concerning whether or not a product should be fully commercialised. The third model is where pharmacoeconomists, in addition to the previous two functions, also get involved in the corporate planning process such as involvement in acquisitions and licensing but this is extremely rare. Most pharmacoeconomic functions get involved in product development only. Unfortunately, however, this survey was carried out on pharmacoeconomists with a global role and probably reflects the lack of attention given to the very important post-launch activities such as the communication and dissemination of the results, and the incorporation of the results into local business cases in order to provide real-life healthcare solutions. In this context, the inclusion of pharmacoeconomics at the operational level is vital to the successful use of pharmacoeconomics with customers.

This leads into a discussion about where pharmacoeconomic resources should be best concentrated. The models described above tend to apply mainly to the corporate role of pharmacoeconomics. A central pharmacoeconomics capability is important but, time and time again, the central role, when working in apparent isolation of the operating companies, have failed to deliver useful results for the markets that can be turned into business solutions to the customer. The question therefore remains as to whether the role and responsibilities of the central function have been correctly defined.

Most companies seem to concentrate pharmacoeconomic resources into the corporate function (up to 60 personnel in some cases) with the bare minimum in the operating companies (1 to 4 staff). This imbalance has largely risen out of the belief that pharmacoeconomic data ideally needs to be captured alongside randomised controlled clinical trials despite the overwhelming evidence that such models are far from ideal.

Prior to launch, models of reality are the only valid designs for economic data capture and they tend to have greater credibility when constructed by independent academic groups with the appropriate specialist skills. These models can show what the drug can achieve against a set of assumptions but the real effort should be on showing what the drug will achieve in real-life practice through phase IV studies and integrating this data into providing healthcare solutions to customers. Quality of life instrument development should be contracted out to specialists because the considerable amount of research that is still required in this field would make it infeasible for an industry pharmacoeconomics function to encompass. This should also be seen as a separate speciality from pharmacoeconomics although obviously an important ingredient in the latter.

Companies with a small corporate function and an equally small number of pharmacoeconomists at the operating level is likely to find itself with some significant problems. On the other hand, the advantage of such a set-up is that some sharp prioritisation is likely to be required which could improve overall efficiency. However, one may also have to prioritise launched products to the detriment of new product development. This may have negative long-term implications. Contracting out is also not necessarily a significant labour saving device since such studies still need to be monitored quite carefully to ensure that the quality of the work meets its target objective and that the results are successfully communicated.

The central pharmacoeconomic functions rely on input from the operating company into their development plans. The pharmacoeconomist in the operating company is also responsible for communicating the messages from those studies to the external customers, in a timely manner, and in a way that is readily of use to them in their decision-making. However, these vital links into pharmacoeconomic research may not work well if there is considerable under-resource in the pharmacoeconomic function. Under-resource may show up in a failure to communicate effectively between the central pharmacoeconomic function and the operating company pharmacoeconomist. This may result in more pressure being put on the latter to contract out more of the work to local pharmacoeconomists and/or to 'partner' with customers. On the other hand, this is more likely to produce work that is business focused and credible but may also lead to an under-utilisation of central resources.

If the major hurdle for pharmacoeconomics is communicating studies to the customer in a way that supports a business case and provides real solutions to healthcare problems, then it makes more sense to put more pharmacoeconomic resources at the operational level where these hurdles are very real and immediate. The pharmacoeconomists in the operating units could then feed in their requests for pharmacoeconomic data directly to the central clinical team or through the central pharmacoeconomic function as well as setting in place procedures for local data capture prior to launch. However, if more resources were shifted to the operating level, it would mean that the primary responsibility of the central pharmacoeconomic team would then be to provide global co-ordination of pharmacoeconomic activities in order to ensure best practice and a co-ordinated strategy.

Large teams of pharmacoeconomists at the corporate level may seem a luxury but is likely to lead to an attempt to do much of the work in-house at the central level which may not be in the best interests of the operating units. The operating units need credible, timely, business-focused data and this is unlikely to be delivered by a central function that is unfamiliar with the customer base and their requirements. Although this knowledge gap can be partly filled by the pharmacoeconomist in the operating company, only by working closely with the customer on a regular basis can the research be accurately targeted to the customer's needs.

A further decision needs to be made as to where the pharmacoeconomic function should be located. Should it be located in medical, marketing, both divisions or some other division? A pharmacoeconomic function requires ready access to a wide range of information if it is to function effectively. Ideally, this would require an environment where divisions between the various functions in the company either do not exist or are very flexible. However, in an environment where such divisions do exist, careful considerations needs to be given to the benefits of closer physical and administrative links with the various divisions relative to the time and effort required to forge such links.

A location in marketing has a number of benefits. This would provide pharmacoeconomics with much closer access to market research and customer information, with greater assurance of being more aligned and responsive to marketing and customer needs and with a more established infrastructure for communicating the results of the research to the end-user. In countries, where pharmacoeconomics is still largely being used for promotional/communication purposes, this is likely to be a very important benefit since one of the main criticisms of most pharmacoeconomic functions is the problem that they appear to have in identifying and delivering the sort of information that customers need and communicating that information in a timely and readily useable form. A location in the marketing division would be ideal for this purpose. On the other hand, marketing still tend to get involved relatively late in product development, and can be rather dismissive of a function that can't deliver useful data and messages rapidly. Since pharmacoeconomics, is very much a research-based function that requires a protracted period of research to produce credible data, pharmacoeconomists may find that they become re-active to marketing needs rather than pro-active. Also, remoteness from the medical division could lead to separation from potential sources of data and missed opportunities for collaborative work with clinical researchers and external investigators, and possibly some loss of contact with the science-base.

A location within the medical division may be ideal for ensuring good science and would allow pharmacoeconomic research to be carried out alongside the clinical development program, thus ensuring timeliness of information for launch. It would also mean that the pharmacoeconomist would be in constant touch with the medical issues and the practical difficulties surrounding the capture of the data that they require. It would allow them to have contact with the key opinion leaders, although not necessarily the key decision-makers, during product development. This would allow the data to have more meaning and greater credibility in their eyes. On the negative side, a location within the medical division could lead to pharmacoeconomic research being remote from the real market needs. On the other hand, if the infrastructure is in place that would allow free and easy exchange of information between the divisions with plenty of opportunities for formal contact, then it may be incidental as to where the pharmacoeconomic function is located, provided clear lines of communication are in place.

Some companies have recognised a strategic advantage in having a group in both divisions, in order to maximise the benefits from both divisions. This could work if the pharmacoeconomic teams work effectively as one department, straddling two divisions, with one head of department who would be responsible for co-ordinating activities across the divisions. Otherwise communication and exchange of information between the teams could be problem. On the other hand, centralisation of the pharmacoeconomic function, whether it be in marketing or medical, can be efficient in terms of ensuring that pharmacoeconomic activities are streamlined throughout the product's life-cycle.

There is still no universally agreed location for a pharmacoeconomics team. It seems to make sense perhaps for the corporate team to be based in marketing. That would put the corporate team in the best position to co-ordinate operating unit activities in order to ensure alignment with global marketing strategy. Similarly, for many operating units where pharmacoeconomics is still very much a part of the marketing mix, the ideal location would again appear to be in marketing but with close collaboration with medical in order to provide input into phase IIIb/IV studies. Some companies have even absorbed these functions into other functions such as managed care or health promotion. Ultimately, the ideal location will be determined by the prevailing regulatory status of pharmacoeconomics and the established strucutre of the pharmaceutical company.

THE EXPERTISE AND TRAINING NEEDS OF A PHARMACOECONOMICS FUNCTION

Company pharmacoeconomists require a multitude of skills of which technical skills is not necessarily the most important. An ability to communicate the ideas, concepts and results of economic evaluations, in a language that customers can understand and find meaningful, is also an important requirement.

In the current environment of suspicion and scepticism of industry-sponsored evaluations, industry may not be the most appropriate setting for conducting economic research in support of one's own company products. Economic research into the economic value of the company's products may be more appropriately carried out and more satisfactorily done by academic departments who are more geared up for this type of activity. Furthermore, their apparent independence may give them greater credibility in the eyes of the customer. On the other hand, backgrounds in clinical research, healthcare administration, pharmacy, statistics, or epidemiology are still very important areas of expertise for company pharmacoeconomists. The company pharmacoeconomist needs to be able to develop a programme of pharmacoeconomic activities to support the marketing strategy and customer requirements. The company pharmacoeconomist also needs to be able to communicate the results to the different customer groups in an easily understandable language, tailored to meet their different needs. Given that it may be difficult to find a pharmacoeconomist with all these skills, it is important to have a team with a multi-disciplinary background.

Nevertheless, the in-house pharmacoeconomist may still require some in-house training. A team with diverse experience and expertise seems to be the ideal although as pharmacoeconomics matures as a business discipline it's possible that academic pharmacoeconomic courses will develop a sharper business edge to suit the needs of industry. Such courses will produce pharmacoeconomists with a broader and more detailed understanding of such areas as statistics, epidemiology, trial design, pharmaceutical product development, clinical research, pharmacy, business analysis and applied health economics.

Good communication skills and a breadth of understanding would be required in order to interface with many other internal functions notably medical and marketing, but also commercial development teams at the operating level. The interface would be required with both the central and local clinical teams.Externally, interfaces would be required with customers, through company representatives, and with external consultants and collaborators who may also be customers.

As the science becomes more rigorous, or as rigorous as it can be, a higher level of numeracy will become a key requirement. As long as the bulk of data is being captured in clinical trials with its rigorous statistical requirements then such expertise is likely to be useful. However, clinical trials will continue to provide only short-term data based on intermediate or surrogate end-points because of the commercial pressure to get a licence as early as possible. On the other hand, decision-makers are increasingly demanding longer-term data in order to demonstrate that not only are the short-term benefits maintained but that the intermediate and surrogate data translate into meaningful longer-term outcomes that have significance for all the stakeholders. This can be done through prospective outcomes studies but the data is unlikely to be available at launch. Therefore, at the time of launch, models may need to be built in order to 'predict' the longer-term benefits. These models could be based on retrospective data that establish the link between the risk factors and the longer-term outcomes so that an hypothesis can be made about what the drug can achieve in real-life clinical practice. In-house epidemiologists who can understand the clinical requirements and the statistical techniques required would be invaluable for such purposes and are likely to grow in importance in pharmacoeconomics. Certainly, from the point of view of preventative care, such as vaccines, an epidemiologist who can understand the sorts of studies required to generate incidence and prevalence data and who understands the natural history of diseases would be a useful member of the multi-disciplinary team.

A member of the pharmacoeconomics team with a background in clinical research would also be invaluable, since randomised controlled trials, which are traditionally regarded as the gold-standard for evaluating the efficacy and safety of new medicines, are also regarded, although controversially, as the gold-standard for economic data. Clinical researchers can also appreciate the practical difficulties of trial design associated with more pragmatic studies or naturalistic trials.

Pharmacoeconomists bring to the table the techniques and concepts of economics that are required to assess 'value for money' of healthcare interventions. They also have a broad understanding of many of the techniques described above and of healthcare systems generally. Pharmacoeconomists who have had experience working in the healthcare system whether as a purchaser or provider would clearly be in a favourable position to understand the needs and perspectives of the customers for health economic studies. One of the reservations about pharmacoeconomic studies is that these messages do not appear to be getting through to the customers. However, this is a part of a much broader concern of how to put evidence into practice in healthcare. One of the main reasons for this situation is probably associated with the fact that the studies do not meet the customers' needs or are not understood by customers. This often stems from insufficient understanding, by the pharmacoeconomist, of the funding dynamics and funding issues associated with a new product launch. In this context, an understanding of the healthcare system is essential to anyone planning to carry out an economic evaluation. To know the stakeholders, and to understand their role and responsibilities within the decision-making framework, would enable the right study to be targetted at the right audience with optimum effect.

WHAT CAN PHARMACOECONOMICS DELIVER?

The science of pharmacoeconomics seems to have been one of the main catalysts responsible for a growth in the interest in outcomes research. Outcomes research can be defined as the science of identifying and measuring the end-points of a health technology that are meaningful and relevant to a range of stakeholders. Outcomes research can be captured in a number of ways; such as 'piggy-backing' on clinical trials or through dedicated outcomes studies. As an alternative to prospective trials, outcomes data can be captured through retrospective database analyses or through meta-analyses of existing studies. It is anticipated that outcomes research could demonstrate significant added value to pharmaceutical products that cannot be fully appreciated from an examination of intermediary or surrogate markers of benefit alone. Some companies have perceived outcomes research as a separate discipline from pharmacoeconomics and have created an outcomes research function that is distinct from pharmacoeconomics/health economics. It may be that this is an appropriate split since it is debatable whether pharmacoeconomists/health economists are necessarily the best qualified or have the correct aptitude for detailed involvement in outcomes research, such as the design of quality of life measures. This may be more appropriately carried out by a team of clinical researchers, psychometricians, and statisticians. Marketing would provide the catalyst for such studies based on customer requirements with the pharmacoeconomist providing the necessary guidance as to how the data should be used and communicated. Pharmacoeconomists, as one of the internal customers for such data, have a role to play in ensuring that the outcomes data is used to add significant value to the product in a way that is relevant to the different customer groups.

Epidemiology is often the focus of evidence-based medicine. An epidemiologist's primary role is to investigate the factors that influence the risk of developing a disease. Consequently, epidemiology is an integral part of most economic research involving modelling. For instance, economic modelling of chronic diseases often requires considerable epidemiological data since it may not be practical to capture longterm data prospectively for such a disease. Economic modelling has its strengths and limitations but is an important vehicle for delivering messages about a product's economic value prior to the availability of data on the product's performance in actual clinical practice. Its main uses are therefore during product development where it can be used as a tool for assessing the potential cost-effectiveness of a product and to 'predict' the benefits of the product in actual clinical practice. It can thus provide useful estimates to the payer as to the future impact of the product when real-time data is not yet available.

Economic models can be further developed into disease management tools that incorporate all aspects of treatment and funding of that disease throughout the disease's entire natural history. The model would therefore have a much broader objective than merely demonstrating the relative cost-effectiveness of specific interventions and would thus be of greater relevance to healthcare planners and decision-makers. Such models can provide the basis of constructive dialogue with customers during the development and roll-out phases. The results of the model can provide an integral part of a business case to the customer by helping customers manage their budgets. It would show customers the budgetary impact of particular policies and provide solutions to specific policy issues particularly in relation to funding.

It is anticipated that pharmacoeconomics could be used to justify premium pricing to customers by demonstrating through scientifically validated research the added benefits of the product. In some cases, enhanced clinical benefit may be sufficient to justify price, but in the real world with finite budgets and real economic pressure to contain costs, even a life saving therapy may not be sufficient to justify routine use because of lack of available financial resources. In this event, pharmacoeconomists have a role to play in providing evidence of monetary offsets and/or providing solutions that can overcome the funding hurdle and address issues of affordability. In this sense, economic research can't remain as a stand-alone piece of economic work but needs to provide solutions to healthcare problems that would otherwise provide a barrier to product uptake. The problems need to have been identified through market assessment and through contact with customers. In particular, consideration needs to be given to the possibility of carrying out economic research on a collaborative basis with customers and developing an effective communication strategy.

ISSUES WITH WORKING WITH CONTRACTORS

In many cases, through lack of internal resources or because of the necessity to keep the research independent of the sponsor, the economic research may need to be carried out by external contractors. This leaves a number of decisions to be made as to the type of contractor to deal with and the basis for the relationship. There are certainly pros and cons associated with the contractor route for carrying out economic research. For instance, academic groups have credibility and technical expertise. However, they may lack an understanding of the healthcare environment and customer needs. The nature of the ownership of the research could also be unclear and the right to publication can lead to conflict unless clearly set out in a contract. On the other hand, commercial contractors, whilst tending to offer more control over the research to the client, are likely to be considerably more expensive and may lack credibility. Dealing with external agencies gives studies a measure of independence and thus greater credibility in the eyes of the customers. However, until there are clear rules of engagement between the sponsor and the researcher that are understood by all, then such relationships are likely to remain difficult.

Credibility is a key issue in economic research that involves cost-effectiveness assessments of the sponsoring company's products. This has been further aggravated by the suspicion that only positive studies are currently being published. This of course may mean that either all new drugs are described as cost-effective or the evidence is inconclusive because quality economic data is unavailable for many evaluations. However, until such evaluations are made mandatory with proper registration of all pharmacoeconomic studies then the non-publication of negative studies will always remain an issue, as it is with clinical data.

In all dealings between the pharmaceutical company and the researcher, confidentiality of key drug information such as launch plans, needs to be ensured. Economic methodology is still under-developed and data for the study may be scarce. Consequently, every study requires a feasibility assessment in order to ensure that funds are used efficiently.

A legally binding contract needs to be drawn up to ensure that quality targets and deadlines are achieved and that mutual rights to the finished product are clearly laid out. The publication rights need to be clearly established and the target journal should be agreed early on since the researcher and sponsor may have different publication/communication strategies that may be in conflict. For instance, for the sponsor, the speed of turn around of publication may be more important than the credibility of the journal, whilst from the perspective of the researcher, credibility may be the most important criteria.

ISSUES WITH WORKING WITH CUSTOMERS

Every pharmacoeconomic study needs to be aligned with the marketing strategy so that it becomes an integral part of the marketing mix. Furthermore, every study needs to be based on established clinical claims. Many studies are criticised for the unacceptable or erroneous clinical claims on which the pharmacoeconomic studies are based.

Good communication also needs to be established between the company pharmacoeconomist and the company representatives who deal with the external customers on a regular basis. These are the people who will ultimately be responsible for communicating the pharmacoeconomic messages to the customer so they need to be trained to interpret the study results correctly.

For all major pieces of economic research, an environmental analysis needs to be carried out and this can best be done through the market research function. The Medical Information Department can also provide the vital background information on which many of the modelling assumptions and clinical claims will be based. Last but not least, management needs to be clear about the purpose of the study and the expected deliverables.

Communication with external customers needs to be handled with great care. Pharmaceutical companies can benefit from educating customers into the meaning and uses of pharmacoeconomic data. Many products can be under-valued if not enough attention is given to communicating all the benefits of a product in a way that is understood by customers. To this end, pharmacoeconomics and outcomes research can identify and measure the added value of new products to the marketplace. Pharmacoeconomists would educate the customer into the meaning and significance of the data. It is also important, in this context, and in the current climate of suspicion of industry-sponsored economic studies, for company pharmacoeconomists to build trust with customers through involvement in high-profile expert meetings and methodological debate and 'face-to-face' meetings with the end-user. It is through such activities that one can develop mutual professional respect and understanding.

Once respect and understanding have been established, then partnerships for carrying out research projects become feasible. These partnerships have to be carefully managed and conflicts of interest clearly identified. Some types of studies may be clearly inappropriate for partnership. For instance, where there are clear and unresolvable conflicts of interest. The partnerships should have the objective of providing solutions to healthcare problems that impact on both the industry and the customer. These solutions may not directly involve the company's drugs but may simply create the right environment for creating opportunities to enhance sales.

MEASURING THE RETURN ON INVESTMENT

When pursuing an initiative as significant as setting up a pharmacoeconomics function, one would need to ensure that there will be a fair return on investment. However, if the return on investment is measured by volume of sales or monetary return on sales, then it may be difficult to separate out the effects of pharmacoeconomics in isolation of all the other factors that can influence sales particularly as many of the decisions that affect prescribing policy are often made behind closed doors.

It is also evident that the impact of pharmacoeconomics will vary from country to country depending on the local environment for pharmacoeconomics. For instance, in countries where it is mandatory or strongly recommended to provide economic data to achieve the desired pricing and reimbursement of pharmaceutical products then the issue over the need for pharmacoeconomics is largely irrelevant. Furthermore, although the impact of pharmacoeconomics on decision-making (or the failure to have an impact) may still be investigated under such settings, the outcome of such an investigation is unlikely to lead to a decision to abandon pharmacoeconomics as a core competency. On the other hand, it is in those countries where it is not mandatory or where there are no clear messages from customers as to whether such data are likely to influence their decision-making, where the need for and the impact of pharmacoeconomics becomes contentious.

There will be some clear-cut cases where good quality, credible economic data could certainly have an impact such as where direct and short-term cost savings can be demonstrated for a higher priced but clinically superior product. However, there will also be cases where it could be argued that the clinical data are sufficient justification on their own, such as with products with substantial clinical benefits and where the price is 'right'. The pressure to include a new drug on formularies may be further enhanced by public/media pressure and in some countries, notably USA, and increasingly UK, the fear of litigation.

In assessing impact on the bottom-line, one must be clear as to the distinction between the need for pharmacoeconomics and the deliverable itself. Industry will need pharmacoeconomics to support its products and increasingly so. For some products it may not be essential to provide pharmacoeconomic data, namely for those products with significant clinical benefits that are considered 'reasonably' priced, or conversely those products which are perceived as 'me-too' and yet more expensive. However, more and more products are falling into the grey zone, where there is a small but incremental benefit due to the new product but at a premium price that would have a significant impact on funding. In this case, costs may become an issue, and pharmacoeconomics can help in these circumstances. On the other hand, it is important for the pharmacoeconomist to handle expectations carefully by reminding requesters that economic benefits are, in general, closely

161

correlated with the magnitude of the clinical benefit. Therefore, if no significant clinical differences exist (or are perceived to exist) between competing interventions, then price becomes the primary differentiator. The provision of discounts and rebates is an easy, but potentially very expensive, option, for pharmaceutical companies to adopt when pharmacoeconomics is available as a more cost-effective and persuasive tool. However, while there may be cases where the cost-offsets from a new technology are clear, the quantification of that benefit may be decisive.

On the other hand, while the need and usefulness (or potential usefulness) of pharmacoeconomics may be evident, although this will vary from country to country, it is still not clear that pharmacoeconomics has fulfilled its potential. There are probably many reasons for this situation largely associated with the relative novelty of the science in healthcare and in the pharmaceutical industry in particular. The infrastructure/culture may not yet be in place in both the industry and in the healthcare system to make the most of the techniques. The change in environment does not happen overnight and as with any new science there are often key people in key positions who will remain sceptical or fearful of its influence and will restrain its development.

A cautious start to building a pharmacoeconomic team seems appropriate. Yet, this leads to a dilemma. A small team of pharmacoeconomists, perhaps initially under-budgeted, may be expected to deliver quick 'wins' to justify investment. This is difficult to do with a research-based discipline where studies can take several months to complete. On the other hand, if sufficient relevant data already exist, then persuasive pharmacoeconomic claims could be readily developed and communicated. Furthermore, the nature of the discipline requires the right environment to work effectively and this can only take time and resources. The team will need to influence other internal customers to provide support through educational programmes.

Pharmacoeconomics will need to identify its areas of influence within the company and outside the company and develop the interfaces/relationships between the various functions and bodies that it will need to work with. Pharmacoeconomics cannot function in isolation of either its internal or external customers.

Pharmacoeconomics will need to determine the critical factors for its success and ensure that these factors are in place. These factors include the presence of an expert team, adequately resourced, a supportive internal environment and an external environment that is concerned with rational cost-effective prescribing to achieve optimal efficiency in the delivery of healthcare. Pharmacoeconomics will add value provided that these conditions are met.

THE FUTURE OF PHARMACOECONOMICS IN THE PHARMACEUTICAL INDUSTRY

Pharmacoeconomics will only be credible as a practical discipline while it remains responsive to the changes in the healthcare environment. In particular, pharmacoeconomists will need to be constantly aware and responsive to changes in the market for their services. In this context, one issue that remains a continually recurring theme in the environment for pharmacoeconomics is the issue of bias in pharmacoeconomic studies and particularly in industry-sponsored studies. The logic behind this controversy is that because of the commercial advantage that pharmaceutical companies can gain from showing their drug to be more 'cost-effective' than their competitors', and because of the current lack of adequate regulation of the design, conduct and reporting of 'cost-effectiveness' studies, there is a potential for biasing studies in favour of the sponsor's drug. Suggestions for reducing the potential for bias have included recommending codes of ethical conduct between researchers and their sponsors, recommending adherence to published methodological guidelines and recommending audits of pharmacoeconomic research on the lines of the accountancy profession. In this article, I am not going to address the issue of the extent of bias in industry-sponsored studies since any further speculation in this area is likely to be fruitless. However, I do wish to caution against over-reliance on some of the remedies for preventing bias described above. While these remedies may be helpful, I also wish to propose that a more fruitful area of research would be in developing better methods to identify, measure and correct for bias rather than focusing entirely on prevention. The reason being that the preventative measures, while reducing the potential for bias, will not eliminate all the bias in economic evaluations since much of it is inherent in study design and methods of data capture. It is beyond the scope of this article to suggest ways and means of identifying, measuring and adjusting for bias in economic evaluation (and sensitivity analysis is not helpful here). The main point is that while there has been a lot of talk about practice guidelines and methodological guidelines, the development of methods for actually measuring and correcting for bias appears to be lagging behind and this state of affairs needs to change if pharmacoeconomics is to remain a credible science.

It certainly is not in the interests of pharmaceutical companies to have an environment where bias is prevalent. Economic evaluations exist for the purpose of providing a rational objective basis for making choices between competing therapies. It is in the interests of pharmaceutical companies to ensure that the 'science' is credible so that new innovative drugs can be fairly assessed. For every bias in favour of one drug there often exists a favourable bias for an alternative therapy; claims and counter-claims lead to confusion and ultimate disbelief in all such studies and we're then back to square one where decision-makers make subjective assessments of their own. Prevention is fine but reality requires sophisticated tools to identify, measure and adjust for bias. Too much emphasis on prevention detracts from this essential need. Once these are in place, and are understood, issues of authorship should cease to be a major issue and guidelines may have a less pivotal role in assessing the quality of a study. However, for those countries where this suspicion of bias is widespread, the feasibility of pharmaceutical companies independently doing their own studies or to be seen to be a principal driver, would seem to be limited if it is to retain its acceptability with customers. Using credible and independent researchers to carry out the studies or partnering with customers to develop solutions to their healthcare problems, is likely to be the way forward in the current environment. Consequently, if the research is carried out by in-house pharmacoeconomists this may significantly limit its acceptability unless there was an independent group that could do the auditing. Peer-reviewed journals address some of the issues of acceptability but their remoteness from the needs of specific customer groups is still a barrier to their use.

There are other changes taking place. Many countries are seeing a shift in decision-making from providers to payers, purchasers and patients. This would inevitably increase the interest and demand for economic evaluations as an aid to priority setting, budget planning, and the choice of investment.

Another change is already happening. Decision-makers are increasingly voicing discontent that the traditional randomised controlled clinical trial, the backbone for clinical research for a number of years, is not reflecting what actually happens in practice. They are demanding longer-term follow-ups that will reflect more closely how the drug will actually be used in practice. In fact, the randomised clinical trial is almost becoming a tool for restricting the market rather than increasing it, as purchasers see the narrow inclusion/exclusion criteria as an opportunity to restrict the drug's use although obviously off-patent use will still be around. Decision-makers are, going one step further, by not only asking for longer-term data but are recommending that this data should focus on meaningful and relevant outcomes with real impact for the patient and other stakeholders.

Furthermore, as the difference between products reduces to marginal increments of improvement as they become the fifth or later entry into the class, monetary offsets may no longer be sufficient to justify the price, and pharmacoeconomists will need to turn their attention to other options for making the product marketable. This may even involve assessing the economic value of non-product offerings. For instance, the cost-effectiveness of add-on services or packages of care, such as diagnostic kits, nursing support, and disease management tools, may transform a product that, on its own may be no more or less cost-effective than any other alternative, into an intervention that is good value for money.

Pharmacoeconomics is the application of micro-economics to pharmaceutical products and services. Whether they be called pharmacoeconomists or health economists, their principal role is to assess the economic value of the company's pharmaceutical products and to show that it has superior economic value to alternative interventions for that indication. However, as therapeutic areas become crowded, clinical differentiation between many products will become so small as to provide no basis for claiming superior economic value and price will become the main economic differentiator. On the other hand, this difficult situation could change for the better once the full impact of pharmacoeconomics is felt.

The environment is changing faster than the training of new pharmacoeconomists can keep up with. In the current climate, the traditional role of the health economist will soon become largely redundant as the number of products on which economic differentiation is feasible becomes less and less. This will be particularly true for those products being launched into an increasingly genericised market or where parallel importing is rife and the indications are that both of these are on the increase. So with the predominance of largely me-too drugs or at least with differentiation being based more on marginally superior safety and convenience rather than on efficacy, with little economic differentiation apart from price, what will now be the principal role of the pharmacoeconomist in that sort of environment? The pharmacoeconomist may now need to apply those skills in a different way or to learn new skills. The cost-effectiveness of packages of care and services, either associated with the pharmaceutical product or not, may become the norm. On the other hand, the arrival of pharmacoeconomics, with potential cures for specific, identifiable patient groups, could lead to the dawn of a whole new era of medicines which are highly cost-effective.

It's likely that pharmaceutical companies will never be in a position to manage whole disease areas unless they change the nature of their business fundamentally. However, it may be feasible for companies to manage parts of the disease management process and to provide solutions to healthcare problems. This requires a much broader and deeper understanding of the healthcare system and much closer partnerships with the customer. This will undoubtedly go hand-in-hand with a much greater need for health economic skills at the local level where true partnering can be cultivated and where studies will increasingly involve the design, monitoring and evaluation of pilot projects that compare current practice with the new reality.

Pharmacoeconomists employed in industry have often been criticised for being too academic in their outlook. This often implies an inability to see beyond the technical detail with a consequent inability to adapt the techniques to real-life problem-solving. Pharmacoeconomists are largely there to provide credibility to the work they do and to get acceptability for the research by peers. However, even this is largely naive, since the environment is clearly suspicious of anything produced by the industry, even if peer-reviewed, no matter what the academic qualifications of the individual. However, while the ability to recognise the type and quality of research that will or will not be acceptable by peer-reviewed journals, is an important function of the in-house pharmacoeconomist, the ability to carry out the study itself, in every detail, may not be an appropriate function for the company pharmacoeconomist. In any event, the study itself should only be considered a part of the entire project and the bulk of the effort should be devoted to identifying the problem and, subsequently to communicating the results of that study, and providing meaningful solutions for the end-user. The communication aspect of the study has been sadly neglected and remains one of the prime reasons for the failure of pharmacoeconomics to have a significant impact in the marketplace. Until this is realised and accepted by industry pharmacoeconomists, people within the company, who work with pharmacoeconomists, will be continually frustrated by their failure to grasp the bigger picture.

In this context, pharmacoeconomists need to think of economic studies as providing solutions to healthcare customers to enable them to overcome some of the barriers to prescribing. This may involve identification of savings that could be generated from using the product, or identification of areas of inefficient spending, that would allow some shifting of budgets. It may also mean identifying add-on services and packages of care that could be provided that would make the overall offering more attractive. It may also mean carrying out studies that could be used to identify non-product related areas of business.

The increasing complexity of the marketplace in terms of the diversity of stakeholders, the decentralisation of healthcare, the complexity of the funding dynamics and the diversity of treatment practices and availability of healthcare would increasingly make it difficult to conduct relevant studies at a distance from the local marketplace. However, while there appears to be some harmonization of the marketplace within Europe, in the sense that the markets may become more competitive and localised with some elements of US-style managed care, it is likely that this will increase the quantity and diversity of pharmacoeconomic studies required. There will be more freedom of flow of pharmaceutical products and services between countries, and regulatory and patent rights will be more harmonized. However, while certain rules and regulations may be more harmonized, and the overall economic system may become more broadly similar, the localised nature of that system will make any involvement at the detailed local level critical to the success of pharmacoeconomic studies.

Pharmacoeconomic studies that are non-customer specific will struggle to have an impact in the marketplace in the current environment. It is now widely accepted that while randomised controlled trials are the norm for demonstrating the safety and efficacy of a drug, it is to be seen whether such trials have any relevance at all for predicting real-life outcomes and whether local outcomes study will ultimately be the norm for supplying added-value claims.

The relevance of non-localised economic data is even more questionable given the widely different management practices, healthcare resources used and more particularly unit costs. Certainly, there will be generic, qualitative arguments that could be used that would form the basis of an hypothesis for a proposed local study. Interactive models used at launch may overcome some of the problems associated with heterogeneity of care but it is not until local studies are carried out, (in partnership with customers), that address real-life local issues, that progress will be made in gaining acceptability of these studies.

It is crucial for the company pharmacoeconomist to make the step from carrying out studies in isolation of the end-user to working in partnership with them from the early concept stage to the final deliverable. Until there is a proper infrastructure in place for ensuring the validity and reliability of all pharmacoeconomic studies, in-house studies carried out by in-house health economists or even in conjunction with a third-party group of researchers and consultants, will be viewed with some suspicion. Working with the end-user in developing these studies is critical to their acceptability and their usefulness. Need has to be identified and the problem which the study is meant to be addressing should also be identified. However, it is understood that such partnerships may be difficult to forge where there are clear lines of conflict. However, each party needs to identify those areas of conflict and either assess the risks and benefits of such joint studies or avoid the areas of conflict and find areas of common ground that would be mutually beneficial to explore.

CONCLUSION

The short answer to the question 'Should pharmaceutical companies be encouraged to establish a pharmacoeconomic team?' is a resounding yes. However, there are still some unresolved questions concerning the ideal number of pharmacoeconomists, how they should be organised, where they should be located, the skills required, their role and responsibilities (now and in the future), and the expected return on investment.

I hope it is clear from the preceding discussion that in-house expertise in pharmacoeconomics is necessary if pharmaceutical companies are to adequately address the challenges raised by the prevailing environment of cost containment and where economic factors are and will be an important determinant in prescribing policy decisions. Customers in healthcare, like customers in almost every other economic sector, have to be concerned about the budgetary impact of their purchasing decisions. Customers are coming to terms with the idea that, if the goal is to achieve optimal healthcare for all, seeking 'good value for money' is not just an economic necessity but an ethical requirement.

However, while in-house expertise is necessary, the benefits of that expertise will not be fully realised until pharmacoeconomics is integrated into the culture of the company and the appropriate supporting infrastructure is in place. Just as it is important for everyone involved in drug development and marketing to understand the role of clinical research, so everyone, particularly the decision-makers within the company, needs to understand the economic imperatives that exist in the external environment and the role that the company pharmacoeconomist plays in trying to provide solutions to the purchasing dilemma.

Pharmacoeconomics straddles across many areas of the company's business. For instance, pharmacoeconomists, in designing their studies, need to consider both the medical and marketing issues facing a particular product or service. The pharmacoeconomist also needs to understand the dynamics of the healthcare system, and the results of their studies must always address the specific needs and concerns of the customer and offer business solutions where these are required.

Pharmacoeconomics is a broad sweeping discipline and is therefore unlikely to function effectively unless it can gain appropriate support from other internal and external functions. For instance, it would be impractical, inappropriate and unnecessary for any company to put together a pharmacoeconomics department that embraced all the necessary skills and attempted to conduct all the studies in-house. Close links with market research, medical information, customer and commercial development groups, and with marketing and medical/clinical groups are essential for pharmacoeconomists to function effectively. There are external academic departments who would be much better positioned to handle technical detail, to have specialist skills, and to carry out methodological research. Clearly, in-house experts need to understand the technical detail but studies can be protracted and labour intensive with questionable external credibility, and therefore it would not be in the company's interests to devote large resources to such activity. The best use of in-house economists is to identify where there is a need for such studies, what the chances of success are, how will it be used, and what impact will it have on prescribing policy. Active involvement, with bringing customers to the table to discuss the uses of such studies, preferably in 'face-to-face' meetings, is a key role for the in-house pharmacoeconomist. In this connection, it will be important for the in-house pharmacoeconomist to build a network of key contacts within the healthcare system — people who can be trusted and who are open to the idea of partnerships.

Once the investment has been made in pharmacoeconomics, it is reasonable for the company to expect a return on its investment. On the other hand, it would be rare for the effects of a pharmacoeconomic study to be clearly distinguishable from all the other factors than can affect product uptake. Nevertheless, while the strategic importance of pharmacoeconomics may not be in question, questions concerning its ability to fulfil expectations, or of ways of enabling it to fulfil expectations, are still much in debate. However, reasons for failing to meet expectations, are likely to be a combination of things. For instance, expectations could be too high because of poor understanding of the nature of the subject. The appropriate infrastructure and culture may be lacking and the function may be inadequately resourced with insufficient time and resource devoted to the much neglected area of communication. The reasons for failing to deliver may be as much due to the above set of circumstances as to any intrinsic inadequacies of the science or its practitioners.

REFERENCES

Drummond MF. (1994). Issues in the Conduct of Economic Evaluations. *PharmacoEconomics* **6** (5) : 405–411.

Hillman *et al*. Avoiding Bias in the conduct and reporting of cost-effectiveness research sponsored by pharmaceutical companies. (1991). *New England Journal of Medicine.* Vol **324** No.19.

Maynard A. (1994). Pharmaco-economical with the truth? *Pharmaceutical Times.* June.

Stemeroff, Gagnon, Goulli. (1997). The evolving structure of health economics. *Scrip Magazine.* March.

Smith H. Value arguments leave US customers unconvinced. (1997). *Pharmaceutical Times.* May.

Slate AE. How to value the health economist. (1997). *Pharmaceutical Marketing.* March.

Wells N. (1997). Planning an approach to pharmacoeconomics. *Scrip Magazine.* July/August.

Grabowski H. The effect of pharmacoeconomics on company research and development decisions. (1997). *Pharmacoeconomics.* **11**(5): 389–97.

The Impact of Cost-effectiveness on Public and Private policies in healthcare: An international perspective. (1997). *Social Science and Medicine* : Vol **45** No.4 August.

Notes

Notes

Notes

Notes

Notes

Notes

Notes

Notes

Notes